The
St. Lawrence River

QUEBEC, LOWER TOWN.

The
St. Lawrence River

Historical—Legendary—Picturesque

By

George Waldo Browne

Author of "Japan : The Place and the People," "Paradise of the Pacific"
"Pearl of the Orient," "Wood-Ranger Tales," etc.

———

Weathervane Books • New York

To

SIR JAMES McPHERSON LeMOINE, D.C.L.

THIS VOLUME OF

THE STORIED ST. LAWRENCE

IS MOST RESPECTFULLY INSCRIBED

BY THE AUTHOR

Preface

WHILE the St. Lawrence River has been the scene of many important events connected with the discovery and development of a large portion of North America, no attempt has before been made to collect and embody in one volume a complete and comprehensive narrative of this great waterway. This is not denying that considerable has been written relating to it, and some of this told in an interesting and painstaking manner, but the various offerings have been scattered through many volumes, and most of these have soon become inaccessible to the general reader. Sir J. M. LeMoine, F.R.S.C., of Quebec, who has done so much to give the St. Lawrence place in the literature of Canada, says of this noble river :

It lies for a thousand miles between two great nations, yet neglected by both, though neither would be so great without it,—a river as grand as the La Plata, as picturesque as the Rhine, as pure as the Lakes of Switzerland. . . . The noblest, the purest, most enchanting river on all God's beautiful earth . . . has never yet had a respectable history, nor scarcely more than an occasional artist to delineate its beauties.

The writer of this volume has undertaken as far as he could in a single work, to present a succinct and

unbroken account of the most important historic incidents connected with the river, combined with descriptions of some of its most picturesque scenery and frequent
selections from its prolific sources of legends and traditions.   He has not hoped to treat so vast a subject fully
in one volume, but he trusts that he will meet the expectations of the majority.   In writing a work of this kind
the difficulty has not been in finding sufficient material,
but rather it has been in the selection of those matters
which most closely concerned the subject in hand.
Thus, he has felt obliged to pass over in silence, or
describe hastily, many scenes that appear to deserve
greater recognition.   It does not seem practicable to
make a continuous narrative in a work of this kind, but
this plan has been followed as nearly as possible, and at
the same time to give an intelligent account of the
incidents in their order.   When and where original
documents and papers have not been available for
consultation, only the best authorities have been accepted and then not without comparison with others.
It is hoped that but few errors have crept in, while it
must be borne in mind that no two historians ever
exactly agree on the local history of a place.

The author wishes to acknowledge his indebtedness
to the numerous persons whose works have proved
especially valuable to him in his study of the subject.
Among these it is a pleasure to mention Cartier's *Bref
Récit*, Champlain's *Narratives*, *Jesuit Relations*, Haldimand Papers, Colden's *Iroquois Nation*, Prof. Grant's

Picturesque Canada, Willis's *Canadian Scenery*, Charle-
voix's *History of Canada*, The Johnson Journals, MSS.
of M. Fère, Winsor's *Cartier to Frontenac*, Haddock's
Picturesque St. Lawrence, LeMoine's *Maple Leaves*,
Parkman's *Pioneers of France in the New World*, and
many others, besides those credited from time to time
in the following pages, not forgetting the numerous
fugitive articles that have materially assisted him.   He
also wishes to record his appreciation of the valuable
assistance given him by his friends who have so generously lent their aid in securing data which was not
always easy to obtain.

In producing the hundred illustrations that accompany the work care has been taken to give as wide a
scope as possible to the views belonging to the river.
In this department many thanks are due to the artists
and photographers for their efforts toward making the
work attractive and interesting.   The thanks of the
publishers are due the Department of the Interior at
Ottawa for a plan of the river.

G. W. B.

Contents

CHAPTER I

CHAPTER II

CHAPTER III

CHAPTER IV

CHAPTER V

Contents

CHAPTER VI

CHAPTER VII

CHAPTER VIII

CHAPTER IX

Contents

Contents

Contents

Illustrations

Illustrations

Illustrations

The St. Lawrence River

Chapter I

From Lake to Gulf

Physical and Picturesque Features of Canada's Remarkable River—Fifty Miles of
Islands—Scenery of "Les Mille Iles"—A Hundred Miles of Rapids—
Shooting the Rapids—The Bright Path of Peril—Romantic Montreal
—Twin Rows of Towns—Historic Quebec—Long Miles of Tide-Water
—Then Out to Sea!

RIVERS play an important part in the history
of a country. They reflect more clearly the
character of the settlers than any other natural boundary. They were, in truth, the one dividing line acknowledged by the American aborigines,
and by them, as a rule, the limitations of the tribes became fixed, so far as it was possible for a people with
unwritten laws to establish their domains. Along the
banks of these unmapped streams clustered their conical
tents; here they held their councils of war; here they
celebrated their festivals of peace; here they fished and
hunted; here they staked their fates, and won, and
lost. These streams became their main highways of
travel. Along their sedgy courses they sped their

light canoes, leaving in their wake no stone disturbed, no twig turned, and scarce a ripple upon the surface of the water. The same boulders and smaller stones that strewed the pathway of the earliest voyager remained in the path of the last. Upon reaching the fountain-head of a river recourse was had to a land journey to the nearest water, the craft which had been their means of transit, as well as their rude "baggage," borne on their shoulders over the intervening portage, known for this reason as a "carrying-place."

Upon the advent of the white man these rivers again became the natural paths of the explorers, their banks the homesteads of the pioneers; later, the sites for cities builded through the industries arising from the mills and manufactories whose power was furnished by their waterfalls. Thus, in many ways, they became closely identified with the progress of civilisation.

The history and description of a river should be written, it would seem, by starting at its fountain-head and following its course to that larger body of water where it yields its life and treasures. Unfortunately for this purpose, the tide of human events runs counter to the current of most rivers, and the storied St. Lawrence is no exception. If this is true the series of incidents that have helped form its history will be better comprehended after an outline of its natural career from lake to gulf; each rapid, lakelet, rocky bluff, and tributary, having a double interest when linked with its ancient and now silent glory, is the story of human achievement, some deed of heroism, sacrifice, or suffering endured by the brave race that led the way along its trackless aisles bordered by mighty forests.

The St. Lawrence River, in its most limited bounds, begins at the foot of Lake Ontario, opposite the city of Kingston, and flows generally in a north-easterly direction about 750 miles, when its flood mingles with that of the gulf by the same name. Treated in a more extended manner, according to the ideas of the early French geographers, and taking either the river and lake of Nipigon, on the north of Superior, or the river St. Louis, flowing from the south-west, it has a grand total length of over two thousand miles. With its tributaries it drains over four hundred thousand square miles of country, made up of fertile valleys and plateaux inhabited by a prosperous people, desolate barrens, deep forests, where the foot of man has not yet left its imprint.

Seldom less than two miles in width, it is two and one-half miles wide where it issues from Ontario, and with several expansions which deserve the name of lake it becomes eighty miles in width where it ceases to be considered a river. The influence of the tide is felt as far up as Lake St. Peter, about one hundred miles above Quebec and over five hundred miles from the gulf, while it is navigable for sea-going vessels to Montreal, eighty miles farther inland. Rapids impede navigation above this point, but by means of canals continuous communication is obtained to the head of Lake Superior.

If inferior in breadth to the mighty Amazon, if it lacks the length of the Mississippi, if without the stupendous gorges and cataracts of the Yang-tse-Kiang of China, if missing the ancient castles of the Rhine, if wanting the lonely grandeur that still overhangs the Congo of the Dark Continent, the Great River of Canada has features as remarkable as any of these. It has its source in the largest body of fresh water upon the globe, and among all of the big rivers of the world it is the only one whose volume is not sensibly affected by the elements. In rain or in sunshine, in spring floods or in summer droughts, this phenomenon of waterways seldom varies more than a foot in its rise and fall. By this statement it should not be understood that the river maintains every year the same depth of water, as from other causes it varies somewhat. One of the historians of its upper section, Mr. J. A. Haddock, says:

The level of the river differs, one year with another, the extreme range being about seven feet. These changes are not the immediate effects of the excessive rains, such as cause floods in other rivers, but appear to be occasioned by the different quantities of rain falling, in some years more than in others, and which finds its way down months afterwards. A series of several years of high water, and others of low water are known to have occurred. The level of the river is also affected by strong prevailing winds, blowing up or down the lake, and several instances of rapid fall, followed by a returning wave of extraordinary height, have been reported.

While favoured with America's Great Lakes as the reservoir from which to draw its supply, the St. Lawrence has not been niggardly treated in the offerings of tributary streams, some of which are themselves noble rivers, the largest being the Ottawa and Saguenay. Hundreds of streams, many of them deserving the designation of river, come winding down from the region of the northland, or from the great watershed of the south. Canada is a country of cañons and waterfalls, and the streams that seek the St. Lawrence run tortuous races before they reach the parent river. Some come tipped up edgewise, like the mysterious Saguenay; others come flattened like the Montmorency, rolled so thin that the sunlight breaks through ; but one and all roll and tumble, toss and twist, and wear the white veil of mist. Beside Canada, New England, with her rivers and mountains, must be content to take a second place in the matter of waterfalls.

Where the great Laurentian chain of mountains, running from east to west across Canada, swings southward to enter Northern New York, it drops a link, as it were, so as to allow the last of the big lakes an outlet in the channel of the St. Lawrence, which moves sluggishly among the thousand islands helping to form the most picturesque archipelago in the world, its nearest rival being that other section of lakes and islands, Finland. The actual number of the islands of this Lake of the Thousand Isles is really nearer two thousand, though this discrepancy would not be noticed by the new-comer into this enchanting realm. Nor can it matter greatly to the daily voyager, as he threads the winding passages of the interior, or glides along the broader way leading into the American channel. This was the old Indian trail, and along this course followed the adventurous Champlain, who was the first white man to gaze upon this entrancing scene.

Leaving the city of Kingston, which stands upon the site of that frontier town, Cataraqui, with its Martello towers and decidedly military appearance, the course of modern travel leads to the lively American town, Clayton, noted as a summer resort. Below this thriving village, island after island studding the placid lake rises into view, the finger-tips of the great mountain range. On one of these larger isles is located the " Thousand Island Park," while a little below is the fashionable resort known as the " Saratoga of the St. Lawrence," Alexandria Bay, its shores the foreground for many elegant villas and summer hotels. Gazing upon the numerous cottages now dotting the islands, the mind of the thoughtful observer quickly spans the years that have seen this beautiful region opened to the admiring sight-seer ; to the period, not so very remote, when this lovely expanse of river and isles was known to the romantic red man as Manatoana, or " The Garden of the Great Spirit." As usual, the Amerind expressed in fitting term the natural beauties of the spot named. Covered with the ancient forest, fitting haunts for the wild deer, the little bays and inlets the common resort of water-fowl, it must indeed have been a paradise for the dusky hunter and fisher. It is well that all of these natural attractions have not vanished, for still many of the isles

MODERN ATTRACTIONS OF THE THOUSAND ISLANDS.

From a photograph by W. Notman & Son, Montreal.

LONG SAULT RAPIDS.

From a drawing by W. H. Bartlett.

are bristling with firs and pines; others lie open like a level field awaiting the husbandman's care. Some are but arid rock, as wild and picturesque as those seen among the Faroe Islands; others have a group of trees or a solitary pine, and others bear a crown of flowers or a little hillock of verdure like a dome of malachite, among which the river slowly glides, embracing with equal fondness the great and the small, now receding afar and now retracing its course, like the good Patriarch visiting his domains, or like the god Proteus counting his snowy flocks.

From Clayton to Chippewa Bay the river, with its clustered isles, is like a fairyland, the thousand and one gems brightened by the fantastic imagery of the beholder. Now an island comes into view which bears a happy resemblance to some spot known in childhood. Yonder is a bit of rock-landscape diamond-shaped, the gleam and glitter of the gem in its setting rather than in itself. Close by, in marked contrast to the other's barren aspect, is a star-pointed plot of greensward, adorned by three trees whose interlacing branches form the outline of a cross. Below, like a huge hand laid upon the waters, is the green-bordered isle of the "lost lover" of Indian legend. The pointing finger of this island hand still shows the way the dusky maid went in search of her recreant lover, never to return. And everywhere art has combined with nature to enliven if not to enhance the scene. Upon a tiny island, barely large enough to afford it standing room, is a modest cottage. Over the brown shingle of the rocky beach of a larger island loom the dark grey walls of a western-world imitation of the Castle of Chillon, but happily the white face of its prisoner, made immortal by Byron, is not to be seen at its windows.

The last of the Thousand Islands are called " The Three Sisters," on account of their resemblance and intimate relations to each other, a beautiful trio that have been the silent witnesses of the coming and going of the races of men claiming lordship over the wonderland of the noble river.

Brockville, " the Queen City of the St. Lawrence," named for General Brock, is situated on the Canadian shore, below the last of the islands, with Morristown on the New York bank nearly opposite. Below these, Ogdensburg, on the American side, and Prescott on the other, stand also *vis-à-vis*, like sentinels long on duty. Then the Massena Landing is passed, and the approach to the famous rapids is begun.

There is a concealed velocity to the current of the St. Lawrence which we do not realise, though at times conscious of passing along swift water, until we are forcibly reminded of the troubled condition of the river, and are told that we are entering the first of the series of rapids marking the downward flight of the waters. The Galops are passed when we come in sight of du Plat, thrilled with the pleasant sensation of excitement, and longing for a repetition of the exhilarating experience. We may be cowards at heart, but there is a fascination in this mild form of danger which arouses our interest. Aware that the descent just made was merely the prelude to the grand march ahead, as if nature were alive

to the best effect to be produced, we approach with
quickening pulse the nine miles of rapids known as the
Long Sault. The river is now divided by a string of
islands. The roar of the surges now breaks solemnly
upon the ear, and the gaze is greeted with whirlpools of
foaming waters and curved lines of yellow flood charg-
ing some hidden enemy which flings it back with furious
defiance, only to receive again and again the rallying
legions forever beating its rock-ribbed front. Farther
than the eye can reach extend these series of rifts, now
capped with white plumes, anon darkling with rage; at
one moment rushing madly past jutting headlands, and
then leaping with bounds the broken barriers in its
pathway.

The engineer shuts off the steam, but the current
carries us on at the rate of twenty miles an hour. The
pilot, a descendant of the dusky boatmen who navigated
the river in their light barks long ere the coming of the
white race, stands with confidence at his post, every
sense on the alert, and the most timid feels safe under
his guidance. Thus one and all give their undivided
attention to watching the progress of the steamer gliding downward amid the pitch and toss of the broken
current, the froth and foam upon the dishevelled waters,
the bended breakers that wind about her pathway like
the fateful combers of some reef-bound coast. Upon
getting better command of ourselves, we are surprised
at the smoothness with which the great boat follows its
winding course, and the swift and faithful compliance it

yields to the man at the wheel.   Upon one hand a big
white cap of foam covers a snarly head of rocks ; on the
other, a granite arm reaches out to seize us as we sweep
past, and though we can see it is a dozen fathoms too
short to reach us, we breathe easier when it is left astern.
Held fast in the granite teeth of a ledge an ill-fated raft
is seen not far away, the sight an unpleasant suggestion
of what might happen to us.

At last, with pleasure and regret striving for the
mastery over our feelings, calm water is seen in the
distance, and we realise we have passed the long rapids,
while the steamer moves gently on where the reunited
streams mingle their waters with a tranquillity quite
remarkable considering the recent display of violence.
Below the Long Sault the river widens so as to form
Lake St. Francis, five and one-half miles in width and
twenty-five miles in length.   Here and there an island
dots the placid surface.   This soon proves to be the
training-ground for another charge in its downward
march from the lake to the gulf, the preparation for a
series of plunges down four rapids known as Couteau,
Cedars, Split Rock, and Cascades, the quartette so
closely connected as really to form one continuous
rift.

Upon reaching the foot of this watery stairway, we
come upon another body of calm water, another muster-
ground, named Lake St. Louis.   The distant range of
mountains — a spur of the Adirondacks — which has
loomed so long and plain upon our view, now grows in-

distinct, and we turn from its peaceful outlines to watch the river-banks gradually drawing nearer, as if fearful of giving their charge too great scope of freedom. Soon the misty form of Mount Royal appears on the horizon.

Then the quickening current again speaks of rapids, of the running of a swift and furious race with fate, as if the elements were forever fleeing from gaolers that would bind them in fetters of granite. The water is whipped into serpents of foam, coiling about the rocky heads thrust above the surface, betraying with added ferocity the rage they would seem to conceal. Borne on once more solely by the current, the boat settles under our feet as if it were slipping from under us. The thrill, the exhilaration, the excitement, the hazard, the fury of the eddies, the foam of the surf, the twists and mazes of the turgid stream that tend to bewilder the onlooker, the efforts of the man at the wheel, the watchfulness of the pilot, the anxiety of the captain, —all these are doubled against our previous experiences, and we have run the famous rapids of Lachine!

The river again widens and assumes a tranquil appearance. The wood-fringed shores of Nun's Island are passed, and then the steamer sweeps proudly under the far-reaching spans of Victoria Bridge, over two miles in length, and considered one of the great engineering feats of the nineteenth century. Then Montreal, Canada's great metropolis, the city of churches and cathedrals, massive business buildings, commodious hotels, and

magnificent parks, with the yet more magnificent
mountain rising in the background, comes into view.

Tried no more with rapids, the great river, like the
mighty stream it is, sweeps calmly and majestically between high, precipitous banks, or where the shores are
low and level, with continuous rows of white-walled
cottages, with groups of these dwellings at regular
intervals forming a well-ordered hamlet, from among
whose tree-tops rises the spire of a church, proving
the inhabitants to be a religious people. Forty-five
miles below Montreal, at the mouth of the Richelieu
River, stands the thriving town of Sorel.

Another broadening of the river forms Lake St. Peter,
nine miles wide and twenty-five miles long.   Then the
St. François River, flowing down past the picturesque
and historic Indian village by the same name, enters
the St. Lawrence ; on the north another stream joins
the larger river through three channels, giving name
to the bustling town of Three Rivers; then the namesake
of a famous Indian chief, Batiscan, the inlet of Jacques
Cartier River, an increasing ruggedness of the river-
banks ; the mouth of the Chaudière ; and then, more
conspicuous than all else, rises upon the view the
ancient stronghold of New France,—the Gibraltar of
America,—Quebec.   Here is more history wrapped in
the silence of grey battlements ; more romance buried
under antique walls; more mystery veiled by the atmosphere of departed centuries, than is to be found
elsewhere in America. Here the luxurious splendour of

SHOOTING THE LA CHINE RAPIDS.

From a photograph by W. Notman & Son, Montreal.

VIEW OF THE CITY OF QUEBEC.

the Old World mingled with the barbaric simplicity of the New; here was cradled a new empire for France; and here, upon her battlefields, was decided the fate of nations.

Quebec is about midway between the lakes and the gulf, and with still four hundred miles to journey the St. Lawrence sweeps on toward the sea, its current now the servant of the ocean tide, passing leisurely in succession islands strung upon a broad band of silver, picturesque villages under the dedication of church spires, an occasional tributary stream, the grandest of which is the deep-volumed Saguenay, frowning points of land and rock, mountains whose ruggedness is softened by the enchantment of distance.

Rivers have at least one human trait. They are invariably loath to render over their treasures, to yield unto the sea the tribute they have brought from hills and woods through many a difficult passage and perilous rapid. As the end draws near they move with increasing sluggishness. The Great River of China, after leaping dizzy mountain cliffs and running a furious race along a thousand leagues of rapids and gorges, slows its gait at last, and finally, in its desperation, heaps up bars of sand in a vain effort to save itself from the hungry sea. The Amazon deploys right and left over the adjacent country, as if bent upon swallowing instead of being swallowed, until it is difficult to distinguish between river and ocean. The Mississippi, after overflowing its banks for miles, creeps sullenly over sand-bars it is constantly building up, and pours its flood into the gulf through several avenues. The Great River of Canada forms no exception. Gradually widening after leaving Quebec, at Point de Montes it suddenly makes a broader pathway than ever, but if moving through Amazonian portals it still clings to well-defined shores for another two hundred miles—

Then out to the sea with a stately sweep,
.   .   .   .
It mingles its tide with the mighty deep,
As it has for a thousand years.

Chapter II

In the Wake of Cartier

His Voyages of Discovery—Planting the Cross at Gaspé—From Gulf to River—
Scenery along the Lower St. Lawrence.

THE St. Lawrence is the only large river traced upon *Novus Orbis*, which is claimed to be the first general atlas of the Western Hemisphere; and whether done from the knowledge of actual exploration or from imagination, it became in Europe the most famous waterway in America before the Hudson, the Mississippi, or any other stream had created a ripple on the surface of discovery.

In regard to its navigation, tradition says one Thomas Aubert sailed up the river, in the early part of the sixteenth century, as far as Tadousac, and brought back an Indian captive. This seems, at first glance, to be the earliest account of an ascent by a European, still there is strong evidence to show that before this adventurous explorer from Dieppe made this voyage the Normans, Basques, and Malouns had ascended the river as far as he claimed, to fish and to trade with the natives for furs. How much farther these rugged fishermen went there is nothing to show, though it

is quite likely they went as far as the present site of
Quebec, where there was an Indian town known as
Stadaconé.

Apropos of this interesting subject, Mr. W. H. H.
Murray wrote of these voyages of the Basque, while he
was enjoying a yacht trip up the Saguenay :

There is reason to think that before the Christ was born the old
Iberian ships were here ; and their descendants, the Basques, continued the commerce which their progenitors had established, and
who had rendezvoused here 1500 years after the Galilean name
had conquered kingdoms and empires. The Norsemen were here,
we know, a thousand years ago, and many a night the old sea kings
of the north drank out of their mighty drinking horns good health
to the distant ones and honours to Thor and Odin. Then, late
enough to have his coming known to letters, and hence recorded,
Jacques Cartier came, himself a Breton, and hence cousin in
blood to the Basque whalers, whom he found here engaged in a
pursuit which their race had followed before Rome was founded or
Greece was born, before Jerusalem was builded, or even Egypt,
perhaps, planted as a colony. St. Augustine, Plymouth Rock, Quebec—these are mushroom growths, creations of yesterday, tradition-
less, without a legend and without a fame, beside this harbour of
Tadousac, whose history, along a thin but strong cord of sequence,
can be traced back for a thousand years, and whose connection
with Europe is older than the name !

Passing into the more substantial structure of history
we find three names standing out with prominence in
the narrative of our river : Cartier, the Pathfinder ;
Champlain, the Father of French colonisation ; Frontenac, the Saviour of New France. Fortunately the first
two left very full accounts of their discoveries, that of
the second being especially valuable in the detail and
fulness of his descriptions of the new country and its

denizens. Even if not as complete, no narrative given to the eager seekers after knowledge at that anxious period threw so much light upon the New World as the *Bref Récit* of the redoubtable Breton who was foremost of this trio.

The opening of the sixteenth century was the dawning of a new day upon the long, moonless night of the Middle Ages. Columbus had startled Europe with the outcome of his hazardous voyages, and Spain, reaping the glory, stood at the head of the leading Powers of the civilised world. What Rome had done in the van of conquest Castile promised to repeat. In his overflow of exultation her king very magnanimously divided the earth with the king of Portugal, who was disposed to believe he had a joint interest in the matter, and their popes issued a papal bull to that effect. The spirit of the times and the audacity of kings is shown by the ruler of France, who went Ferdinand one better by laying claim to all of the New World. Thus we see marked upon the maps and globes of that day the continents of North and South America under the name of " New France ! "

The assumption for this bold claim was based upon the discoveries of Verrazzano in 1524, and those of Jacques Cartier, 1534–36. As the first of these intrepid navigators only sailed along the coast of the unexplored country, I have no occasion to speak of the fruits of his voyages. Those of the latter have a direct bearing upon the subject in hand, for he penetrated so far into the interior as to become not only the discoverer but the explorer of the St. Lawrence.

Little is known of Cartier outside of his voyages to America. He belonged to a race of hardy fishermen, and had, it is claimed, made several fishing voyages between St. Malo and the shores of Labrador, until he had become imbued with the idea that it would be worth his while to penetrate into the interior of the country, whose shores, if inhospitable and forbidding, yet beckoned him hither with the finger of mystery. Others speak of him as a corsair. Let which will be right, or both for that matter, it is certain he was a bold navigator, who had sailed the seas to such an extent he had created for himself a confidence among his friends and patrons that he was equal to the undertaking of leading the way for any enterprise France might undertake in the unknown West. He was in the prime of life, being forty-three years of age at the time he proposed his daring scheme, and the opportunity was propitious. Central Europe was shaken by the spirit of a religious revolution. Germany was under the rod of Luther, and France was trembling before the attacks of Calvin. In both cases Catholicism was the sufferer and it was argued that the success of Spain was due largely to her fidelity to this church. Thus Francis the First, King of France, whose piety was equalled only by his political ambition, eagerly seized upon the prospect of recompensing his church for its loss in the Old World by opening up a field in New France.

JACQUES CARTIER.

THE VOYAGE OF JACQUES CARTIER TO CANADA, 1534.
From an old print.

St. Malo stood upon a peninsula, whose point ran out into the water so as to form a small harbour, left nearly dry at the ebb of the tide, which went out with a roar and rush quite terrific. Naturally the men of such a place were experienced sailors, and it is certain none stood higher than the master pilot, Jacques Cartier, who upon the morning of April 20, 1534, felt his heart bound with freedom as the tide lifted upon its mighty bosom his small vessels, and bore them resolutely away upon their long voyage. Among the friends who bade the departing sailors a hearty god-speed, not even the most sanguine could have dreamed of the outcome of the undertaking.

The passage of the Atlantic was made without serious delays, but off the shore of Newfoundland, Cartier experienced such stormy weather that, after going as far as the Strait of Belle Isle, he was fain to turn south, by this manœuvre accomplishing the first navigation of the coast. Rounding the Magdalene Islands he entered the gulf, and sailing along the shore of Prince Edward's Island, he made on the 8th of July the Bay of Chaleur, giving it the name by which it is now known from the excessive heat of that day.

The exact course followed by him after this is not clearly shown, though this is a matter of small importance. Where the land juts out into the gulf as a sort of dividing line between that body of water and its generous affluent, he landed to implant the first cross upon the shores of the New World. To appease the fears of the wondering natives he explained that he was doing it as a beacon-post for other voyagers likely to follow him.   Then, enticing two of the men on board and impressing them as pilots, he sailed away from the solitary but magnificent shore, whose scenery has not yet been appreciated save by an occasional artist who has reached the ancient hamlet of Ste. Anne des Monts and Cape Gaspé.   It has its own peculiar attractions, however, and the day cannot be far distant when the southward tide of tourists will find them, and the quiet simplicity of the humble fisher- and farmer-folk will be swallowed up in the train of modern fashion and revelry.

Highly elated over his pious accomplishment at Cape Gaspé, Cartier sailed proudly up the gulf, coasting along the shore of the island of Anticosti.   But he failed to realise that he was within the sweep of the flood of the St. Lawrence, and thus missed the knowledge of a discovery of the great waterway bringing its offerings from its vast system of inland seas nearly two thousand miles distant.   He was nine weeks in making this exploration, and, after repassing the lonely strait which had led him into the gulf, bore away for his homeland. If he carried with him little to encourage his King in another enterprise of the kind, he had accomplished, in fact, from having paved the way for future voyages, more than he could have foretold.

The following spring Cartier started on his second voyage, his one aim and instruction this time being to carry Christianity to the heathen. One cannot help speculating, without intending sarcasm, as to whether there was not quite as much necessity for this work upon his ships, inasmuch as his crew was made up largely of criminals pressed into his service. Letting that, which is really none of our concern, alone, the weather on this voyage was adverse, so his little fleet of three caravels was scattered before he could bring them safely to the shores of the new country. It was late in July when he again entered the Strait of Belle Isle, on the Labrador coast, and sought safety in a small harbour he christened the " Bay of St. Lawrence " (Saint Laurens), the first appearance of this name which was later to be applied to both gulf and river.

Soon the doughty Breton resumed his onward course, hugging the southern shore, along a river eighty miles in width. With what awe he watched the surrounding scene may be imagined, believing, as he did, he had at last found the passage to Cathay, the Mecca of the dreams of every voyager of that day. As his brave little craft plunged boldly along the coast frowning cliffs, bleak, barren, forbidding, frowned down upon him, and then he came abreast of the stern bulwarks of the Gaspé range, whose watchmen, the Shicksaws, tower like huge giants vainly climbing to reach the sky that bended low over their crests as if eager to meet them half-way. Over all hung the silence of forest and mountain, the restless sleep of river and sea.

Farther away, upon the other hand, rose rocky walls

that formed mighty barriers to the mysterious wilderness beyond. Broken here and there with huge rents, gorges, and chasms, these defiles only served to reveal the mightier breastworks beyond thrown up by nature in her defence against the incursions of explorers. What a grand sight! Grey rocks, piled tier upon tier; sombre forests, looming terrace above terrace; the vague, mist-like outline of mountains beyond. Over all hung the shifting tints of light and shade. Now the bright-hued beams of breaking day illuminated pine and spruce, brilliant maple, dazzling poplar, and the deep green of the cedar. At noontide this crimson and pink became intensified with the gorgeous brightness of midday. Anon, the atmosphere of evening glorified all with many tints, splashing the landscape with an added transparency of gold and silver upon green and brown, russet and purple, the lighter shades swiftly taking on the deeper hues as the sun sank behind the distant ranges, each halo forming a distinct band of shadows. These, too, proved of short life and shifting shades, for the rising moon touched them with her magic wand, sending them deeper and deeper into the gorges and ravines from whence they had sprung, as she ascended the stairway of the sky.

As he progressed, bold headlands thrust, ever and anon, their solemn fronts far out into the water, and then these gave way to long, level reaches, marking the outer boundaries of some bay or deep swamp, the resort of innumerable birds, the most prominent of which were great flocks of crows, whose flight darkened the sun. Then the mountain breeze, tempered with the aroma of a perennial forest, kissed away the damp of the salt-sea spray from his brow, and exchanging the plaintive swish of the moaning tide for the soughing of the west winds through the groves of fir and pine, he passed boldly through the open gate to Canada, leading the way into the primeval fastness for the bold *voyageurs* who were to follow in his wake.

"What river is this?" asked Cartier, of his dusky pilots,—the two natives whom he had taken captive the year before,—as he stood with uncovered head, beginning to realise that his dream of a passage to India was fading away. The red man, with solemn dignity becoming his reply, answered:

" A river without end."

Now Cartier moved slowly and cautiously along the great river, which he felt certain must come from the interior of the continent. His dark-hued companions told him many wonder stories of the strange region to the north, over which roamed the tribe of Montagnais, or "mountaineers," so frequently written of by the Jesuit missionaries in after years. These Indians had been long at war with the Innuits. They evidently had come at some remote period from the north and west. To the south-west of the Ungava district dwelt the Little Whale River Indians, more mild in their conduct than the others. They were boatmen of extraordinary skill. In their birch-bark canoes, which had a higher curve at prow and stern than others gave to theirs, so as to cut better the foaming current, they outrode winds and waves that would appall the hearts of braver, but less skilled, canoe-men. Then there were the Koksoak Indians, whose leading trait was their ability to carry on a long-distance conversation. Through an inflection of speech, peculiar to them, they could raise their voice to such a pitch that they could make themselves understood by their companions who might be more than a mile away, while each alternate word would sink to a whisper. These Indians were also, and are still, noted for their exactness in imitating the cries of wild geese. In doing this some of the men will make one note, and others follow with the variations. It is claimed by ethnologists that all of these families of Amerinds belong to the Cree stock, their difference in customs and language being due to their environments.

The scene along the south shore was less suggestive of the sublime and fiercer elements which reigned over the northern country, the realm of the foaming torrent and the warring wilderness. Here were to be seen at times wide breadths of lowland forests, with a framework of mountains in the distance. To-day there is an almost continuous chain of fisher hamlets, farm-houses, villages, diamonded by church spires, marked by windmills, groves of trees, and green meadows, whose bosoms are knotted with silvery streams winding sluggishly down to the sea.

Chapter III

The Lower St. Lawrence

The Oldest Town in America—Legend of Percé Rock—A Glimpse of the Saguenay—Cartier Reaches Stadaconé, the Original Quebec.

THIS lower section of the Great River of Canada
is the birthland of the gods and heroes of
the picturesque Amerinds, whose myths and
legends have not yet fled before the searchlight of civilisation, so there is not a spot without its warrior
dream and some allusion to that day when the land was
peopled by a race with an unwritten history.   Here,
long before the coming of Cartier and his successors,
the most poetical and chivalrous of the explorers of
America, was waged many a sanguinary battle for the
lordship of. these fruitful hunting-grounds and fisheries
between the Micmacs, Malecites, Abnakis, Montagnais,
Souriquois, and others.   Nor did these tragedies cease
with the coming of the white conquerors, themselves
made up of many families.   From where lies grim
Anticosti, swathed long nights in its cloaks of mist, disclosing with the sunlight desolate shores strewn with the
wreckage of good vessels driven upon its rocks under
the stress of the furious gales prevalent off this coast,

25

there is not an island, point of mainland, or indentation of water where some wonder story does not cling, some wraith of old-time adventure does not hover. We see signs of these imprinted upon the rugged features of the inhabitants,—singular compounds, it would seem, themselves of the ancient *voyageur* and the latter-day farmer- and fisher-folk.

The oldest French name on the continent is "Breton," supplied by a Portuguese cartographer in 1520, in memory of the hardy fishermen from Brittany, who had been in the habit of visiting, for an unknown period, the place on their fishing trips. Gaspé can claim a greater honour, as it has reason to be considered the most ancient town founded by Europeans in America, if it is true the Vikings had a fishing station here in the tenth century, five hundred years before Columbus went forth to rediscover the New World. Velasco, the Spanish navigator, is supposed to have visited the bay in 1506. Cartier, as I have already shown, was there in 1534, taking possession of the surrounding country in the name of the King of France, and leaving as a monument of his easy conquest a cross thirty feet in height, decked with the fleur-de-lis of his native land. If the Latin race proved poor colonisers, so did the Gallic adventurers, and it was left for the Anglo-Saxons to accomplish what the others had failed to do. Fortunately the earlier feelings of racial dislike have gradually softened, and out of the union has come a strong and virile people, working harmoniously together for their common good toward building up a nation destined to become a power in the world.

Gaspé Bay is about twenty miles in length, and ends in a basin large enough to shelter a fleet of a thousand vessels, so it is worthy of the notice it attracted in the days of exploration, when the first object desired was the safety of the ships.

It is easy to imagine the feelings of these doughty voyagers as they gazed for the first time upon that grey obelisk five hundred feet in length and nearly three hundred feet in height, known as Percé Rock. Rising from the water in the distance like a pillar of solid stone, when they drew nearer a lofty arch opened, as if the massive walls had been swung ajar by the Omnipotent Hand. Some rocks lose their startling shapes upon closer approach, and the air of mystery melts into the clear sunshine, robbing each point and fissure of unlikely pictures. But this one manages to increase the vividness of its setting, until it requires no grievous strain of the imagination to feel that you are gazing upon the outer wall of some old granite castle long since depleted of its tower and temple. This illusion is enhanced by the dark broadsides of a mountain in the background, whose top is as square as if it had been chopped off by a single stroke from the mighty axe of Glooscap or some other weird deity of the aborigines of this vicinity. As usual where nature reigns supreme, rock and water and mountain blend together so as to form one grand and perfect whole. Throw over this the broad bars of the setting sun, and an atmosphere that only the clear air of this hyperborean temperature can produce, and you have obtained a most remarkable effect of a remarkable scene.

Beyond this the same sunset is flooding a long, huge pile of brownish ledge of rock, cutting in twain a tide that rolls majestically over fifty fathoms of water. This last is Bonaventura Island, which has been beating back for unnumbered ages the white-maned cavalry of the sea, until its high walls bear the marks of the inroads of these invincible legions, which in the end must become its conquerors though that day is still far removed.

Romance delights to cluster around such spots, and Percé Rock is not devoid of interest in this direction. The sweetest, saddest, of these stories still told by the fishermen of this locality is the account of the fair Breton maid who lost her life here, and whose white wraith is still to be seen hovering over the fateful place at certain times when the sun's light dips just so far and no farther over the rim of the distant mountain. She is seen but a moment, and sharp and quick indeed must be the eye of him who catches a glimpse of her. Those who have been so fortunate declare that her form is clearly outlined, and that she is very beautiful.

It has been nearly two hundred years since her earthly figure assumed the spiritual. Her lover—for, like most of the delightful folklore of this region, hers is a love-story—was among the early voyagers who came to seek his fortune in the wilds of the American wilderness in the valley of the storied St. Lawrence.

GASPÉ BASIN.

PERCÉ ROCK.

She was his promised bride, and fain would have accompanied him upon his hazardous journey, but he deemed it best for her to remain behind until he should send for her.   Upon reaching Quebec he soon arranged for her coming, and sent her word to come by the next vessel.   She obeyed gladly, but the ship upon which she sailed was captured by Spanish corsairs, and she of all the crew was spared, as it proved, for a worse fate. Her beauty had so captivated the pirate captain that he soon announced his purpose of making her his wife. She refused to comply with his demands, and, finding his threats could not move her, he swore that she should never reach Quebec.   Furthermore, he would sail past the town upon the rock, and in sight of its walls and the home of her lover she should be put to death.   This fate so preyed upon her mind that as the vessel entered the waters of the Great River she escaped her watchers and sprang overboard.   The efforts put forth to effect her rescue were in vain, but later, as the ship was sailing past this rock, the lookout discovered what appeared to him as a woman just arisen from the water, her clinging garments dripping with the salt spray.

It was the hour of sunset, and attracted thither by some mysterious power, the vessel slowly approached the figure luring them on.   In the midst of this advance it was discovered that the ship was slowly sinking, though she had appeared to spring no leak !   In vain her frantic commander shouted his orders to wear away from the haunted spot.   In vain did his frenzied crew

endeavour to obey. It was soon found that the hulk of
the ship and themselves were turning into stone! The
masts became uplifted pillars of iron, and the sails were
transformed into sheets of slate! While she drifted
with invincible power toward the fateful rock she continued to sink deeper and deeper into the tide. Before the seamen and their officers could leap overboard
they were changed to bodies of stone. Then, as the
doomed vessel collided with the rock, in some mysterious manner she became a part of it! Yonder point of
ledge is said to have been her bowsprit, but time and
tide have dimmed her outlines somewhat, though there
was a day when she could be plainly discerned. If the
ship has lost its identity in the rock the wraith of the
unfortunate maiden still lingers over the place. It is
believed now she, too, will depart when the last vestige
of the ship shall have vanished. The fisherman who
tells you this legend of Percé Rock may vary its details
somewhat, for no two tell it alike, but in one respect all
will agree. No one will hazard his luck by dropping a
line for fish at the sacred hour when its white visitant
is expected to appear.

Even this has come since that distant day when
Cartier, still wondering, still anxious, kept on his lonely
way, the swish of a leaping fish clearing at a bound yards
of water and air, the calling of a pair of gulls in the language known only to them, the deeper call and answer
of a couple of loons far out over the water, the plashing
of some white whales disporting in the tide, plunging

about like porpoises, while giving utterance to a deep, lowing sound like a cow calling to her calf, the sounds breaking upon the solemnity of his lonely advance. As he sailed on, the distant walls of the forest, which Ruskin has compared to a mighty cathedral, with painted windows and hung with illuminated manuscripts, gradually drew nearer, the silence unbroken by the clink of a surveyor's chain, and where the industrious beaver, which was unconsciously to become such a potent factor in opening up this wilderness, now plied its craft undisturbed, save when that being, half-human, half-satyr, silently set his traps for it and clothed his dusky form in its skins.

In turn the bronzed and bearded voyager passed the silent places where stand to-day the quiet hamlets of Ste. Anne de Monts, named for another bold navigator as well as in memory of a saint, past Cape Chat, Metis, the favourite resort of romantic lovers, Rimouski, noted for its cathedrals, picturesque Bic, and many other places of modern interest, to stay his progress at last where a tremendous break appeared in the mountain range on the north, making a gigantic gateway opening into the mysterious region beyond, a fitting passage to the underworld.

He had been looking for this gloomy passway, for the Indians of Gaspé had awakened his curiosity with wild stories of marvellous mines and stores of gems lying behind the rock-wall, to be reached only by a river that flowed through a cavern. His Indians with him

told him this was that river,—the Saguenay,—and on the
1st of September, 1535, he anchored his little fleet
in St. Catherine's Bay around Point Noire.   His pilots
told him the country far to the north was inhabited by
a race with white skins, and who clothed themselves in
wool.   Great wealth lay hidden in the earth in that
region.   Seeing little evidence of it here, and having
little relish to brave the frown of the hills about him
by entering the silence of the sublime gateway, Cartier
speedily headed up the river, until at last he came in
sight of that rocky escarpment which was the site of the
first settlement of natives he had seen since entering
the river.   This he was told was the "great town of·
Stadaconé," where dwelt the mighty chief Donnacona
and his followers.   He saw only a cluster of bark camps
covering the rocky outpost of barbarism, clothed in the
majesty of supreme silence and breathing the stern
poetry of the wilderness.

Passing the Isle of Orleans, which so abounded
with grapes that he named it the Isle of Bacchus, the
ships, which already had awakened the keenest interest
of the dusky watchers on the lookout, glided to anchorage.   In an incredibly short time the water swarmed
with the birch-bark boats of these amazed Indians, who
climbed upon the decks of the new-comers with undisguised curiosity, even the chief forgetting the dignity
of his kingly position and joining his rabble of followers
in their childish wonder at the strangers, who they
were inclined to believe were superior beings.   A few

trinkets, some wine and cake, were sufficient to secure their friendship, and without loss of time Cartier, with a few chosen companions, approached the rocky promontory in a boat, soon reaching that harbour which has since been the port of so many inland ships. Guided by the dusky natives he made the summit by a circuitous path, when for the first time upon record a European gazed upon that wonderful panorama of country unfolded to this day to him who stands upon the embattled heights. He saw, as one sees to-day, far below him the harbour, sparkling like a silver buckler in the clear northern light; beyond, the bold front of Cap Tourmente; on the north and east he looked upon a crescent of primeval forest where we look calmly down upon the farms of peaceful people, framed in now, as then, by the mountains whose blue vies with the azure of the horizon; on the south-east, with the Isle of Orleans forever breasting the current of the mighty river a little to the left, he gazed upon the unpeopled highlands of Point Levi; from above, and of greater interest to him than all else, moved the slow-coming stream, bringing its tribute from the great storehouse of the west. A nobler or more picturesque expanse of country was never disclosed to the gaze of an explorer. But even he could not foresee that this spot was to become the site of America's greatest fortress, where the proudest warriors of the Old World were to be marshalled in after years to decide the fate of the empire of which he was to lay the corner-stone of discovery.

Chapter IV

The Primitive Capital of Canada

Cartier Keeps up the River to Hochelaga—Ascends Mount Royal—Description of the Stronghold of the Amerinds—Returns to France—Coming of Roberval—His Failure—Romance of the Isle of Demons.

CARTIER had already been informed that a town larger and of more importance than Stadaconé was situated farther up the river, and was known as Hochelaga. Received here with friendliness, and having a lingering hope in his bosom that he was still on the broad road to Cathay, the bold pathfinder soon pushed bravely ahead, promising the dusky chieftain of the town upon the rock that he should return. It is possible this promise afforded the aged king little cause for rejoicing, as it is said that he displayed evident feelings of relief when he saw the strangers heading away in the wake of the westering sun. Be that as it may, their minds were too deeply engrossed with the wonders of the new land to take into consideration the effect their coming or going might have upon a small confederation of untutored men.

Upon the morning of October 2nd he was warned of his approach to the primitive capital of the wilderness by the appearance of a great crowd of half-naked

RIVIÈRE DU LOUP FALLS.

CARTIER'S VISIT TO HOCHELAGA, 1535.
From an old print.

natives, who rapidly gathered along the banks upon sighting them, and began to display wild antics which he easily imagined to mean both surprise and welcome. In the background was a high eminence of land, and at its foot they saw fields of maize, melons, and beans, showing that the people were to a certain extent agriculturists. Some of the early writers describe them, as well as those at Stadaconé, as belonging to the Iroquois. Others say they were Hurons. It does not seem to matter which were right, as another race occupied both towns when, years later, Cartier's successor visited them.

Cartier described his reception as most cordial by the natives, who seemed to look upon him and his followers as superior beings. The best they had was placed before the visitors, while the sick and crippled were brought to be healed. The chief went so far as to place upon the brow of Cartier his crown of wild vines, thus acknowledging the latter as his sovereign.

The primitive town stood at the base of a hill, encircled by corn-fields, with the river and forest beyond. The village was surrounded by high palisades, after the rude form of protection common among the Amerinds. The following day, with some of his officers, and a body-guard of twenty men, Cartier visited the fortress. As they were escorted through a gate into the inclosure they found on the inside a gallery built to afford a vantage-ground from which the defenders could hurl missiles over the fence upon an

attacking enemy.   A pile of stones was placed to be in
readiness for immediate use.   In describing this stronghold of these wildwood warriors, Parkman, in his picturesque language, says :

> An Indian path led them through the forest which covered the
> site of Montreal.   The morning air was chill and sharp, the leaves
> were changing hue, and beneath the oaks the ground was thickly
> strewn with acorns.   They soon met an Indian chief with a party of
> tribesmen, or, as the old narrative has it, "one of the principal lords
> of the said city," attended with a numerous retinue.   Greeting them
> after the concise courtesy of the forest, he led them to a fire
> kindled by the side of the path, for their comfort and refreshment,
> seated them on the earth, and made them a long harangue, receiving
> in requital of his eloquence two hatchets, two knives, and a crucifix,
> the last of which he was invited to kiss.   This done, they resumed
> their march, and presently issued forth upon open fields, covered
> far and near with the ripened maize, its leaves rustling, its yellow
> grains gleaming between the parting husks.   Before them, wrapped
> in forests painted by the early frosts, rose the ridgy back of the
> Mountain of Montreal, and below, encompassed with its corn-fields,
> lay the Indian town.

Cartier spoke in glowing terms of the height of land
behind this lodgment, and the thought of the view from
its summit must have been in his mind during his visit
to the palisaded town, as he improved an early opportunity to make its ascent, led by a few of the red men,
and followed by a mob.   He had named it at first sight
"Mont Royale," a designation since easily transposed
into Montreal, the name of the city that stands upon the
site of ancient Hochelaga, the primitive metropolis of

the Canadian wilds.   From its crest he looked out over
the great green roof of the boundless west, which was
for centuries the battle-ground of rival races.   No voice
of prophecy came up to him from the savage silence
saying that the canopied desert at his feet was destined
to produce in its time the towers, domes, and spires,
congregated roofs, and bright walls of the city of a
civilised people.   While he gazed up and down the
broad river rolling toward the sea, and its tributary, the
tumultous Ottawa,—if smaller, scarcely less impressive,
—he must have seen but dimly the realisation of any
hope to reach that Cathay, for ever in the minds of the
early voyagers.

It was now too late in the season for him to dally
longer here, as much as he may have wanted to do so,
and on the 11th of October he was back again at his
station on the St. Charles River, just below Stadaconé,
and called by him Havre de Sainte Croix, in many
respects greatly pleased with his trip.   He now prepared to spend the coming winter here.

The experiences which followed, during what he
termed " the white winter," were severe enough to have
discouraged a less energetic leader.   Soon after the cold
weather had set in, which was a revelation in itself to
these men of France, a disease resembling the scurvy
broke out among the natives.   This dread malady soon
spread among the French, until there was scarcely a
man able to keep about.   Before the warm weather
brought relief twenty-five had perished.   Probably the

lives of the survivors were saved by drinking a bever-
age prepared by the Indians which they called *ameda*.
This was supposed to have been brewed from pine
boughs and bark.   Beyond question it had a soothing
and beneficial effect.

With the coming of spring the handful of emaciated,
disheartened French found courage in the thought of
returning to France, and as soon as the river began to
clear of ice they prepared to make the homeward trip.
One of their vessels was so badly disabled in coming
that it was looked upon as quite unseaworthy.   But
this made little difference, as there were really barely
men enough left to man the other two.   So they decided to give the condemned ship to the natives.

Feeling it his duty to leave here some monument of
his visit, on the 3rd of May Cartier planted a new
cross upon the shore of the river and placed upon it a
notice of his claim to the country in the name of his
king, couching his notice in the following words:
"*Francis Primus, Dei Gratia Francorum Rex
Regnat.*"

Having accomplished this purpose he next performed an act less humane.   This was nothing less
than the seizure of the poor king of the little band who
had treated him in such a friendly manner through the
most trying winter of his life, and four of his subjects,
having enticed them on board of his ship under the
pretence of friendship.   Perhaps he excused this deed
to his conscience upon the ground that it would be

necessary to have some proof of the kind to offer his sovereign at home.

Though indignant at this outrage the Indians offered first to ransom their chieftain. This being firmly declined, they resorted to force, when Cartier outwitted them by compelling Donnacona to stand up in sight of them, and declare that he was not displeased with the treatment given him. Another year they might look for him back again, with wonderful stories to tell and laden with many beautiful presents. These artful words, with a few simple presents flung to them, together with the proffer of the abandoned vessel, so far appeased the red men that they allowed the abductors to depart without further molestation.

This act closed the more noteworthy incidents of Cartier's second voyage. Certainly this time he had not made any discovery that was likely to benefit his King. While there had been held up before the gaze of Cartier at all times the alluring picture of a land abounding in gold and precious gems, covered with a forest filled with wonderful creatures, not the least among them being a race of white men who walked on one leg and lived without food, he had really found a country clothed most of the time under the white mantle of winter, peopled by a race of savages; and, if he had made strange discoveries, he had reaped a whirlwind of disease and disappointment. So his mind was not wholly free from trouble, any more than the abused king and his companions who had accompanied him as captives, the one party looking back with bitter regret at the cabin walls they were never to look upon again, and the other with mingled joy and sadness upon the lonesome emblem of Christianity entwined with the fleur-de-lis of their native land, all they had left to speak of their year of hardships.

Cartier designated the stream which he had discovered "the river of Hochelaga," or "the great river of Canada." The former term was no doubt an Indian word, applied by them to a collection of cabins or wigwams; as we should use it, a town or village. In the journal of this voyage he says explicitly, " *Ills appellent une ville Canada.*" This word belonged to the Iroquois tongue, with this meaning, and it was the same in the speech of the Mohawks, which was a dialect of the other. Cartier limited the application of the name "Canada" to the country about Stadaconé, while he designated that below as "the country of the Saguenay," and that above as "Hochelaga."[1]

In his description of the river he had discovered the voyager from St. Malo declared it was "the greatest river that is ever to have been seen." So his narrative

---

[1] The cartographer Ortelius published in 1572–73 a map of America, upon which he applied the name of "Saguenai" to the country about the river which still bears that name; "Canada," to the country above and reaching to the Ottawa; "Moscosa," to the district south of the mouth of the St. Lawrence and east of the Richelieu; "Chilaga" (Hochelaga), that near the mouth of the Ottawa; "Avacal," to the south and west of the Moscosa country; "Norumbega," to Maine and New Brunswick. He followed others in giving the name of New France to all of North and South America.

flashes out with wild visions of the country, the whole inflated with superstition, which was a prevalent leavening in the accounts from most of the explorers of that period. He brought, too, specimens of the gold and diamonds that were said to abound so plentifully in the land. But his former patron, Charbot, had fallen into trouble; his King had all he could do to look after his wars and affairs nearer home. His "gold" proved spurious; his "diamonds," valueless quartz. So Cartier's account did not find sufficient response to enable him to return on his third voyage, as he had hoped. In fact, so slowly did the importance of his discovery impress itself upon the King and his subjects that it was not until 1544 that the first fruit of his work appeared as a map, while the narrative of his second voyage was not published till a year later. Neither seemed to have afforded the Government any satisfaction, and the publication of both was not only suspended, but all copies that had been put out which could be found were secured and destroyed. It is now supposed that only one copy of the map and his *Bref Récit* of 1545 have been preserved. The first of these is to be found in the Library of Paris, having been recovered in Germany, and the other still exists in the British Museum. (Parenthetically, it may not be out of place to say that the map is believed by some to be a copy of the original.) It was in reality sixteen years after Cartier had completed his voyages that the French people were made acquainted with his work, and

then through an Italian author named Giambattista
Ramusio.

In the meantime Cartier was not inactive.   At Fontainebleau, January 15, 1540, Francis signed the papers
which made one of his favourites, Jean François de la
Roche, a Picard seigneur better known by the designation of his vast estate as Roberval, Vice-Royal over
the country discovered by Cartier.   What was of more
importance than this, he placed to his credit 45,000
livres.   Even under such encouragement this nobleman
from Picardy dallied so with starting upon his enterprise that the King felt obliged to return to Cartier,
whom he had neglected, and he appointed him pilot and
captain-general of the expedition.   The latter showed
that he was equal to the trust, and, though Roberval
still delayed, on the 23rd of May, 1541, Cartier, in command of three vessels, set sail on his third voyage,
leaving his superior to follow at his leisure.

Again he met with a stormy passage of the Atlantic,
and his ships were scattered, but fortunately reunited
before making the "great river."   For the second time
he drew near the tower of rock overlooking the foam-
flecked water at its base.   There had been no apparent
change in the scene.   On the summit of this natural
lookout, commanding a wide view of the surrounding
country, under the oak and walnut trees, still stood the
primitive dwellings of the people who were the keepers
of the wilderness.   It was evident they had been looking for him a long time, and had discovered the sails of

his caravels from afar, as they flocked upon the shore and swam out to meet him as he drew near. Their first demand was to meet their King, whom they had missed for over five years.

Cartier told the truth when he informed them that he was dead, adding, as a saving grace, that he had died strong in the faith of the white man's religion. The French captain dared not risk too much upon the truth, so he denied that the others had also fallen victims to disease, but declared that they lived, had married white women, and were so well contented with their new life that they had refused to come back. They had, however, sent kindly greetings to their old companions. These answers served their purpose, though the astute commander could see that he had lost largely the confidence of the red men.

This time he selected a harbour twelve miles farther up the river, near Cap Rouge, where he established a fort he named Charlesbourg. Rumours reached him of an intended attack on the part of the Iroquois at Hochelaga, and, while these did not prove true, he passed a rather uncomfortable season. As soon as their fortifications were completed, leaving the command here with one of his trusty followers, Cartier started up the river with two boats to continue the exploration he had begun on his previous voyage. His discoveries did not add materially to his knowledge, but it was late in October when he returned, to find his followers gloomy and distrustful. Nothing had been seen of Roberval; the

Indians had continued to hold aloof, if not displaying
open hostilities; and with the winter already setting in,
it was natural a spirit of homesickness should prevail.
Nothing more hopeful, however, could be done than to
wait until spring, when their leader promised them to
return to France.

Fortunately they were better prepared for the cold
weather than on the previous occasion, while the winter
seems to have been less severe. At any rate they
apparently suffered less, and another May-day found
them sailing once more down the river on their homeward voyage. Again the grand scenery of the lower
St. Lawrence was passed, the rocky islets nearly hidden
behind clouds of screaming sea-fowls left behind, and
their staunch little ships stood boldly down the gulf.
Upon approaching the harbour of St. John, whither
they had been attracted by several fishing vessels lying
at anchor, Cartier was taken aback to discover the fleet
of Roberval, who had left France upon the 16th of
April, with three ships and two hundred colonists.

Cartier was quickly ordered to retrace his course, the
Viceroy assuring him that, with the large number of
colonists aboard his ships, little trouble would be experienced in establishing a settlement. But the homeward-
bound Breton, for reasons of his own, had no mind to
return to Stadaconé. Wisely keeping his peace, under
cover of the following night he stole away toward the open
sea, leaving his superior to continue his expedition as
he chose.

CARTIER ON HIS WAY UP THE ST. LAWRENCE.

MANOR DE CARTIER, ST. MALO.

Upon finding that he had been deserted, Roberval resumed his course steering toward the Strait of Belle Isle, passing on the way those ill-fated piles of rocks denominated " the Isle of Demons," believed by the aborigines to have been from time immemorial the abode of a giant, with more of the monster than of the human, and his satellites, who lived upon children and young women.   Over the ill-fated place hovered, in the forms of birds and beasts, the spirits of the slain, forever haunting the dead slayers.   It seemed destined that the French explorer was to add another wonder tale to the gruesome list already accumulated.   This time it was a love romance, which doubtless had some groundwork of reality, as it is told with great gravity by the historian of this expedition, M. Thêvet.   Shorn of its superstitious adornments the story runs somewhat as follows :

Among the Viceroy's passengers was his niece, an extremely comely maiden by the name of Marguerite, who had a lover upon the vessel.   When this fact was made known to Roberval he was so enraged that he declared that she must either forswear her lover or suffer banishment from the ship.   This she refused to do, and soon after, coming abreast of the haunted isle, he caused her to be put into a boat.   Giving her four arquebuses with which to defend herself from demons, and a scanty allowance of food, she was set adrift, accompanied by her old nurse who would not be torn from her.   While this was being done her lover, proving himself as faithful as she, managed to escape the

watchful eyes of the commander, and followed her to
the island.   Exulting over what he had done, a deed
that the old chroniclers say doomed him to everlasting
disappointment, Roberval sailed on his way up the St.
Lawrence.

Letting alone the imaginary perils from the haunting
demons ever trying to assail them, the fortunes of the
marooned lovers, and their faithful old friend were
extremely hard to bear.   With their arquebuses they
managed to kill enough of the birds and beasts to live
upon during the long months that followed.   Then
came the sufferings of the long, intense cold of the winter.
Then another spring, and with it came another life to
care for, and the Crusoes grew doubly anxious.   Wilder
and fiercer than before did the demons wage their
ceaseless warfare to get possession of the babe, which
they seemed to look upon as their especial prey.   But
the mother's heart was strong, and the Virgin, to whom
she prayed almost constantly, had pity upon her.   The
child was spared for a time to cheer their loneliness,
but the father lost courage, and, sickening, died that
summer.   As well as they could the two women laid
his worn-out form to rest.   Soon after the little one,
too innocent for such a life, pined away, and its little
body was laid beside that of its father.   The elder
woman lived through another winter, and then she laid
down her burden, when poor Marguerite was left alone
with her sorrow.   Several months later she descried the
sail of a fishing vessel, and, by building a fire, finally

succeeded in attracting the attention of the fishermen, who drew near the island with great reluctance, until they discovered the figure of a woman in strange attire, beckoning frantically to them. So Marguerite eventually found her way back to France, where she told her strange story, and the island became known among the French voyagers as " l' Ile de la Demoiselle."

Whether or no the curse of the demons followed Roberval for his cruel treatment of his niece, whose only sin seemed to have been artlessness in her love, he and his followers had a sorry time of it in the end. Cap Rouge, Cartier's last stopping-place was reached, and here the new-comers built their rude fort, patterned roughly after some Old - World castle, the while the dusky inhabitants of the country looked on with askance. Well they might, had they been invested with higher intellect, for never was there a stranger compound of human beings than those gathered there under one roof: officers and soldiers, artisans and sailors, noblemen and felons, women and children, for the first time undertaking their important part in the colonisation of the New World.

If they had builded well in their minds they soon found experience to be a hard taskmaster. If they had shown good judgment in preparations of defence, they had overlooked a matter of even more importance. This was in the matter of provisions. Two vessels were sent back to France with the proud tidings of their successful beginning in colonisation, but the sails of

the outgoing caravels had barely faded from the blue
expanse of the distant St. Lawrence before they discovered that the supply of food was wofully short. So
winter and famine came hand in hand, the horrors of
which outweighed the "white winter" of Cartier, inasmuch as a goodly portion of this band of sufferers
were fair women and helpless little ones. Again the
Indians came tardily to the rescue, selling them fish,
and digging roots for them, which they boiled in whale
oil. Disease was inevitable, doubling the horror, and
had it not been for the iron hand of Roberval it is not
impossible but the immigrants would have torn each
other like a pack of wolves. So sorely were they
pressed that the old narrative says the hearts of the
Indians were stirred to pity. The balance of the
account, if ever written, is lost. It could not be pleasant
reading.

Cartier had returned to France, and the following
spring, 1544, the King, getting anxious over the protracted absence of his favourite, sent Cartier to find him.
The latter was successful in so far that he succeeded
in bringing back to France a handful of wretched
survivors of an expedition which had set forth with
such enthusiasm and under such auspicious circumstances. Of the fate of Roberval there are conflicting
accounts. That he was among those rescued by Cartier
is certain. One writer says that he had not got his sur-
feit of experience in the new country, and that in 1549,
after the death of Francis the First, accompanied by his

brother Achille, he made another voyage, landing this time at the mouth of the Saguenay. From here the natives declare that he and his men passed up this river, but never came back, and that they are wandering yet somewhere in the interior. Another says he was killed in a mob in Paris. The latter is doubtless right, though he may have undertaken a second voyage to the St. Lawrence.

Cartier had made his last voyage to America. His King, in recognition of his valuable services, gave him a manor on the coast shortly removed from St. Malo, where he seems to have passed his remaining years contented and peaceful. He died September 1, 1557. Among the sea-rovers and wonder-seekers of his age, when adventurous voyagers and daring explorers were braving the perils of the trackless oceans, no one ranks higher among the French. While he had not established a single colonist in the vast country claimed by his King, to him belongs, more than to any other man, the honour of leading the way in that colonisation which was to awaken Europe to the possibilities of the new continent.

Chapter V

The Coming of Champlain

I T is not necessary to dwell upon the successive explorations that followed in the wake of Cartier, as none of them were of lasting importance until we come to the beginning of the seventeenth century. France had quite as much on hand as she could well look after during the latter half of the sixteenth century. Great Britain was now bending her energies toward establishing a foothold in America. This aroused Henry the Fourth of France to action, and the struggle between the rival Powers to gain the prize of the new country began in earnest.

By this it must not be supposed that the interval had been wholly a waiting time. The Norman and Breton fishermen had continued to ply their vocation. The sight of their sails was a common occurrence to the Indians, and they often sought them with their spoils of the hunt, eager to barter these for such trinkets and gewgaws as the strangers might offer them. In this way began an industry which was to supplant in a large measure the craft of fishing. Here were possibilities the other calling did not hold forth, with far less of danger and uncertainty. Among the early fur-traders we find two nephews of Cartier. The seekers after bearskins and beaver pelts built rude huts for their comfort on the inhospitable shores of Anticosti, while others went up the river as far as Tadousac. But in the infancy of this enterprise bitter jealousies and intense rivalries entered, until these fortune-seekers not only abused the dusky hunters upon whom they depended for their wares, but they abused each other.

The attention of men of speculative minds at home was attracted by the gaining of a monopoly of the business for twelve years by the two Cartiers, who seemed to possess something of the indomitable spirit of their uncle. Finally, at the beginning of the seventeenth century, an enterprising merchant of St. Malo, named François Gravé, but commonly spoken of as Pontgravé, undertook to colonise and explore the country upon his own account, with an eye to the profits of the fur-trade. He engaged as an associate one M. Chauvin. Pontgravé made two successful voyages, ascending the St. Lawrence as far as Three Rivers. Then, in 1603, his partner died. They had already enlisted in their interest another in the person of Pierre du Gaust, Sieur de Monts, a Gentleman of the Bedchamber to Henry the Fourth. Through his influence a patent was obtained allowing the exclusive trade of the territory between the 40th and 54th degrees of latitude.

De Monts immediately began to fit out an expedition equal to the purpose in hand. Even while this was being done, another, with a commission from the King in his pocket, was sailing up the St. Lawrence with the destiny of New France, in spite of all others, in his keeping. His name is one we shall not forget, as there is scarcely an incident in the following years with which it is not connected. He was a native of a small seaport of Brouage on the Bay of Biscay, in his thirty-sixth year, a captain in the royal navy, a favourite of King Henry the Fourth, fresh from adventures in the West Indies. Fortunately his activity, daring, and enterprise were equalled by his firmness, honesty, and cheerfulness. No one understood better than he how to relieve the tedium of a long sea voyage of that day, and no one seemed to exercise better judgment in following up his explorations and in founding his settlements. Always faithful to the charge reposed in him by his patrons, he was just to those who crossed his path. In addition to the good qualities mentioned and many others, none of which were too abundant in those trying days, he wrote with a fluent and accurate pen, carefully recording all that he saw and did. He was a Catholic without being bigoted; a soldier without being tyrannical; the one man equal to the task of founding an empire in the dream of New France. Perhaps enough has been said to recognise the sturdy figure of Samuel de Champlain.

With him was Pontgravé, who had yielded some-

SAMUEL DE CHAMPLAIN.
From the O'Niel copy of the Hamel Painting.

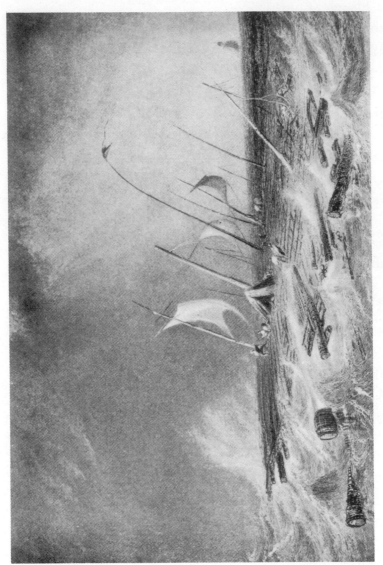

A SQUALL ON LAKE ST. PETER.
From a drawing by W. H. Bartlett.

what his ambition to De Chatte or Du Chaste, who had obtained a patent, and, as Champlain says in his journal, "though his head was crowned with grey hairs as with years, he resolved to proceed to New France in person, and dedicate the rest of his days to the service of God and his King."

With the memory of the little colony of sixteen that Chauvin had left a year before to found a trading post at Tadousac in his mind, Pontgravé desired to stop at that place. Reaching here without mishap, they found the mountains capped with fog, and the mist hanging low over the broad expanse of water, but the only sign of life which greeted their gaze was the sportive porpoises at play in the silver-crested waves. A rocky point reaching out to the south-west formed the outer wall of the bay, in which their vessels could find anchorage. Down from among the deep shadows of the lofty crags, whence the dusky canoeists had been wont to come with their freights of furs, rolled unpeopled the dark Saguenay. From out of the solitude of the place no friendly voice greeted them ; no hearty welcome from men who had long waited for their coming. Of all of Chauvin's little band of colonists, not one was ever found. It was learned from the Indians afterwards that a portion had perished of famine or disease, and the others had gone into the interior of the country in comradeship with some of their race.

As eager to escape this bleak shore as his companion, Pontgravé gladly consented to have Champlain hold his course resolutely up the St. Lawrence, looking in vain for evidence of the native population that Cartier had found sixty-eight years before. Solitude reigned primeval on every hand. The rock of Stadaconé was desolate of its bark cabins, and when they had come under the dome of Mont Royale they looked in vain for the palisaded walls of ancient Hochelaga. A few Indians, of a different tribe from those who had occupied the town, were roving about the region, like shadows haunting some beautiful vale. These greeted them with friendly frankness, and in answer to the questions of Champlain, traced for him upon pieces of bark rude outlines of the river above, with its rapids, lakes, cataracts, and islands. Then, finding himself baffled in his attempt to ascend the chain of rapids, the indomitable explorer was fain to retrace his course down the river, delaying, rather than abandoning, his resolution to penetrate the mysteries of the country that lay beyond.

Upon reaching Havre de Grace the weather-beaten voyagers learned with sorrow that their commander, De Chatte, was dead. Already Sieur de Monts had obtained his grant and been made Lieutenant-General of the vast territory stretching from the St. Lawrence to Cape May, known under the name of *L'Acadie*. Though the apparent purpose was to colonise the new country and Christianise the aborigines, it was known to be a gigantic monopoly of the fur-trade. Hence the merchants of St. Malo, Rouen, Dieppe, and Rochelle, all of which had been sending out their claimants for these privileges, raised such a remonstrance that De Monts was fain to include in his corporation De Chatte's company.

De Monts set forth upon his mission in four ships upon the 7th of April, 1604, taking Champlain along as pilot, and leaving Pontgravé to follow with supplies. Champlain's narrative goes on to describe the incongruous medley of passengers that De Monts took with him to begin his colonisation. Along with noblemen, the most prominent of whom was the Baron de Poutrincourt, were the occupants of prisons; with Catholic priests were Huguenot ministers, for De Monts was a Calvinist, though he pledged himself to convert the Indians according to the rites of the Church of Rome. Showing themselves to be more human than divine, these last fell to arguing on questions of faith, and from angry words often came to blows.

Having had a taste of the more northern clime, De Monts did not steer directly for the St. Lawrence, but, shaping his course more southerly, entered the Bay of Fundy, on the northern shore of the peninsula of Nova Scotia, where he established a post that afterwards became the site of Port Royal. Poutrincourt was so pleased with the country that he asked for a grant, that he might settle here with his family. De Monts, with half a continent at his disposal, could well afford to part with this plot. With singular infelicity De Monts selected for the site of his capital an island at the mouth

of the River St. Croix, giving the name the stream now
bears to his capital in the wilderness. Before winter
had set in willing hands had constructed a row of houses
around a square, where a solitary tree had been left
standing. In this square were the storehouses, a maga-
zine for the powder, workshops, and lodgings. De
Monts had built a more pretentious dwelling for himself,
and Champlain had followed his example. This was
barely completed when November's chill blasts began to
warn them of what was to come. Pontgravé had come
and gone to trade with the natives at Tadousac. Now
Poutrincourt started for France, promising to return in
the spring. This left De Monts's little colony by itself.
Says Parkman, in describing the situation :

> From the Spanish settlements northward to the pole, no domestic
> hearth, no lodgment of civilised men through all the borders of
> America, save one weak band of Frenchmen, clinging, as it were for
> life, to the fringe of the vast and savage continent. The grey and
> sullen autumn sank upon the waste, and the bleak wind howled
> down the St. Croix, and swept the forest bare. Then the whirling
> snow powdered the vast sweep of desolate woodland, and shrouded
> in white the gloomy green of the pine-clad mountains. Ice in
> sheets, or broken masses, swept by their island with the ebbing and
> flowing tide, often debarring all access to the mainland, and cutting
> off their supplies of wood and water. A belt of cedars, indeed,
> hedged the island; but De Monts had ordered them to be spared,
> that the north wind might spend something of its force with whist-
> ling through their shaggy boughs. Cider and wine froze in the
> casks, and were served out by the pound. As they crowded around
> their half-fed fires, shivering in the icy currents that pierced their
> rude tenements, many sank into a desperate apathy.

That disease which proved such a scourge to the
colonists, scurvy, before spring had claimed as its victims

thirty-five out of the seventy-nine. The survivors, mere wrecks of humanity, now thought only of the promised succour. In this respect they were not disappointed. On the 16th of June Pontgravé reached them with a reinforcement of forty men, and, what was yet more needed, a supply of provisions.

De Monts now lost no time in pushing the exploration which he had begun so anxiously. Champlain, who had been the one among them to face without flinching their desperate situation during the long, bitter winter, had the previous fall explored the adjoining country to a considerable extent, making a detailed account of what he saw. His commander, hoping to find some more desirable place to remove to, taking Champlain along with him, besides several of his most distinguished companions, a crew of twenty sailors, and an Indian pilot, in a bark of twenty tons, sailed down the coast of Maine and Massachusetts as far as Cape Cod, which they named Cap Blanc. Landing almost daily, the natives had treated them upon friendly terms, until one day a party of sailors, in seeking for a fresh supply of water, lost the kettle which they had taken with them. Three or four Indians had followed them, and these they accused of stealing it. Enraged at this, the natives fired upon the sailors, killing one. Immediately the crew upon the ship opened a volley upon the Indians. The arquebuse of Champlain burst, and he barely escaped being killed. The red men on the shore fled with nimble feet, and escaped uninjured. Others, who had been on board of the vessel at the breaking out of the unfortunate occurrence, sprang overboard, and all escaped excepting one, who was afterwards released.

Provisions now were running low, and De Monts prudently steered toward his infant settlement, ill-pleased with the prospect he had found. No place suited him as well as the region he had so freely granted to Poutrincourt, and he resolved to remove thither. Arriving at St. Croix in August, he lost no time in carrying out the plan of removal, as he knew only too well he had scanty time in which to make the change before winter should set in. While he was doing this a messenger came from France to inform him that rivals were endeavouring to steal the rights of his company. Leaving Pontgravé to take the command of the new settlement at the mouth of the river Annapolis, called by them the Esquille, and by others, afterwards, the Dauphin, he set sail for France. Champlain and others of his faithful followers offered to remain and brave the rigours of another winter. Fortunately these were not as severe as those of the preceding season, but the next news that reached them from France was the discouraging fact that De Monts had been deprived of his grant. Hence Champlain and his companions returned to their homeland.

If baffled for a time, the indefatigable De Monts soon recovered a portion of what he had lost. Upon the advice of Pontgravé and Champlain he sought for and obtained a monopoly of the fur-trade for one year.

The plan was, for the first, to revive the old trading station at Tadousac, and, for the latter, to establish a new station farther inland.

Two small vessels sufficed for this expedition, one commanded by Pontgravé, and which stopped at Tadousac, as arranged; the other by Champlain, which can claim the distinction of carrying to New France the pioneer colony.   He sailed from Honfleur on the 13th day of April, 1608.   This was a year before Hudson sailed from Amsterdam upon the voyage during which he was to discover the river that bears his name, and only a year after the founding of Jamestown by the English, and which at this very time was undergoing such experiences as only another of Champlain's courage and indomitable will, Captain John Smith, could have saved from utter failure.

While Champlain was not following a course entirely new to him, he having passed that way five years before, with his deep-seated love for nature he scanned closely each point of interest as he sailed up the great river. Leaving his companion at the mouth of the Saguenay, he passed the lofty Cap aux Corbeaux, which name comes from the dismal croakings of the innumerable ravens as they hover over the jagged cliffs and rock-shelves beyond the reach of the most nimble climber; under the pilotage of the Laurentian range he followed the great river up past Cartier's Isle of Bacchus, past the shimmering falls of Montmorency, to which he had given that name on his previous voyage, steadily advancing until he had entered that beautiful harbour which has since become the anchorage of so many fleets of vessels and craft of varied descriptions. His keen judgment had already told him that the site pre-eminently fitted for his purpose was the deserted Indian town upon the rock. The indentation of the river where his ship had come to anchor was protected upon the south by that rugged promotory since named the Heights of Levi, and, on the other hand, by the bold escarpment of Cape Diamond. Under its shadow, on the narrow strip of land covered with its primeval growth, the founder of the great northern stronghold, which was to become the centre of action in New France for one hundred and fifty years, stepped ashore and began his work. The very day of his landing the axes of his labourers broke the solitude of the unpeopled wilderness, their ringing sounds the speaking signals of civilisation arrived at last.

Chapter VI

Founding of Quebec.

Champlain's First Expedition against the Iroquois—Discovers Lake Champlain—
Scenery—Situation of the Five Nations—Rout of the Mohawks—Affairs at
Quebec—the Rival Factors.

THE original Quebec consisted plainly of a few
rough cabins such as a party of adventurers,
equipped with the few implements at their command, could build.   These were constructed in the form
of an open square, near the centre of which Champlain
placed on the top of a pole a dovecote, emblematical of
his peaceful intentions.   Around the group of dwellings
he raised a wooden wall, and outside of this dug a ditch,
the few guns he possessed so arranged as to command the
place.   This was a prudent policy to pursue, though
the deserted lodges of the people inhabiting this country in the days of Cartier alone haunted the rock of
Stadaconé, and the triumphant cry of the dusky warrior,
once master of these domains, found only a hopeless
echo in the dismal croak of the raven or the howl of
the wolf.

If Champlain had little to fear outside of his own followers, it soon proved that he had enemies within his
camp.   Among his men were those who hated him for

his check on the fur-trade, which they looked upon as a
legitimate source of plunder, and a conspiracy was laid
to murder him, and get control of affairs.   Fortunately
not only for the sake of Champlain, but for the weal of
the little colony, this plot was betrayed by one of its
tools, and the conspirators were treated with the usual
vigour of this energetic leader.

Presently the little settlement was visited by some
Indians from the country to the west, who frankly acknowledged that they came in the hope of enlisting the
"man with the iron breast," as they designated Champlain, for their ally in the troublesome wars they were
having with their ancient enemies, the Iroquois.   More
fully than ever before the new-comers came to realise
the deadly feud of long standing between the rival
tribes of aborigines inhabiting the country, a struggle
which had accomplished the ruin of Stadaconé and
Hochelaga.   Champlain listened to their story with a
friendly interest, knowing that it would be impolitic for
him to refuse.   For this act Champlain has been condemned, and even if there was reason to censure him
in this, it speaks in eloquent tribute to him that this
alone stands against him.   But in this it would appear
that he followed the only feasible course open to him.
Having cast his fortunes, as it were, among the Algonquins and their allies, he of necessity must become their
friend, and consequently opposed to that powerful element occupying much of the territory now included in
the State of New York, with an influence felt far beyond

their border. There was in reality no middle policy for him to pursue, though even he could not anticipate the far-reaching result to arise from his choice. This result, however, was destined to be tempered by the strength or weakness of those who were to follow him in his own path. Ay, had Champlain's successors always possessed his rugged honesty and courage of conviction, there would have been no occasion to accuse him of mistakes, or to have written whole pages of the history of New France in tears and blood.

Elated to know that they had secured such a powerful ally, the Indians immediately urged their new-found friends to accompany them upon an expedition against their dreaded enemies, whose name they frankly confessed carried terror to the most remote regions lying between the sea and the sunset plains beyond the Father of Waters and fir fringes of the frozen north. Prompted by a desire to explore the country, as well as to add to his influence with the Indian tribes of the St. Lawrence valley, Champlain joined the Hurons and Algonquins with a handful of his followers in the spring of 1609, to enter upon his first memorable raid against the Five Nations.

This expedition was made along a course afterwards to become famous in the French and Indian wars with the English, as it had been in the annals of the wildwood warfare for many generations. Keeping up the St. Lawrence to Lake St. Peter, they entered that river which lies like a broad arrow upon the landscape, reaching from the lake of the highlands since christened in honour of the leader of this band, to Canada's great river. Cartier did not have time to explore it, and passed it by without giving it a name. Champlain, knowing it had been the main highway of the Iroquois, very appropriately called it *Rivière des Yrocois*, "the River of the Iroquois," which it would have been well to keep. But, later, when the renowned Cardinal-Duke Richelieu became the head of the French commerce and navigation in New France, *Chef, Grande Maître, et Sur-Intendant Général*, it was given his name, which it still bears. In this respect it suffers no more than the lakelet forming its headwaters, whose apt Indian designation has been supplanted by the name (Lake George) of a king whose association with it is meaningless. Champlain pursued resolutely his course, as the poet tells us—

> Through woods and waste lands cleft by stormy streams,
> Past yew-trees, and the heavy air of pines,
> And where the dew is thickest under the oaks,
> This way and that; but questing up and down
> They saw no trail.

Upon getting as far as where is now the great dam of St. Ours, Champlain abandoned the undertaking for the time being. But the tidings was soon brought to him that the Iroquois, exulting over what they believed to be the fear of the allied forces, were planning to make a grand raid to recover their ancient fishing-and hunting-grounds of the valley of the St. Lawrence.

Believing that it would be well to carry war into the enemy's country, Champlain determined this time to follow the River of the Iroquois to its source. Accordingly every preparation needed was made, the Algonquins eager and anxious to encourage the expedition, realising that their possession of the Canadian paradise depended upon the success of this undertaking.

With a flotilla of twenty-four canoes, his own skiff leading the way, Champlain moved silently and cautiously under the overhanging arms of the towering oaks and walnuts that grew abundantly along the riverbanks, and anon under the deeper canopy of the wilderness of Belœil, until he came to where the stream broadens into what is now known as Chambly Basin, with its primeval intervales and deep-sounding woods. Where these last began to assume darker shades the voyagers came upon the rapids, which they were forced to pass around by the old Indian portage where now is the Chambly and St. John Canal. Just above here they came upon an island since christened Ste. Thérèse, which was then covered with a growth of pine that excited the keenest admiration of the doughty leader.

Still on they moved in solitude past where the city of St. John now stands, and then past *Ile aux Noix*, with a stirring history yet to be enacted. Noiselessly the little fleet glided around Rouse's Point, and the unsuspected vanguard of civilisation advanced triumphantly into the very battle-ground of past and future races, Lake Champlain. Now the veteran of sea and land,

the hero of many hard-fought battles, and the explorer
of many strange scenes paused with uncovered head and
unspoken applause to bend his keen gaze over the
sheet of water which was to perpetuate his name.   He
saw, rich in their summer vesture, a scene of glistening
water, wooded islands, shores banked in forests, distant
mountains groined into "great domes of foliage" such
as even he had never found before.   Woods and water
abounded with wild life, and in the lightness of heart
given by the happy mingling of Nature's gifts, he
quickly gave the order to move on into the mystery
ahead, when his swarthy and dusky rowers plied anew
their paddles, sending their light canoes swiftly over
the crystal water, little dreaming, little caring for the
horrors to follow in their wake, the wars and rumours
of wars into which were to be drawn not only the
several tribes of red men then claiming the country,
but the French, British, Dutch, and Americans.

Happily free from the burden of all this, the bold
explorer continued to watch with a critical eye his surroundings, while his rowers carried him on into the heart
of a region which it was fitting such as he should enter.

To the west lay the Adirondacks, the ancient homestead of
the Algonquin warriors who were his companions.   Their forefathers deserted that picturesque wilderness for the gentler shores
of Hochelaga, driving before them the then unwarlike Iroquois, [1]
whom Cartier had found fishing, corn-planting, and road-making.
Contrasting their own better fare with that of the improvident and
often famished Algonquins, the Iroquois had nicknamed them
Adirondacks, "bark eaters."   Once in Canada, the Adirondacks

[1] Probably that branch known as the Hurons.—AUTHOR.

became infused into the other Algonquin tribes that occupied the
banks of the Ottawa ; but the ancient nickname still happily
applies to their old mountain home.   Through Emerson's muse
these peaks have won a name in literature, as well as on maps ; but
on that morning, and long afterwards, they were "titans without
muse or name."   Then away on his left Champlain saw the soaring
peaks of the Green Mountains, which, through the French *verts
monts*, have given name to the State of Vermont.   The discoverer
remarked, though a July sun was shining, that their summits were
white with snow.

Toward midnight an Algonquin scout discovered
an Iroquois encampment at that place since become
famous as Crown Point.   Here Champlain prepared to
wage his opening battle, and just as the rays of the
morning sun were tingeing the distant forest with their
gold he and his two French soldiers stepped out upon
the headland.   Soon after, the solitude of the country
was broken for the first time by the report of firearms.
Watching this audacious approach of their enemies
from their vantage-ground some thirty yards away, the
disdain of the Mohawks was swiftly changed to terror
at the sound of that discharge of powder which sent its
death-dealing slugs into their midst.   A panic followed,
which ever rankled in the breasts of the discomfited
braves, and which was paid for over and over again in
future years, though it could not then save their town
from the ravages of the conquerors.   Considering this
victory sufficient for the time, celebrating the event
by giving his name to the lake he had discovered,
Champlain immediately retraced his course to the St.
Lawrence.

The significance of this rout of the Iroquois at
Crown Point is shown by the fact that the allied nations
of the Indians were not only undisputed masters of the
Great Lakes, but they also commanded all of the prin-
cipal rivers from the Ottawa and the Hudson to the
Mississippi.   It was estimated by La Hontan in 1684
that the Five Nations numbered seventy thousand souls,
and that they could muster nearly eight thousand warriors.   What the allied forces of Rome at the zenith of
Roman glory were to Europe, were the combined tribes
of the Iroquois to aboriginal America.   Thirty years
later a sixth tribe, the Tuscaroras, were admitted to the
league, adding materially to their strength as well as to
their numbers.   Among these shrewd, stalwart sons of
the council and the war-trail, by their boldness, sagacity,
and eloquence, the Mohawks stood at the head.

While the British, as a rule, showed greater wisdom
than the French in not discriminating between native
tribes, it was inevitable that the Five Nations, with the
beginning that had been made, should ally themselves
to a certain extent with the former.   It was also inevitable that the British should arm them, while the
French did the same by the Algonquins and the Hurons.   If the French went farther and taught the last-
named tribes the arts of defence, it was because they
intended them for allies.   Neither the whites of New
York or New England went as far as this, for they never
sought to make the Indians their allies in the full sense
of the term.

OLD FORT CHAMBLY.

From a drawing by W. H. Bartlett.

THE CHAMPLAIN MONUMENT, QUEBEC.

From a photograph by Livernois, Quebec.

The Treaty of Utrecht, 1713, held that the Iroquois Confederacy was under British protection, and through the long and bitter hostilities that followed, as a rule these tribes remained faithful to "Great Father." They proved so true in this direction that they fought against the colonists during the American Revolution, and at its close found themselves in the same situation as the Loyalists or Tories. In this dilemma they sought the protection of the Canadian government, then under British power, and were given reserves along the Grand River. Brant, at this time leader of the Mohawks, selected the fertile and beautiful valley where since the town of Brantford has sprung into existence. It was his purpose to establish here a reproduction of the agricultural community which had formerly made famous the valley of the Mohawks. Unfortunately he did not live to see his dream fulfilled. A period of peace with the red men was pretty sure to be followed by one of war, and after his death in 1807 the relapse of his tribe into paganism was speedy.

We get an inkling of the condition of the Five Nations before the coming of the French and English from the fact that prior to Sullivan's expedition of fire and sword the valleys of the Mohawk and the Wyoming were set with great grain-fields, whose nodding heads whispered of Indian thrift, and the hillsides white with apple blossoms were huge flower gardens. It was to duplicate such a homelike picture that Brant laboured so zealously, when the bloody drama of war was practically over, and if the red men failed to follow the example of their leader it was because they fell victims to their own weakness rather than to the prowess of their enemies. As a matter of fact it was the vices of civilisation which overpowered them and not its manifold strength. It has been so with all native races.

From his first expedition against the Iroquois Champlain had quite as much as he could do in making his journeys of exploration and war against the foes of his dusky allies, to say nothing of the repeated demands made upon him by the home government. Frequent changes in the control of affairs gave him not a little trouble. While remaining in France upon one of these visits he married a girl of twelve, though she did not accompany him to Quebec until 1620, the year the Pilgrims landed at Plymouth Rock. Upon his return from France in 1613 he was stirred by the report that an adventurer named Nicolas Vignan had discovered the passage to Cathay by following up the Ottawa, and thence by other great rivers he claimed to have found in the north. It proved that Champlain, not less than other explorers, still dreamed dreams of this northern passage, and he quickly set about undertaking a voyage into the north, the result of which brought him only disappointment. Still, this failure did not deter him from making other trips of exploration and war into the interior.

One of these incursions into the land of the Iroquois

proved less satisfactory to him than the victory at
Crown Point. This took him and his followers across
Lake Ontario, to where the Onondagas lived behind
the barriers of their stoutly fenced town. Filled with
an unbounded faith in the supernatural powers of their
leader, while ignoring his tactics of war, the Hurons
and Algonquins attacked wildly the defence of their
enemies and were as wildly routed. Champlain had
taught them to construct a movable tower from which
he and his companions might shoot over the walls
of the Onondagas. But, becoming furious the moment
the battle opened, Champlain's orders were drowned
by their maddening cries, and he found himself power-
less to control them. The result of the fight was
disastrous to him. He was wounded in the knee and
thigh, and the attack finally abandoned, very much to the
chagrin of Champlain, who found he had lost, through no
fault of his, the prestige he had hitherto enjoyed among
his allies. Beating a headlong retreat, the disappointed
Hurons then broke their pledge to take their leader
back down the St. Lawrence to Mont Royale. Unable
to make the journey without their assistance, Champlain
was obliged to pass the winter with the Hurons, who
treated him well, and one of their chiefs paid particular
attention to his wounds. In the spring he returned to
Quebec, where he had been looked upon as dead.

During his absence Champlain had learned considerable of Indian character which was to be of benefit to
him and his followers in the succeeding wars. From

the nature of their combats they had been trained only
to meet single foemen, or else to overpower a concealed
body of men by massing themselves.   They drilled for
such encounters by sticking pieces of wood into the
ground to represent the chiefs and their soldiers, a dif-
erence in the size of the sticks used indicating the
leaders and their followers.   Taking a bundle of these
sticks the chief would select a spot suitable for his purpose, and, having chosen his own position, mark it with
a dummy, and then place in the ground a smaller upright to show the position each of his soldiers was to
occupy.   They must then study carefully the position
assigned them.   This simple drill was practised until
every warrior was perfectly familiar with his part.   The
Hurons entered into battle nude, except for the war
paint daubed generously over their lithe forms.   Champlain described the Mohawks, whom he routed upon
the shore of Lake Champlain, as dressed in armour of
cotton fibre, which was arrow-proof.   When he came
to discharge his arquebuse at a distance of thirty paces,
loaded with four balls, he killed two chiefs and wounded
a third.   Small wonder these simple-minded sons of
Mars, who had never witnessed anything like it, should
become panic-stricken, fleeing in wild disorder at the
second shot fired by one of Champlain's men.

Meanwhile the little band of colonists at Quebec
were making exceedingly slow progress.   Fourteen
years after its establishment the colony numbered less
than fifty.   In 1617 an apothecary named Louis

Hébert, who had experienced a season at Port Royal under Biencourt, settled at Quebec, with his wife and two children, this courageous family having the honour of founding the first household in Canada. Three years later, a few months before the Pilgrims made their wintry landing at Plymouth, Champlain brought his own family to Quebec. His wife was a woman of great beauty, enthusiasm, and accomplishments, and she entered heartily into the work of converting the women and children of the Indians, and of helping to raise the standard of morals then prevailing there.

This unhappy condition of the social and intellectual life of the struggling colony was due mainly to the utter lack of honesty on the part of the fur-traders, who from the first had been a disturbing element. Meeting in Champlain a firm and powerful opponent to their nefarious purpose, they seemed to have developed the very worst phase of their character. To add to the perplexity of the situation this monopoly of the traffic was constantly changing hands. Rivals were continually coming to the surface, old favourites were driven out, and scarcely had one set of men or one corporation become established before another would enter the contention. Always were they met by Champlain, doing all in his power to save the common people and the red men from the greed and corruption of the reckless fur-traders, who hesitated at nothing to carry their unjust ends.

Champlain was obliged to cease his explorations, as loath as he was to do so. In the future this must be left to others. He had all he could attend to in looking after the welfare of his infant colony, which was about equally divided between being a trading station and a mission. Out of this bitter rivalry were to spring two factors destined to become powerful in shaping the welfare of the new empire. These can be best treated in separate chapters.

Chapter VII

From Fur-Trade to Commerce

Cardinal Richelieu and his Hundred Associates—First Surrender of Quebec to the English—Comparison of the Settlements of the St. Lawrence Valley to those of Massachusetts Bay—Trade Troubles Increase—Founding of Three Rivers—Death of Champlain—His Character—The Great Company Make Concessions—Laziness Denounced—Fisheries—Lack of Pilots—Early Ship-building—Fairs—Suppression of Knowledge—Ladies of Quebec—First News-paper in Canada—First Steamship to Cross the Atlantic—Commerce of the St. Lawrence To-day.

WHILE the two infant colonies in America that were destined to become intense rivals in years to follow—the Pilgrims at Plymouth Rock and the little band under Champlain at Quebec—were undergoing such vicissitudes as must have disheartened less courageous founders, potent changes were taking place in the affairs of France. The religious wars of the sixteenth century brought to the surface of power a French statesman named Richelieu who had begun his military education as Marquis du Chillon and rose to become the most important political figure in Europe. He was made cardinal in 1622, at the time when Champlain was meeting his trying opposition, and in his ambitious desire to add to the greatness of France, he extinguished the remains of feudalism, subjected the higher nobility to the sway of the Crown, abased the House of Austria, and in his triumph at Rochelle crushed Protestantism. The conqueror now dreamed of bending Europe to his will. Again he dreamed, and this time saw visions of an empire in the New World, which he vaingloriously believed would revivify the grandeur of Old France, and immortalise his name in the wilderness of America.

With vivid conceptions he ran over the names of the gallant discoverers,—the illustrious quartette of C's,—Columbus, Cabot, Cortes, Cartier. Now to these was added a fifth, Champlain, whose glowing accounts awakened his fertile imagination with such plots of conquest as had not stirred others. With less religious zeal than Champlain, he schemed to build upon the interest of the fur-trade. First of all, the complications surrounding this industry must be removed, and instead of many petty factions, quarrelling one with another, there must be a unity of effort. To secure this he caused to be discontinued the honourable office of Admiral of France, and created in its stead the office of Grand Master and Superintendent of Navigation and Commerce. It is perhaps needless to say that he made himself head of this. He then organised a trading company of one hundred influential men. This body became the famous Company of the Hundred Associates, and Samuel de Champlain was its strongest member.

The charter for Richelieu's company carried on its face the possession of all New France—Canada, Acadie,

Newfoundland, and Florida—and its members consisted of priests and religious workers, as well as traders and *voyageurs*. It openly declared that its first object was the conversion of the Indians to the faith of the Catholic church by its zealous teachers, the Jesuits ; in the second place, it was to extend the fur-trade ; and third, and last, to continue the search for a route to the Pacific Ocean. This was exactly reversing the order of purpose controlling the movements of Cartier, whose first object was to find the passage to Cathay.

Under the policy of this company was established that feudal seigniory which so long dominated the methods of colonisation. It thought to end the religious discords which had been such a disgraceful portion of previous efforts. No Huguenot or " other heretic" was to be allowed on its soil. The company was given a perpetual monopoly of the fur-trade, with a control for fifteen years of all other trade, except traffic in cod and whale fisheries. To those who might want to trade in furs, and who did not belong to the corporation, it was stipulated that the company should buy every beaverskin at the rate of forty sous each. The company was pledged to aid colonisation by sending out three hundred colonists the first year, and within the following fifteen years to increase the number to six thousand. As proof of its fealty and homage the company was to present each successive heir to the throne with a crown of gold. The King, as a personal tribute, presented it with two armed

battleships.   Champlain was placed in command.   The
new company then sent out a fleet of eighteen vessels
laden with provisions and commodities for the new
colony.   The command was entrusted to De Roquemont, who sailed from Dieppe for Quebec in the spring
of 1628.

This was an anxious time for the handful of inhabitants by the rock of Quebec, who were languishing
under short allowance of food and with hope at ebb-
tide.   All of Champlain's wonderful resource of tact
and good cheer was called into play in order to keep his
followers under control until the expected succour should
reach them.   But this was not destined to arrive.
England and France, as usual during the long and trying period of American colonisation, were at war, and
an adventurer named Sir David Kertk or Kirke, a native of Scotland, at one time professing allegiance to
the French but now carrying the flag of Great Britain,
sailed boldly into the harbour of Tadousac with his
fleet of six vessels.   Finding this trading station poorly
equipped to resist him, he seized and pillaged the
place.   He then sent a boat up the St. Lawrence to demand the surrender of the starving colony at Quebec.
Upon meeting an enemy seeking to destroy him, instead of some of his own countrymen coming to his
rescue, Champlain answered the new-comers boldly.
Despite the fact that he did not have fifty pounds of
ammunition, and that the walls of his primitive fortifications were sadly in need of repair, he sent word to

THE ST. LOUIS GATE, QUEBEC.
From a photograph by Livernois, Quebec.

THE FRENCH FLAG IN THE TIME OF CHAMPLAIN.

the British admiral that he should defend Quebec to the last.

Deceived by this reply Kertk abandoned for the time his scheme of attack in that direction and sailed down the river. Near its mouth he encountered and captured De Roquemont's fleet of eighteen vessels, taking possession of the supplies so desperately needed at Quebec, whose hope was shattered by this calamity. Reinforced by his two brothers and their ships, Admiral Kertk continued to hover about the gulf for awhile, and then crossed the ocean to England with his prizes.

Learning of the fate of De Roquemont and his transports, Champlain's little colony grew more and more despondent, as well they had reason to be. Their rations were reduced to seven ounces of pounded peas a day, until in May even this scanty supply failed and recourse was had to the roots that grew along the margins of the streams, last year's acorns, and the green, tender leaves of the trees. In desperation some of the inhabitants sought the friendly Indians on the west, or the Abnakis on the east. It is possible that Champlain was contemplating invading the Iroquois country, to seize one of their palisaded towns, and take up his abode there. He would be pretty sure of finding a supply of corn, which was so sorely needed here.

The season wore on into midwinter without any prospect of a relief from their friends, when the sails of three ships were discovered a league below Point Levis. There was no doubt as to the character of the strangers, but even an enemy was not likely to receive a very cold reception.   Champlain, with that display of rugged determination so natural to him, called around him his handful of ragged, hungry followers, now reduced to sixteen in number, and calmly awaited the approach of the English under the cover of a white flag.   It was not difficult to agree upon the terms of capitulation, and on July 20, 1629, the cross of St. George of England was planted for the first time upon Canadian soil.

It proved that negotiations for peace were already well under way, and England thought so little of the prize won surreptitiously by Kertk, that Champlain, still loyal to his trust, but almost alone of his countrymen, succeeded in winning back to France by the skill of his diplomacy all of Canada.   Then, it was said, the honour of France was saved, and her golden lilies were restored to the rock of Quebec.

With the romance that clusters about its name, and the mystery clinging to its history, this fair emblem of French sovereignty—this flag of Champlain—is worthy of more than passing mention.   Not unlike other insignia that have given inspiration to thousands and become the sacred symbol of the virtue of a race, the origin of the iris as the heraldic emblem of France is lost in the obscurity of distance.   So far back does tradition carry us that it becomes evident it antedates the Frankish Government.   But this does not rob the fleur-de-lis of the glory it shares with the prestige of

France. It can even claim to have originated with the beginning of Christian France. According to story, Clovis, the pagan conqueror, before entering upon his battle of Tolbiac, 496, fearful of defeat, pledged his wife Clotilda, the Christian heroine of ancient Paris, that he would accept Christianity if he should gain a victory on the morrow. Pleased with this promise, which had long been her dream, she prayed continually for his success, and her prayer was answered. Clovis continued a conqueror. Within a year he and three thousand of his followers accepted the Christian faith. Immediately upon becoming a believer in her teachings, his beautiful wife presented him a blue banner, that her own hands had embroidered with golden fleur-de-lis, and declared that as long as the kings of France should keep that as their standard so long would their armies be victorious. Others, content to give it less ancient origin, claim that the iris was a device adopted by Louis the Seventh, in 1147, just before undertaking his crusade to the Holy Land, which ended so disastrously. He may have simply revived the emblem that Clotilda gave to her illustrious husband. Let it be as it may, the iris as an emblem of wide-spread influence became popular about the middle of the twelfth century, and was conspicuous not only upon the national flag, but upon church crosses, chalices, windows of houses, seals, and sceptres.

The flag of Champlain, which was, of course, the naval standard, had a blue background, with the fleur-

de-lis in gold.   The fleur-de-lis ceased to be the
standard of France with the abdication of the citizen
King, Louis Philippe, and the rise of the republic in
1848, after an illustrious career of over a thousand
years.   It was succeeded by the tri-colour, which has
held its place through the vicissitudes of French government until the present day.

Immediately upon the signing of the Treaty of
St. Germain-Laye in 1632, Emeric de Caen, one of the
sufferers from the recent war, was sent to receive
Quebec from her captors.   To him was given the
monopoly of the fur-trade for one year, that he might
be reimbursed for his losses.   It was not a pleasant or
prosperous scene that Kertk left when he pulled
down the flag of England and sailed away, glad, no
doubt, to get well rid of his prize.   Parkman, in describing the situation, says :

> Caen landed with the Jesuits, Paul le Jeune and Anne de la Noüe.
> They climbed the steep stairway which led up the rock, and as they
> reached the top the dilapidated fort lay on the left, while farther on
> was the massive cottage of the Héberts, surrounded with its vege-
> table gardens,—the only thrifty spot amid the scene of neglect.

Few Indians remained, having found the companionship of the English less congenial than that of the
French, and those remaining here were rioting under the
maddening effects of liquor.   De Caen's occupancy of
the wilderness capital was not in accord with the aims
of the Jesuits, and when, in the succeeding spring, 1633,
the Hundred Associates again assumed control, rein-

stating Champlain as governor, rejoicing reigned among
them.   The Récollets had removed to other fields, the
Huguenots were expelled, and religious peace predomi-
nated at the settlement under the dark walls of Cape
Diamond.   The two years that followed were the
brightest Quebec had known.   Champlain was now
invested with all the power and prestige of Richelieu
and his Hundred Associates, but he was soon to find
that this could not be fully transplanted to the New
World.   In fact, he was finally forced to believe that he
had no greater expectations from the new company
than from any that had been organised before.   He
made such preparations for a defence from the Iroquois
as he could, and this called for a station at Three Rivers strong enough to check any advance down the river.
Another was needed below Quebec to prevent the English from coming up, as well as a protection against
the Indians in that direction.   It was in vain that he
asked for soldiers from France to maintain these stations.   Two aims were paramount in the minds of those
who turned their gaze upon New France.   One of these
was still the conversion of the Indians by the Jesuits, and
to carry on this work the missions here were strengthened by the coming of four priests, Brébeuf, Massé,
Daniel, and Davost.   The other was the traffic in furs,
which lasted during the summer season.   This was
not materially different at first thought from the
course being followed by the Dutch in New Netherlands,
and the English in New England.   Albany found its

greatest source of revenue from it, and large consign-
ments were annually shipped from Manhattan to
Holland. New England was maintaining its trading
posts on the borderland of the rival colonies at the
headwaters of the Kennebec. But the similarity between the last two colonies ended here. While the entire population of Canada numbered in the vicinity of
only sixty, and could boast of only two households,
fully four thousand English had settled about Massachusetts Bay, and already that tide of immigration had
begun which was to bring twelve thousand more to the
country. What was of even greater importance, these
people were home-builders. They began at once to
build ships and open commerce with distant places.

No one realised this difference more keenly than
Champlain, and in the hope of encouraging enterprise
in this direction, in 1634, he began a new settlement at
Three Rivers. He encouraged the priests in carrying
the gospel still farther west, and Brébeuf and his companions went to establish their missions among the
Hurons. In July Champlain made his last journey westward, in going to see how work was progressing upon
the fort at Three Rivers. Shortly after, Le Jeune went
to take charge of the new post. Then an epidemic broke
out which threatened to destroy the settlement. A
register of the baptisms and deaths in the hand of this
faithful priest now remains as the only document of the
old Canadian days that is in existence. The burning in
1640 of the chapel of Notre Dame de Recouvrance, built

by Champlain to commemorate the restoration of the
town by the English, caused the loss of the early records
of Quebec.

July 22, 1635, Champlain met in his last council with
the Indians at Quebec. According to their practice a
goodly number of the Hurons were present, and the
founder of New France spoke like a father to his
children. Without dreaming that the end was so near
the dusky listeners paid careful attention to all he said,
for no man was so revered among them. A little later
Champlain learned of the return from among the
Indians of the west of the young Norman explorer,
Nicollet, whose story fills so large a space in the *Jesuit
Relations* of those days. On the 15th of August he
wrote his last letter addressed to Richelieu, endeavouring to impress upon him the importance of assisting
the colony. Two months later he was stricken with
paralysis, from which he suffered until upon the after-
noon of Christmas Day, 1635, in his sixty-eighth year,
the " Father of Quebec" found surcease from his troubles in that sleep called death. There was genuine
grief among those who stood around his bier, though
none of his mourners fully appreciated or understood
him. If he had failed in a great measure of reaping the
harvest he had anticipated, it was not his fault. Had
there been more Héberts and Gifarts with his followers,
his disappointment would have been less poignant.
The widow of the first-named still lived, and to this day
can be pointed out to you the spot where this one early

householder of Quebec did more than all other yeomen towards establishing the permanency of New France. At this time across the valley of the St. Charles could be seen the stone manor of Robert Gifart, who had only the year before builded him here a home, where homes were the only thing lacking to make the new empire complete.

The Jesuit Lalemant performed the last service, while Le Jeune delivered the eulogy. Then the body of the hero was laid away to rest in a tomb built by the feeble colony. In the changes which have taken place since then this mortuary chapel has been swept away, and no man can point out the resting-place of Champlain with any more precision than that his sepulture was made where is now an open square in the upper town. It matters little where he may have found his resting-place, so long as it was in the heart of the town he loved so well; where his dust has mingled with the earth, so long as it is with the dust of the streets of that city which he founded with not a little sacrifice. Champlain has many mementoes and monuments, but the greatest and most enduring of these is the great and powerful city of Quebec.

No true estimate of a man can be made without taking into account the influences, environments, and opportunities of his day. Champlain lived in a stormy period, when no man could count upon the friends of the day to stand by him on the morrow, and when corruption entered soon or late into the relationships of

most men.   Above these wrecks rises the sturdy figure
of Champlain, incorruptible and unchangeable.   No man
of his times was more sincerely mourned, and there is
no one whose memory will live longer.   Possessing all
of the qualities needed for such arduous undertakings :
a sublime patience, an enduring frame, a keen foresight,
an unswerving passion for discovery, a mind capable of
discerning the true from the false to a remarkable extent
under his surroundings, a courage that never faltered,
and a good cheer that always animated his companions
with hopefulness, he was an ideal explorer.   He was,
too, a statesman of no mean quality, and if his scheme
of colonisation ultimately failed, it was due to the system
under which it was founded.   The prestige of Richelieu
waxed and waned ; the Hundred Associates yielded to
a weaker combination ; but the influence of Champlain
was still the guiding star of New France for a long
time.   Ay, while governments have changed, and a
nation greater than even he could have conceived has
risen upon the ruins of that he so fondly planned, his
illustrious light kindled by the goodness of his heart
cannot fade from the firmament of stars.

Champlain was succeeded by De Montmagny as Governor, and in 1645 the monopoly of the fur-trade which
had been enjoyed by the Company of the Hundred Associates was made over to inhabitants of the colony,
who assumed all of the debts, and allowed the corporation to retain all seignioral rights and an annuity of a
thousand pounds of beaver-skins.   It was now hoped

many of the evils which had prevailed would be stopped, and the colonists expected to receive direct benefits from the change. Under this arrangement, no private individual was allowed to enter into trade, and he could sell his furs only to the colonial corporation and at a fixed price.

Even here we see the old spirit of monopoly paramount. Individual rights were unheeded. Under this system, the evil was not lessened, while another was fostered. This was a habit of looking to the home government for encouragement in whatever enterprise was undertaken. Appeals of this kind were seldom ignored, more 's the pity. This served to encourage claimants, without materially adding to the trade and prosperity of the country. The result was demoralising. Of all the industries, the people of the St. Lawrence were favoured in the matter of fisheries, as far as Nature had performed her part. But for one reason and another the progress was not made that should have been, in spite of the fact that the King was supposed to be heartily in accord with such an enterprise. " His Majesty," wrote Denonville, in 1688, " desires you [the governor] to unite with the merchants to encourage the inhabitants to overcome their natural laziness, since it is the only way to save themselves from the poverty they are now suffering." Then, after declaring against the young men who "ran wild in the woods" for the sake of a few pelts, " Boston is getting rich out of it [the fishery] at our loss."

SCENE ON THE JACQUES CARTIER RIVER.

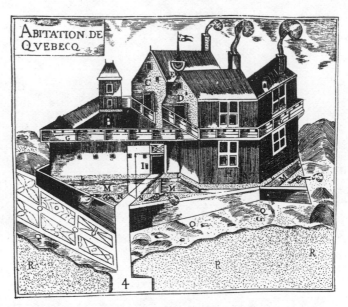

HABITATION DE QUEBEC, FROM CHAMPLAIN'S SKETCH.

Key to illustration : A, Storehouse ; B, Dovecote ; C. Workmen's lodgings and armoury ; D, Lodgings for mechanics ; E, Dial ; F, Blacksmith's shop and workmen's lodgings ; G, Galleries ; H, Champlain's residence ; I, Gate and drawbridge ; L, Walk ; M, Moat ; N, Platform for cannon ; O, Garden ; P, Kitchen ; Q, Vacant space ; R, St. Lawrence.

We find in this same year that the St. Lawrence was
without pilots and sailors.   Twenty-five years later, Engineer Catalogne reported to the government that the
river was dangerous for vessels at many places, but that
it was almost impossible to find a pilot.   De Chalons
writes at this period : " We ought to have a trade with
the West Indies and other countries.   Everybody
agrees that this is true, but no one attempts it.   Our
merchants are too poor, or they are taken up with the
fur-trade."

As early as 1674, the energetic Talon undertook
to encourage shipbuilding, but met with slight success.   In 1714, one Duplessis built a vessel, from
which is dated the beginning of shipbuilding in Canada, which was so well adapted to become a great
maritime nation.   But the day when that glory should
be known was still far distant.   The slight interest paid
to commerce reflected upon agriculture, which has since
become such an important factor in the prosperity of
the country.

The absorbing trade was the traffic in beaver-skins.
It seemed the best adapted to the wild, adventurous
nature of the French colonists.   Says Parkman :

In the eighteenth century, Canada exported a moderate quantity of timber, wheat, the herb called ginseng, and a few other commodities; but from first to last she lived chiefly on beaver-skins.
The government tried without ceasing to control and regulate this
traffic; but it never succeeded.   It aimed above all things to bring
the trade home to the colonists, to prevent them from going to the
Indians, and induce the Indians to come to them.

To accomplish this purpose, annual fairs were inaugurated at Montreal and Three Rivers, when great fleets of canoes laden with pelts came down the rivers. In the former place, upon the day following the arrival of the Indians with their cargoes, a grand council was held on the Common between the river and St. Paul Street; every possible courtesy was paid to the red men; compliments were showered upon them, and then trade began.   For a time good order prevailed, but the result was inevitable.   The fair would become a wild scene of uncontrollable actors.   Indians, clothed only in a feathered headdress, and armed with bows and arrows or a highly painted " trade gun "; French bush-rangers, decked out in gaudy finery, and as untamed and untamable as the wild sons of the forest; greedy merchants ready for any sacrifice to make a *livre; habitans* in their plain, coarse garb, as lookers-on in a scene in which they had the smallest interest; officials in high office, vainly trying to bring order out of chaos; and sedate priests of St. Sulpice, in their dark robes now sadly bedraggled, praying and exhorting,—all these, and many others, became involved in a maddening, but picturesque, medley of human beings.

A great check to the growth of commerce in the valley of the St. Lawrence was the suppression of knowledge.   The government, blind to its own interest, was ever watchful to see that the merchants, and would-be merchants did not meet to discuss the situation, and inform themselves by learning of others.

Hence there was, with a single exception of little account, no bourse or place of exchange; no encouragement from one to another, and least of all from the officials at the head of affairs. The education of those who came to the country compared favourably with others of the times, but their children were not destined to be as fortunate. For the women to learn to any great extent, or to read such few books as had been brought from the homeland, was looked upon as a sinful waste of time. From such literature as was at their command, the latter deprivation could have been no serious loss, as it could not have afforded them great benefits. The complaint does not seem strange, under these circumstances, that the greater portion of the ladies in Canada took too much care of their dress, and squandered money upon it, with too little regard for the future comforts of the home. Professor Kalm of Sweden, writing in the middle of the eighteenth century, says of them with a hint of sarcasm :

They are no less attentive to know the newest fashions; and they laugh at each other, when they are not dressed to each other's fancy. . . . The ladies of Quebec are not very industrious. A girl of eighteen is reckoned poorly off if she cannot enumerate at least twenty lovers. These young ladies, especially those of a higher rank, get up at seven and dress till nine, drinking their coffee at the same time. When they are dressed, they place themselves near a window that opens into the street, take up some needle-work, and sew a stitch now and then, but turn their eyes into the street most of the time. When a young fellow comes in, whether they are acquainted with him or not, they immediately set aside their work, sit down by him, and begin to chat, laugh, joke, and invent *double entendres ;* and this is reckoned very witty.

So far as the matter of frivolity goes, there is little to show that the sterner sex had any reason to claim greater industry.   The daughters of families of all ranks did not disdain to go to market, and to carry home whatever they had purchased.   With all their faults, real or imaginary, it seems that the young ladies of Montreal felt "very much displeased because those of Quebec get husbands sooner than they !"

Returning to the subject from which this is a digression, there was no printing-press in the colony to spread intelligence.   It is true, one was brought to Quebec early in the eighteenth century, but it was looked upon as a dangerous experiment and sent back from whence it had come with all the despatch possible.   The first newspaper did not appear until after the British conquest, and its founder came from Philadelphia, as did another a few years later to begin the publication of a paper in Montreal, the second of its class in Canada. The enterprising young man in this venture was named William Brown, and his sponsor was the Rev. William Dunlap, a relative of the wife of Benjamin Franklin. Thinking there was a fertile field here for him to work, he took in as partner another young man named Gilmore, and the two prepared at once for their undertaking.   The latter went to England to buy material, while Brown started for Quebec to make a beginning. Upon reaching Boston, and disappointed in not finding a boat to take him to Quebec, he started on horseback for an overland journey.   Upon reaching Albany, he completed his trip by boat, going down Lake Champlain, the Richelieu River to Montreal, and thence by the St. Lawrence to his destination, which he reached September 30, 1763. He then began a canvass for subscribers, and made all preparations for carrying on the business, learning during the interval the French language. In due season Gilmore arrived from London with a press, type, ink, paper, and other articles needed. The initial number of the paper, called the *Quebec Gazette*, appeared upon June 21, 1764, the first newspaper printed in Canada. Great credit belongs to the young men, who paid every dollar of debt they had incurred, and were very successful in their endeavours.

Before the British conquest, Quebec had become quite a shipbuilding place, and as many as fifty vessels, varying from five hundred to two thousand tons burden, besides many smaller craft, were built here in a year. The oak used in the construction of these ships had to be brought from the highlands between New France and New England, as that growing about Quebec was too small and inferior in quality. French war-ships were built here for a time, but finally the order came not to build any more, as American oak did not have the lasting quality of the European species.

As a great maritime highway, however, the St. Lawrence was not really appreciated until within half a century. But a quarter of a century before this, in 1831, Quebec sent from her stocks, with Montreal furnishing the machinery, the *Royal William*, the first steamship to cross the Atlantic from the St. Lawrence. To Canada belongs the credit of originating the pioneer line of ocean steamers, the Cunard Line, founded by Samuel Cunard, of Halifax, in 1840. The first line of ocean steamers plying directly between Quebec and Liverpool was the Allan Line, founded by Hugh Allan, and his first ship was the *Canadian*, built at Quebec in 1852–1853. Mr. Allan met with great obstacles in carrying out his plans, but through his indomitable perseverance won, and was eventually knighted in honour of his achievement. To-day the St. Lawrence is one of the greatest maritime highways of the world, and her commerce extends to the most distant ports of the globe. Montreal alone has a shipping trade amounting to 3,500,000 tons annually, and fifteen transatlantic steamship lines. At present Quebec has to take a second place in this department, though her citizens look hopefully forward to the day when she shall become the " Empire City " of that great maritime nation, Canada, and her sister across the way become her Brooklyn.

Chapter VIII

The Wilderness Missions

Four Récollet Priests Come to Quebec—Were Explorers as well as Missionaries — First Missions — Encouragement of Agriculture — Récollets Forced to Abandon their Work—Taken up by the Jesuits—Work Interrupted by the English—Westward from the Ottawa—The Thessaly of Olden Canada—The Huron Missions — The Mission of the Martyrs — College Established at Quebec.

ENTION has been made of those who came to the valley of the St. Lawrence as religious teachers, and no narrative of the great river would be complete without their story and that of the wilderness missions founded by them. No story in the annals of history is of more thrilling and pathetic interest. It is filled with such personal sacrifices, trials of fortitude, and patient suffering as make the tales of the most adventurous explorers read like commonplace incidents. If it often showed confidence misplaced, and dreams the most sanguine could hardly expect to be fulfilled, the golden deed remains as a living monument of what man is willing to do, to dare, and to suffer in the zeal of religious work.

The missionary was the saviour of the little bands of colonists in New France at the beginning of the seventeenth century. Champlain, himself half missionary, with the other half *voyageur*, giving him a spirit

Always roaming with a hungry heart,

encouraged the coming of the Jesuits, though even **he** could not foresee, when a few years later he forbade the Huguenots to sing their psalms to the symphony of the St. Lawrence, that within a hundred and fifty years the *fleur-de-lis* he had so proudly planted upon the fortified heights of Quebec would be torn down, and New France, then empress of America, would be represented by a few fishing islands clinging to the coast of the great country he fondly believed was destined to reflect the glory of Old France.

When Champlain brought to New France four priests of the Order of Récollets in 1615, a religious influence in more than name was given to the undertaking of founding the colony. It should be said to the credit of these new agents in the work that they came with words of peace and compassion, and a purpose to do and to suffer. The cruelty of the Spanish missionary in the South, which encircled the word "Christian" with such terrors, was unknown here. The Indian of Canada, with thrice the ferocity of his southern cousin, had no occasion to exclaim to those who claimed to be his salvationists :

" The devil is more kind to us ; we adore him !"

These brave men and their followers were not only missionaries but explorers and discoverers. Not only did they lead the way up the Kennebec from the shores of Maine to the St. Lawrence, but they pierced the wilds of the Saguenay, and pushed overland from

Quebec to Hudson Bay, the Récollet Father Le Caron being the first to carry the cross to the tribes of the Great Lakes. But, faithfully as they went about their work, for ten years these austere soldiers of the cross, in their grey garbs of coarse gown and hood, with wooden sandals on their feet, unused to the severe climate of this country, moving hither and thither through the pathless wilderness upon what they believed to be errands of sacred duty, met with no perceptible success, though others, with far less sacrifice of comfort and personal vanity, were reaping a harvest from trade and from politics.

Humiliated and dispirited, but not lagging in the faith, they felt compelled to ask the succour of that stronger brotherhood, the Society of Jesus, already established in Asia, Africa, and South America. Three of the Jesuits came, among them that giant in figure and intellect, Jean de Brébeuf. His companions were Massé and Charles Lalemant. Even the united efforts of these do not appear to have borne any lasting fruits. Quebec then was indeed but a collection of a few miserable huts. With its surrender to Kertk, the career of the Récollets ended here, and that of the Jesuits for the time was suspended.

Following the restoration of Quebec to the French, the Jesuits reorganised the mission here in 1632, and extended their field of action so as to cover the whole of New France, a country reaching from the gulf to the Mississippi. Interrupted by the fortunes of war, they

continued their herculean task, having first to master
the language of the people they hoped to bring to an
understanding of their teachings. They established
missions at Three Rivers, Montreal, Sillery, Bécancourt,
and St. Francis de Sales. These were intended for the
Algonquins, who had settled along the St. Lawrence,
the Montagnais, and such of the Abnakis as chose to
come within the fold.

Among the most noted and influential of the missions was that of the palisaded station first named St.
Joseph, but later honoured with the name of Commander Noel Brulart de Sillery, who gave liberally
towards its founding. This was established in 1637,
and enjoyed the distinction of accomplishing the first
step towards bringing the Indians to adopt agricultural
pursuits. Here twenty Algonquins were persuaded to
take up the cultivation of the soil, but allowed to fish
and hunt when not actually needed among the growing
crops.

Early in their work, the missionaries had come to
understand that the greatest difficulty they had to con-
tend with was the fixed habit of the red men to follow a
wandering life, fishing, hunting, warring, never settling
in one place, and always lapsing from their pledges by
these frequent changes. Thus the missionaries endeav-
oured to interest them in a more settled pursuit. At first
this worked in favour of that growing power in the new
country, the fur-traders, but they soon saw that if this
idea was carried out it would end or seriously curtail

their enterprise. On the other hand, these "meets" between the dusky hunters and the buyers of their wares brought about several evils, not the least of which was the introduction of rum. So between the priest and the trader, one who thought only of saving souls, and the other of the profit from his traffic, there sprang up a rivalry which, at times, developed into feelings of bitterness bordering upon enmity.

Eventually some Montagnais joined the other Indians at Sillery, and the little hamlet grew gradually into importance. In 1640, its usefulness was increased by the opening of a hospital here by the nuns of Quebec. This was for the benefit of both French and Indians. After an existence of six years, the laudable enterprise had to be abandoned on account of the hostilities of rival tribes of red men. Soon after, the chapel and mission house were destroyed by fire. Then disease broke out among the Indians, the soil, exhausted by its prodigal treatment, refused to yield enough to sustain its meagre population, and the old Sillery was given up. The descendants of its original founders re-established themselves at a new mission named St. Francis de Sales, soon better known as the Mission of St Francis, of which I shall speak more anon.

Father Bateaux established a mission at Three Rivers, formerly a trading station, to fall a few years later, 1652, at the hands of the Iroquois. He made some of the longest, most difficult, and most painful journeys recorded among his Order.

The missionary settlement of Montreal was founded, 1641, by Maisonneuve, but this mission was soon taken in charge by Abbé d' Olier, who established in Paris four years later the " Priests of the Society of St. Sulpice," and this colony was transferred to the Sulpicians in 1656. Afterwards this mission was removed to the Sault au Récollet, and from there to the Lake of the Two Mountains, where it still exists, the oldest in the country. Here several tribes of red men, among them the Algonquins, the Nipissing, and the Iroquois descendants, meet to-day.

No permanent mission was attempted on *le grande rivière*, the Ottawa, though this was for some time the main way of travel by the missionaries into the west. The first Indians to trade with the French from the region of the Upper Lakes were the Ottawas, hence that territory became known as the country of the Ottawas, though several other tribes dwelt within the region. From this came the modern name of the river.

Looking westward, we behold the great battle-ground of the races. Here were lighted the momentous council-fires of the Iroquois ; here was carried from border to border the Huron's tocsin of war ; and here wound the war trails of nations that fought, bled, and perished in the same cause that has wrung tears from the old earth since it was young. This was the Thessaly of old Canada. Here the stately Titanis mustered his dusky legions, and went forth as did Varus of old Rome, to vanish into the night of the wilderness.

CHÂTEAU ST. LOUIS (1694–1834), DESTROYED BY FIRE IN 1834.

THE RAPIDS ABOVE THE CEDARS.
From a drawing by W. H. Bartlett.

Here was the home of the fiery Pontiac, who staked his all and lost on the ebb of the tide. Here, the curtain fallen upon the last act in the terrible drama of war, came the noble Brant to teach his people the ways of peace, dying with his dream a-dreaming. Here the grand Tecumseh rallied his faithful followers in the interest of an alien race, and here he fell, bravely battling for a lost cause. No mean warriors these, worthy to stand shoulder to shoulder with the noblest of the Old World heroes. The door to this magnificent country was the Huron Mission, of which it has been truthfully said :

No men have, in the zealous exercise of their faith, performed hardier deeds than these Jesuits of the Huron Mission ; yet after three years of unremitting toil, they could [1640] count but a few hundred converts out of a population of 16,000, and these were for the most part sick infants or aged persons, who had died soon after baptism. The rugged braves scorned the approaches of the fathers, and unmercifully tormented their converts ; the medicine men waged continual warfare on their work ; smallpox and the Iroquois were decimating the people.

Still they clung to their work, and new missions were undertaken. During the thirty-five years in which they carried on their labours here, twenty-nine missionaries entered the field, five of them sacrificing their lives on the altars of their ambition. But the end was inevitable. The time came, in the summer of 1650, when the few survivors of the unfortunate missions abandoned their last resort on some islands in Lake Huron, and with their flocks gladly accepted the hospitality offered them by the founders of a small village on the Island of Orleans, just below Quebec. Even here, they soon found that they had not escaped the vengeance of the Iroquois, and they saved themselves only by making a desperate stand at Lorette, also near Quebec, where are still to be found reminders of the faithful band.

At this time the dusky allies of the French against the Iroquois,—the Montagnais, the Hurons, the Algonquins, the Petuns, and the Neutrals,— had suffered so from the inroads of their enemies, not the least among which was that of disease, that the colonists of New France were threatened with complete extinction at the hands of the Five Nations. Not only had the Jesuits reasons to be disheartened, but the *coureur du bois* had found his forest trade ruined, and the settlements of Quebec, Three Rivers, and Montreal were sorely oppressed by an enemy that knew neither mercy nor the limit of human endurance.

In 1653 came an unexpected overture. This was nothing less than a proposal on the part of the Iroquois for peace, and an invitation to the Jesuits to establish a mission in their country. It was a shrewd act on the part of the Five Nations, as they were anxious to distract the French from helping the routed Hurons, Algonquins, and Petuns to rally against them. This was essential to them, as they had about as much as they could attend to in stemming the tide of the Eries coming in upon them from the west, and of the Susquehannas from the south.

The first missionary to enter the territory of the Five Nations had been Jogues, 1642, who went as captive of the Mohawks. The second was Bressani, 1644, who had a similar introduction, and who, like the first, after a series of hazardous hardships, eventually returned with the forlorn hope that he could Christianize these warlike people. These two, with a companion in each case, suffered torture and death at the hands of those whom they would fain have converted to milder ways. In 1659, the Iroquois formed a conspiracy to kill all of the French within their country, and then to blot out of existence the settlements in the St. Lawrence valley. Fortunately, this plot was betrayed by one of their number, and the missionaries then among them managed to escape and reach Montreal after a series of adventures of the most hazardous nature. Though baffled at the outset, the Iroquois actually massed to carry out this far-reaching plan, the sequel of which will be told in another chapter.

In the midst of this unstable condition, they again, as a subterfuge possibly, in the person of a Cayuga sachem, asked for another visit from the black-robed Fathers. As usual, the appeal was not made in vain, the fearless, patient Le Moyne answering the summons this time. He passed the winter with them. It was not until five years later, however, when the French had become strong enough to subdue four of the allied tribes, the Cayugas, Oneidas, Onondagas, and Senecas, that the missionary could go among them without fear and trembling. The Mohawks, still stubborn, were humbled and humiliated only when their village had been laid in ruins. Among the converts of this period was one at least worthy of mention. She was an Iroquois woman known as Catharine Tegakouita, "the Iroquois saint." She afterwards founded a native mission on the banks of the St. Lawrence.

The French did not wholly retire from this field until 1687, when the English had become so strong that they felt obliged to abandon an enterprise which at its most prosperous period was barren of great result. The New York Indians who had been attracted to the valley of the St. Lawrence were cared for at a palisaded mission, nearly opposite Montreal, known as the St. Francis Xavier. This mission, which was originally an outpost against the marauding Iroquois, was subsequently removed to Sault St. Louis, and is known to this day as Caughnawaga.

The accounts of the sufferings and hardships borne by these pious followers of the cross surpass the belief of the most humane, and overleap the imagination of those who have not read them. It would seem as if the savage mind invented every form of cruelty that was possible to punish these heroic men who were sacrificing everything for them. Among them, none could exceed the Mohawks in their ingenious and devilish atrocities, hence the labour undertaken in their midst has appropriately been distinguished as "The Mission of the Martyrs."

So assiduously did they apply themselves to the task in hand, that within seven years of their second arrival they had accomplished the exploration of the country to the borders of Lake Superior, and thence down the Mississippi to the Gulf of Mexico. On the shores of the Great Lakes, they established their outposts of civilisation while yet the battle-cry of a savage race was awakening the fastnesses of the wilderness,— all this before the sturdy New Englander had cared to push away from the seacoast, and while the slow-moving Dutch were occupied within their limited domains. Before Eliot, of New England, had addressed a single word to the Indians within six miles of Boston Harbour, Le Jeune, Brébeuf, and others had mastered the Algonquin and Huron tongues, and were preaching to the dusky congregations in their own language.

Neither the conversion of souls nor exploration was their paramount purpose, for the education of the young was ever in their mind. In 1637, while the English were debating the building, upon the banks of the river Charles, of Harvard University, a Jesuit named René de Rohaut established a school for Indian children and a college for French boys at Quebec. The first pupil came from the Huron country, under the charge of Father Daniel, who, in 1648, fell with half a dozen Iroquois bullets in his body, the second Christian martyr in New France. Nicollet, who had spent so much time among the Indians to learn their language, succeeded in furnishing several subjects for

the training of the pious teachers. But these dusky
seekers after knowledge came with little aspiration for
light, and Father Le Jeune confesses that some ran
away ; one was kidnapped by parents who could not appreciate the golden opportunity open to their offspring,
while two others met more ignoble fates by gorging
themselves to death with — not overstudy, but over-
eating ! The college building, which was a wooden
structure, was made into a soldiers' barracks upon the
occupation of the city by the English.

It is fortunate for those who seek for a knowledge
of the scenes in which they figured that the missionaries
were faithful chroniclers of what they saw and did, and
that the French Government required them to render
such reports from time to time. The style of these
writers was simple in the extreme, while a pathetic interest pervades all they say. There is no other source of
early history which contains so much of the customs,
religion, legends, and language of the native races. The
Jesuit Relations was originally published in forty small
octavo volumes, and is now (1904) being reprinted, in
Cleveland, in a definitive edition comprising 73 volumes.

THE INDIAN VILLAGE OF CAUGHNAWAGA.
From a photograph by W. Notman & Son, Montreal

MARIE GUYARD (MÈRE MARIE DE L'INCARNATION.)

Chapter IX

The Beginning of Montreal

Founders of the Ursuline Convent in Quebec—Maisonneuve, the Champlain of Montreal—The Heroines of Ville-Marie—A Canadian Regulus—The Holy Wars of Early Montreal.

I T must not be supposed by those reading the story of the wilderness missions that all of the heroism of founding the Catholic Church in New France belonged to the sterner sex. From among the gentler followers of the cross came spirits equally brave and self-sacrificing. The touching and beautiful pictures the devout Fathers sent home, in spite of the pain and the burden they had taken upon themselves, found sympathetic hearts in court ladies and youthful nuns. Many young and beautiful maids and matrons promptly vowed themselves ready to help in the grand work of upbuilding the missions of the St. Lawrence.

"A charitable and virtuous lady is needed here to teach the word of Christ to little Indian girls," wrote Father Le Jeune, nothing discouraged by the obstacles constantly rising in his path of trying to educate the dusky youths. No sooner was his touching request heralded across the water, than thirteen nuns from one convent pledged their lives to work in the good cause in Quebec, or wherever they should be called. This same appeal awakened the religious ecstasy of another, even as the religious zeal of the young and beautiful Madame Champlain had been stirred twenty years before into a determination to devote her life to the work. This good and pious woman was the widow of the lamented De la Peltrie, and, left childless, she resolved to become a nun. In vain her father, to force her to marry again, threatened to disinherit her. Upon the advice of a Jesuit she did allow arrangements to be made for the form of a marriage, but the death of her father, soon after, left her free to carry out the purpose which now absorbed her life. From the convent at Tours she easily secured three nuns to help her in founding an Ursuline convent at Quebec. One of these companions became the noted Marie de l'Incarnation, then a tall, regal woman of forty, with a romantic and pathetic history. She was both a widow and a mother, having been married at seventeen, and left without a husband at nineteen. It was only after long and earnest meditation, severe discipline, and devout supplication to the power upholding her that she could finally separate herself from her child. When she had at last concluded to take the veil, she was received by the Ursulines of Tours with great rejoicing. She was made Superior of the new convent at Quebec, and proved herself to be worthy of the hopes of her associates.

M. de Montmagny, a Knight of Malta, had become

the successor of Champlain, and though lacking the other's resourceful enthusiasm he did fairly well. He rebuilt, in stone, Fort St. Louis, close to the precipice; he restored the fallen tenements of Champlain's first habitation; he saw the first Hôtel-Dieu rise on the cliff commanding the valley of the St. Charles; and he looked with satisfaction upon the progress of Quebec's lonely farmer, Louis Hébert. He had encouraged the brave Ursuline sisters to found their mission at Sillery, where they nobly contended with disease and dangers such as must have discouraged less brave hearts. A memorial of their unselfish work endures to-day in the cloisters of Garden Street, where in the sweet repose of seclusion gentle followers of their faith minister still to the maids of French-speaking Quebec; and yet another exists in Palace Hill Hospital, where the suffering are cared for as tenderly as in the dark days of Indian invasion when their Order undertook the humane work of establishing itself among the wilderness missions of 1639.

Not alone was Quebec the scene of womanly devotion to duty and religion, but already the gaze of some of the religious spirits of France was turned upon the island situated at the vortex of two rivers, both important waterways for trade with the natives of the interior. The very fact that this was in the midst of one of the most troublesome periods of Indian invasions made it the more imperative that an outpost should be established here. Mention has already been made of the founding of the mission of Montreal by Maison-neuve, under the patronage of M. Dauversière and M. d'Olier, who established, four years later, the Order of St. Sulpice. The island of Montreal then belonged to M. Lauzon, one of the Hundred Associates, who was induced to transfer his title, with the reserve that they should not engage in the fur-trade nor build forts. The Society of Notre Dame de Montreal was then organised, and the leadership of the undertaking intrusted to that brave Christian knight, Paul de Maison-neuve, who was worthy to wear the mantle of Champlain, and by his untiring efforts linked his name inseparably with the queen city of Canadian commerce, no little honour.

Neither does all of the credit belong to this brave man. Among those who became interested in the laudable enterprise was a devout lady, Mademoiselle Mance, who joined the mission, and encouraged three other women to go with the settlers. Forty-two men, besides Maisonneuve and the three women, after meeting at the church of Notre Dame, at Paris, to consecrate the new settlement, which they had christened Ville Marie de Montreal, set sail for New France.

Delayed in getting started, they did not reach Quebec in season to continue up to their proposed stopping-place. Here they met with an opposition they had not expected. Montmagny opposed the scheme upon the exceedingly plausible ground that the settlers were needed at Quebec; that it would be folly to try and

establish another settlement in the very teeth of the
enemy, when he had all he could do to defend his own
flock.   The governor knew whereof he spoke.   Only a
short time before had the Iroquois, grown bold and
sinister with their previous successes against their rival
tribes, sent two Frenchmen, whom they had captured,
in advance of their large force, to demand the surrender
of the post at Three Rivers.   The terms proposed were
for the French to accept an armistice of peace, and
leave their Algonquin allies to the mercy of their foes.
The messenger, whose name was François Marguerie,
under a flag of truce, did as he was bid in delivering the
infamous message intrusted to him.   Then, seeing his
countrymen wavering in their duty, knowing the fearful
odds they were facing, he broke forth into a defiant statement of their duty to the allies who had always stood
by them, and who would be butchered in cold blood by
the Iroquois did they accept such conditions of peace.
His bold words saved the honour of New France, and
it was decided that a desperate stand should be made
until the last.   Marguerie was then advised to remain
with them, as it was known he would be put to the
most fiendish torture should he return to his captors
after having betrayed them in this manner.   But this
modern Regulus pointed out that if he did not go back,
his companion, who was held as hostage until he should
return, would have to suffer in his place.   Under these
circumstances Marguerie heroically bade adieu to his
companions and went back to meet his fate.   Fortun-

ately, the delay caused by this parley enabled the governor to send a small body of reinforcements to the post, and upon learning of this the Iroquois abandoned the siege. They also consented to let Marguerie and his companion go free upon a ransom, and thus the hero was spared the fate that he expected when he decided upon his bold stand.

Maisonneuve was equally firm in his purpose. He showed how he was simply an agent with an appointed duty before him. " I have not come here to deliberate," he declared, "but to act. It is my duty and my honour to found a colony at Montreal; and I would go if every tree were an Iroquois." That autumn, October 14, 1641, the site of Ville-Marie was dedicated, but the settlers wintered in Quebec, where their leader was looked upon by the governor as his rival in power. He softened somewhat in his attitude with the coming of spring, and accompanied the colonists upon their trip in May to their future homes.

Over the route that is now accomplished by one of the river steamers in as many hours, Maisonneuve's little fleet forged its way for fifteen days, when, on the 17th of May, the rounded slopes of Mount Royal, clad in the delicate green foliage of spring, burst into sight, stirring the hearts of the anxious beholders with new-found joy. They were delighted with the scenery, the fragrance of the springing forest permeated the balmy air, and, what was dearer far to them, over the water and over the landscape rested an air

of peace quite in keeping with their pious purpose.
There was nothing save rumours of an enemy that never
allowed their vengeance to sleep, to forewarn them of
the bloody deeds so soon to be enacted upon that fair
scene.

As belonged to him, Maisonneuve was the first to
step upon the land, and as the others followed him,
Mademoiselle Mance next to their leader, they fell
upon their knees, sending up their songs of praise and
thanksgiving. Their first work was to erect an altar at
a favourable spot within sight and sound of the river-
bank, the women decorating the rough woodwork with
some of the wild-flowers growing in abundance upon
the island, until the whole looked very beautiful. Then
every member of the party, from the stately Governor
Montmagny, in his courtly dress, the tall, dignified
Maisonneuve, the fair, brave women, with their female
attendants, lending grace to the scene by their presence,
to the humbler persons,—the artisans, soldiers, and
sailors,—knelt in solemn silence while M. Barthelemy
Vimont, the Superior of the Jesuits, in his dark, ecclesi-
astical robes, performed the ceremony of high mass.
As he closed, he addressed his little congregation with
these prophetic words:

"You are a grain of mustard seed that shall rise
and grow till its branches overshadow the earth. You
are few, but your work is the work of God. His smile
is on you, and your children shall fill the land."

Speedily the site of Ville-Marie was surrounded by

a palisade, but the hospital erected by them was set outside of this wall. This was a stone structure, looking more like a fortress, which it proved to be in the battles to come. The summer passed quietly, while a little village of small wooden houses sprang up around the spot. A small chapel was built over the altar. Happily the band remained in ignorance of the bitter strife being waged all around them.

As yet the Iroquois had not discovered the presence of this party of brave colonists daring to invade territory they claimed belonged to them. Certainly they had shed blood enough to possess it. But all too soon the discovery was made, when they patrolled the woods in large bodies and in small, waiting for the opportunity to strike the blow which should sweep this new outpost from existence. The stockade was deemed insufficient to meet such an enemy, and it was replaced by solid walls and bastions. This summer was passed in anxiety and alarm. The cultivation of the soil had to be abandoned, except as it was done under the protection of arms. The fuel needed to keep them warm during the cold weather had to be procured under cover of arms. Cut off from intercourse with the posts below, that were experiencing equal extremities, Ville-Marie was little better than a prison-pen. The Iroquois held a rough fort at Lachine, and had openly declared that they would not rest until they had cleared the country of both French and Algonquins. Some Hurons, falling into a trap of their setting, to save themselves betrayed their allies, and assured them that it would be an easy matter to capture Ville-Marie, which was too poorly equipped to stand a siege.

Another winter passed in inactivity. Now and then the enemy had been seen, and an occasional skirmish took place, but Maisonneuve counselled prudence. As might have been expected, some of his men began to murmur, saying that a bold onset would scatter the foes. Their sagacious leader replied that a single defeat would ruin all. Better to remain inactive and watchful than to hazard their fate by overconfidence in their strength. That fall the little colony had received from France several watch-dogs, which proved remarkably intelligent and useful. One, named Pilote, was especially helpful, acting as scout and sentinel, leading her train in evident enjoyment upon her round of duties.

One morning in early spring, while the snow still lay deep upon the ground, Pilote was sent out upon her daily round of reconnoissance. She had not been gone many minutes before she came bounding back, barking furiously, as much as to say, " The enemy are skulking in the woods." " Let us prove if the dog be right or not," said the soldiers among themselves, and Maisonneuve answered promptly that they should have the opportunity to see all the fighting they would care for.

Eagerly the men, whose bravery over-ruled their better judgment, armed themselves with guns, and fastened snow-shoes upon their feet. As there were not enough of the latter for all, some went without. Thus, in battle array, Maisonneuve marched his band of thirty out of the fort into the clearing, covered deeply with the melting snow.   Entering the deep forest they could see no sign of the enemy, and the soldiers began to think that Pilote had given a false alarm.   Then a volley of bullets and arrows whistled around their heads, and the words of Maisonneuve proved a prophecy of truth, when every tree became an Iroquois!

The suddenness of the attack, the outburst of yells coming from throats of demons, fairly paralysed the soldiers, who were unused to Indian warfare.   Massed in a bunch they must have fallen easy targets for the arms of the Iroquois, who were exultant over their surprise, had not their leader proved himself wise enough to order them to get behind the trees.   Three or four were already killed and several wounded.   The brave fellows returned the fire of the Iroquois, and, reloading their firearms, poured a second volley into the forest, though few, if any, of their bullets took effect.   Maisonneuve was shrewd to see that such a fight, if continued, was sure to end disastrously to them, so he ordered a retreat, instructing his men to bear off the dead, and to gain a sledge-path leading to the fort.   Nothing loath they obeyed, while the gallant Maisonneuve covered their retreat with his pistols, the Indians following upon their steps, while they dodged from tree to tree.   Upon gaining the sledge-track the soldiers fled in such disorder to the fort that they were mistaken by the occupants for the enemy, and, but for a timely warning from one of the women would have received a volley of bullets from their friends.

With a pistol in either hand Maisonneuve slowly followed his men, keeping his eye upon his foes, who refrained from shooting him, as they now considered it a great honour to capture such an enemy alive. Warwise in this course of action, the brave captain kept them at bay, until the last of his soldiers had got within the gate, with the bodies of the dead and the wounded. Then he began to look to his own safety, when an Iroquois chief, seeing their last opportunity of capturing him slipping away, sprang boldly forward to intercept him. But Maisonneuve proved that he was alert for such an act, and before the other could close in upon him he sent a bullet through his brain. The next moment he leaped inside of the gate, gladly opened to him by his anxious companions, who shouted for joy over his escape. Henceforth no man ever questioned the courage of their leader, who had shown himself a hero.

The death of the chief threw the Iroquois into such confusion that his body was dragged away without further attack being made. The spot where the valiant Maisonneuve stood when he fired the shot that saved himself and his friends is now known in commemoration of his deed as *Place d'Armes.* And so prophetic have the words of the Jesuit Father proved that it lies in the heart of a great commercial city and near to that noted church, Notre Dame, the largest cathedral in

America, with the exception of one other standing on the site of the ancient Aztec pyramid of Mexico.

While a period of comparative peace followed for a time, this little outpost of civilisation was never free from concern over its safety. Making the Richelieu River, as they had always done, their main entrance into the valley of the St. Lawrence, the Iroquois would lie in ambush along Lake St. Peter to intercept the fur-traders coming down from the upper country, or send their scouting parties farther down the stream to waylay whomever they could find. As has been mentioned, Montmagny built a fort at its mouth, but this, though meeting successfully an attack upon it, the wily red man found many ways to get around, and maintain a barrier of armed forces between this upper outpost on the St. Lawrence and the settlements below. This state of affairs lasted for over ten years without an abatement of its terrors and its horrors. During the interval the Jesuits, in the person of Father Jogues, had their first experience in the homeland of the Iroquois. In the west the Huron missions had suffered beyond the power of description, until finally the few survivors fled toward Quebec, finding a place of refuge at Sorel.

At this time the colonists of New England were enjoying peace and a rapid growth of population. The confederacy known as "The United Colonies of New England" was formed to secure such protection as could be obtained from a union of interests. Hitherto, and in the years to follow, however, the settlements in New

England and those in the valley of the St. Lawrence
might flourish, whether planning war upon each other
or enduring internal strife at home, neither knew, or
seemed to care, what the other was doing. At this
time, however, the eyes of the prosperous New Englanders became turned upon the region along the St.
Lawrence, and a treaty of perpetual amity was proposed between New France and New England. Coming in the midst of such distress as the former colonists
were enduring it was received with joy by them.
Montmagny had been succeeded as governor by D'Aille-
boust, and he immediately sent as a representative to
act in their behalf Father Druilettes to confer with the
English council at Boston. Smarting under the terrible
blows being dealt against them by their unswerving
foes, the Government at Quebec stipulated that one
condition of the treaty should be that the colonists of
New England should join with them in exterminating
the Iroquois. This the latter stoutly refused to do.
An armistice of peace had existed between them and
the Five Nations which they had no desire to break.
The emissary from Canada was firm in his demands,
and so the negotiations came to naught. Disappointed
in this direction Druilettes resolved to secure an ally
elsewhere, and so astutely did he manage matters that
he won over to his cause the Abnaki tribes in the east,
who had shown but little disposition to be unfriendly
to the English. So, instead of averting bloodshed as
they had hoped, the New Englanders were drawn into

a series of struggles and bush battles which, with few and short cessations, lengthened into a war lasting over a hundred years.

Nor were the French able to escape what they had hoped to throw off in a large measure. Learning of this intrigue the Iroquois became more bitter than before in their hostilities. Their lonely settlements in the heart of New France never rested in peace. Under the canopy of the great forest skulked a foe that never slept, and so bold did he grow that his war-plumes danced under the very guns of St. Louis on the fortified rock of Quebec. If the brave hearts at Quebec fairly hushed their beating, how silent it must have been behind the walls of Ville-Marie! Fasting, penance, and prayer reigned supreme among these brave, but well-nigh hopeless, colonists, only fifty in number, and environed by a wilderness that was a veritable beehive of dusky foemen.

In 1653, while the Iroquois were busy in exterminating another tribe of red men, the Eries, the colonists of the St. Lawrence were given a breathing spell. The missionaries were brought into renewed activity, being called among the rival tribes to carry on their work of building missions and saving souls. But the cloak of promised protection held under its folds the viper of death. The Five Nations of the Iroquois were agreed to unite in exterminating the missionaries and attendants in their midst, and then sweep the St. Lawrence valley clean of Frenchmen, which has already been mentioned. The hero of this scene in the drama of races was the intrepid Dupuy, who was in command of a little band under the supposed protection of the Onondaga Mission. Learning from secret sources of the plot of the Indians, he had his men construct some very light boats within cover of the fort. As soon as these were completed he invited the Onondagas to a feast, which was so liberally furnished that the Indians ate and drank themselves into an unnatural sleep. While they slumbered their entertainers stole away with their boats upon their shoulders. Reaching the Oswego River, though it was in mid-March they succeeded in making their passage to the lake, and from thence down the St. Lawrence to Quebec.

In the meantime at Ville-Marie, Mademoiselle Mance, though beginning to feel the infirmities of years, with her associates, was kept busy caring for the sick and wounded at her hospital. Another brave woman, young in years, and with a good inheritance had she remained at home to enjoy it, came to Ville-Marie to teach the children, opening her school in a stable, lodging herself in the loft. In fact, others of the gentle sex found their way upon this stormy scene, lured hither by intoxicating stories of the good they might accomplish among the poor and needy. Many of these came through the agency of that arch-scoundrel, Dauversière, whose name has already been mentioned. It was even claimed that he had kidnapped and sold them into this life of sacrifice.

As well as men and women the missions needed money, and in 1658 Mademoiselle Mance and Marguerite Bourgeoys, a young teacher, visited France to solicit aid.   They were so successful, through the aid of the Sulpicians, that a large body of emigrants came with them upon their return, and an energetic Sulpician Father, the Abbé de Queylus.   The latter established the seminary which had long been the dream of the colony.   The dwellings were increased to fifty well-built houses, compactly situated, and protected by a fort and stone windmill where is now St. Paul Street.

The brief term of peace which had allowed this hopeful upbuilding now proved but a lull in the storm of what has passed into history as the "Holy Wars of Montreal."   The Iroquois again took the war trail, fiercer, stronger than ever.   Victims were scalped within sight and sound of the only stronghold within New France.   Thither fled the frightened nuns from their stone convents, and thither the fur-traders and *voyageurs* looked for succour.   In the midst of this thrilling situation intelligence was brought of a great war-party of Iroquois descending the Ottawa River to hurl itself upon Ville-Marie.   Under its impending doom, amid the prayers of priests and women, rose the hero of this occasion, a young nobleman named Adam Daulac, Sieur des Ormeaux, since frequently called Dollard, who had come to Montreal a short time before, as it would seem, for just such an opportunity as this. His story is worthy of a separate chapter.

SIEUR DE MAISONNEUVE.

THE JUNCTION OF THE OTTAWA AND THE ST. LAWRENCE RIVERS.

From a drawing by W. H. Bartlett.

Chapter X

Spartans of Canada

The Story of Daulac and his Heroic Band, Every Man of whom Died for New France—How Twenty-two Heroes Held Seven Hundred Iroquois Warriors at Bay.

THE pioneer days of all countries are filled with deeds of heroism, and the names of many heroes and heroines stand boldly out on the historic pages as conspicuous examples of faithfulness unto death for generations to come, inspiring their descendants with love for homeland. The early history of Canada is especially bright in this respect. But among her many fearless builders and defenders no figures stand forth in bolder relief than Daulac's little Spartan band that dared and did so much for New France in the stirring and perilous period of Iroquois invasion.

Adam Daulac, or Dollard in its Englished form, was only twenty-five years old, but, belonging to an old family of soldiers, he had seen considerable military service as a regular in the army of France. Unfortunately his record was blackened by the charge of cowardice, and his sensitive nature writhed under the accusation, which was really groundless. Smarting under this humiliation he had come to New France with the avowed purpose of washing out by some deed of prowess the stain on his otherwise proud name. In a new country he fondly believed he would find greater field for his desire. Now he believed his opportunity had come.

Thus he watched the uprising of the Iroquois with feelings far different from those who listened to the reports with trembling. Instead of waiting in fear and suspense for the savage enemies to gather their wild forces and hurl them *en masse* upon their homes, poorly fitted to withstand a siege, he favoured carrying war into the others' midst. Such a course, he argued, would do more to disconcert the Iroquois than a hundred fights made on the defensive, however bravely the stand might be taken. Unless something of this kind were done they would grow bolder as the season advanced, and as the men of necessity became more busy about their growing crops the Indians would be given greater opportunity for action.

So, obtaining permission from the governor to raise a party of kindred spirits to take the war trail, Daulac soon enlisted sixteen as brave and dashing spirits as himself. For reasons of his own he accepted only those who had no families depending upon them for a living, and no man older than himself. As far as possible he selected those, who, through some disappointment, had grown reckless and placed a low value on life. He then advised them all to make their wills, if they had any property which they wished to dispose of, in case they failed to return.

The older men of the vicinity asked that the expedition be delayed until they could plant their seed, when they would gladly accompany the others, and thus bring the company up to a respectable number. Daulac met this with the argument that a small body of men could move faster and easier than a large number, and thus be better able to surprise the Indians, which would be the only hope of a success.

After having seen that his little band had taken an ample supply of arms and ammunition, among the former several heavy musketoons, or small cannon, together with as much crushed corn as was deemed best, Daulac was ready to set forth upon his perilous mission. The Sacrament was received and their confessions made in the little chapel, while their many friends, who felt they never should see them again, bade them a tender, tearful good-bye.

A fair April morning was breaking over the north-land as the brave seventeen resolutely set the prows of their stout canoes up the stream, and entered upon the first stage of their arduous and dangerous journey. The river swollen by the floods of spring and still carrying floating cakes of ice, they were six days in stemming the rapids of Sainte Anne, and only the most determined battle with the elements enabled them to enter the furious Ottawa. But strengthened rather than daunted by this difficult beginning they pushed ahead, crossed the Lake of the Two Mountains, and paused for their first respite at the foot of the angry current of Carillon.

Daulac cheered his companions with stories of Champlain on his first voyage up the Ottawa, and soon they gazed upon the stormy rapids where the great explorer had nearly lost his life. Looking upon the rock-strewn waterway where the mad current leaped and roared and flung twenty feet into the air its white and yellow mane, they wisely concluded it would be impossible for them to ascend the cataracts of Long Sault at this time. Even if that were possible, the news which had reached them that a large war-party of the Iroquois were encamped just above warned them that it would be running into a trap. Their leader, whose judgment was seldom questioned, argued that it would be better to lie in ambush near by and attack the enemy when they should come down the turbid stream.

It happened that an Algonquin war-party the previous year had made a small clearing and hastily constructed a fort surrounded by palisades. Though this simple fortification had fallen into a dilapidated condition during the winter, it was quickly decided to make it their rendezvous, and repair it as soon as they had somewhat recovered from the exhaustion of their efforts in battling with the current. So their supplies of provisions and ammunition were taken inside the fort, their canoes dragged up out of the reach of the water, a hearty meal eaten, when they wrapped themselves in their blankets and lay down to the rest and sleep so greatly required, putting off until another day the improvement they intended to give the fort.

The night proved uneventful, and the following morning Daulac and his men were both surprised and pleased at the appearance of a party of Indians, consisting of Hurons and Algonquins, who hated the Iroquois and consequently professed friendship for the French. These dusky allies numbered forty-four, of whom only four belonged to the Algonquin tribe. Daulac himself had little confidence that the Indians would stand by them in case the fight should become close, as the Hurons were not noted for such qualities, having of late several times deserted the French at a critical moment. However, he had no reason to doubt the courage and loyalty of their leader, so he was fain to accept their proffered aid, and the repairs upon the fort were begun with promptness and strong belief in their success against the enemies, who the Huron chief assured them were even then close at hand.

They were in the midst of this work when one of the scouts reported that two canoe-loads of Iroquois warriors were shooting the rapids at that moment. Axes were immediately exchanged for firearms, and the allies waited impatiently for the appearance of their enemies. The suspense was of short duration, and having passed the falls in safety the Iroquois were in the act of landing just below, as Daulac gave the word to fire. But in the excitement so many shots were wasted that a portion of the Iroquois escaped up the bank of the river. These carried the news of the attack to their companions encamped above the rapids,

and preparations were hastily begun to make a raid
upon the French and their allies.

Meanwhile Daulac and his companions, speaking
lightly of what they had done, cooked their morning
meal, and were eating it when they were apprised
of the approach of a hundred canoes of Iroquois!
Quickly as they ended their breakfast, before they could
carry their cooking utensils into the fort the foremost
of the invading Indians shot into sight, borne downward by the wild river with a rapidity that appeared
startling to the beholders.

If the watchers from the fort at first thought it possible they would pass them without molestation, they
were speedily shown the contrary, for upon reaching
the calm water at the foot of the rapids the occupants
of the canoes swarmed out upon the shore until Daulac
felt positive there were not less than two hundred of
them. He was confident it was the same war-party
that was on the way to attack the settlements, and he
addressed a few stirring words to his companions, declaring that the fate of the homes in New France was
in their hands.

The attack of the Iroquois was so stubbornly met
that the latter fell back with considerable loss. Nothing daunted by this they prepared for a second attack, changing their tactics somewhat this time. First
breaking up the canoes of the besieged allies, they
ignited the pieces of bark, and carrying these blazing
torches over their heads hoped to get near enough to

set on fire the palisades. But they were met by such a hot fire from the weapons of the brave men within the fort that the survivors were forced to retreat in wild disorder.

At this juncture, a Seneca chief, who had won great glory in a former campaign for his bravery and cunning, assumed command. It seemed certain that in a short time, inspired by his heroic daring, they would enter the fort in spite of the furious firing of the occupants. This chief had indeed almost reached the palisades, when Daulac sent a bullet through his brain. Upon seeing him fall the others again retreated into the forest, where they held a short consultation.

It proved that this party had been on its way to join another and larger body, and together they were planning to sweep every French colonist off the banks of the St. Lawrence, from Montreal to Quebec. The council quickly concluded that it would be wisest to send for this large party to come to their assistance as soon as possible. In the meantime it was decided to erect a fort for themselves close by, keeping up the appearance of a siege by an occasional attack.

While this was taking place three of the young followers of Daulac determined to bring in the head of the Seneca chief, as an act of defiance to their foes. Daulac not objecting, they set forth upon their daring mission, their companions standing at the loopholes ready to shoot down the first Iroquois that ventured within reach of their bullets. The deed was accomplished without loss of life on their part, and a few minutes later the head of the chief was placed upon the top of a pole close by the palisades.   This aroused the Iroquois to another attack, which proved as fruitless to them as ever.

Between the intervals of the attacks of the Iroquois, while they were building their fort, the French and their allies improved the opportunity to repair and strengthen their fortifications.   Small trees were cut to form a second line of palisades, the space between the rows filled in with earth to the height of a man.   Five loopholes were left on each side of the defence, each sufficient to accommodate three men, so at least sixty men could be employed at one time.

By this time the besieged party had been called upon to meet enemies more to be dreaded than even the fiery Iroquois.   These were hunger, thirst, cold, and the loss of sleep.   There was no water to be had within the inclosure of the palisades, and the only kind of food they had was the dry hominy.   Once half a dozen ventured forth, and succeeded in getting a small quantity of water, but this could not be repeated.   Then they began to dig for it, succeeding in getting a limited supply of muddy water, but in spite of all they could do their sufferings soon became intense.   This fact, with the certainty that sooner or later all must fall into the hands of the Iroquois, caused the Hurons to desert, one after another, until only their chief, the brave Étienne Annahotaha, with the four Algonquins, remained with the little band of French.

Then came the fateful day, nearly a week after the Iroquois had settled down to what seemed the slow process of starving out the besieged men, when the war-whoops of five hundred warriors, hastening to the aid of their brothers-in-arms, came wildly up through the forest, drowning the steady roar of Long Sault. The cheers of the besiegers answered in exultant tones, while the beleaguered ones felt that their last hope was gone.

Soon the siege was resumed in deadly earnest, and for three days and three nights the Iroquois kept up an irregular assault, trying in vain to get inside the walls of earth defended by the twenty brave spirits resolved to fight and die if need be, but to surrender, never! The more fearful of the besiegers would now fain give up the siege, declaring the French were protected by the Great Spirit. Others looked fiercely upon the Huron deserters, as if they would wreak their vengeance upon them. These, knowing their own lives lay in overcoming the French, boldly taunted them of lacking courage. Thereupon a daring chief proposed a scheme by which it could be found just who had the courage to continue the attack. This was to be done by tying together as many bundles of small sticks as there were warriors, and let each one choose if he would pick up one of these or not. Put thus to the test, fearing to be branded cowards if they did not, nearly all of the Iroquois and all of the Hurons caught up his bundle of sticks with guttural exclamations of defiance. All talk of desisting from the attack ended here.

Resolved now to destroy the party within the fort at any cost, a council was held to decide how it was best to cope with so desperate an enemy. Thereupon one of the Iroquois suggested that they make large wooden shields out of small trees fastened together, behind which it might be possible to reach the fort and overwhelm its defenders. This plan was accepted without debate, and preparations began at once to carry it forward. All joining willingly in the work, it required only a short time to fell the small trees and cut their trunks into suitable lengths. These pieces were then lashed together with withes, and the rude defences were ready for use.

Volunteers, eager to distinguish themselves in the fray, were not lacking to lead the charge, while behind those who carried the shields followed the main body of the Iroquois. In this way, without firing a shot, the dusky legion approached the palisades, waiting eagerly for the opportunity to begin their work of annihilation.

In the meantime a more anxious council had been held by the little group of heroic defenders of the fort. Daulac called each man by name, offering him the opportunity to surrender if he chose; but not one, even to the four Algonquins and the Huron chief, hesitated in his decision to remain. In fact, they knew only too well the dread alternative, and a speedy death was preferable to the slower torture that awaited them if they fell into the hands of the enemy alive.

Watching the movements of the Iroquois from the

loopholes they anticipated their intentions and understood the form their next attack would take. Their
only hope now lay in the musketoons, which they had
not used before on account of the greater amount of
powder they required. Now they only wished they had
four instead of two, so as to be able to protect every
side at once. However, these were planted to do the
most effective work, and the approach of the Indians
anxiously awaited.

Realising that the end was near, each brave defender
of New France stood at his post impatiently waiting for
the opening of the battle that was to become the closing act in the tragedy of border warfare. Daulac spoke
a few words of encouragement, and then turned to see
that the musketoon on that quarter was discharged at
the proper moment to do the most mischief.

It proved, indeed, a sort of mischief that for a brief
time threatened to demoralise the Iroquois. As the
double reports rang out simultaneously, many of the
shield-bearers fell, and for a time the wooden walls
proved but poor protection to those exposed by their
fall. Daulac lost no time in having the guns reloaded,
and had there been two more it would have been very
uncertain if the Iroquois, notwithstanding their overwhelming numbers, would have succeeded in their
purpose.

As it was, two sides were left unprotected by these
large firearms, and the advance of the enemies was
unchecked. The brave Huron, Étienne, was on one of

these more exposed positions, and the moment the Iroquois had got near enough to throw down their shields and begin to hack at the palisades with their hatchets, he sprang into the fray hand-to-hand. He was closely followed by others. No quarter was asked or expected. The faithful Huron soon went down with more than a dozen wounds, and his body was quickly covered by two of the Algonquins, while the French died like the heroes they had proved themselves to be.

Finding that their enemies were breaking through the wooden wall at his rear, Daulac, having literally filled to the muzzle one of the musketoons with powder and shot, lighted the fuse, and tried to throw it over the palisades into the midst of the assailants. But it was not lifted high enough to clear the top, and falling back into the inclosure it burst as it struck the ground. Several of the defenders were killed or injured by this explosion, but the others, resorting now to knives and axes, continued to hew down the Iroquois as fast as they showed themselves at the rents they had made in the walls. It had been their orders not to kill any one if possible, but to save all for the torture. But, seeing so many of their numbers slain by these indomitable men, and fearing they would escape after all, the command was given to fire upon them.

Daulac was killed by this volley, though not till he had encircled himself with victims. Of his brave companions only three survived this deadly discharge of bullets, and these were more dead than alive when seized by the fiendish captors, maddened by the fact that they obtained no more captives. In this disappointment they turned upon the unfortunate Hurons, who had deserted the French to fight with them, and more than half of their number were put to death along with the three survivors of the garrison. Of the balance of the Hurons, five escaped soon after to carry to Montreal the tragic story of the fate of Daulac and his heroic band. The fate of the other Hurons is unknown.

The Iroquois had suffered so severely at the hands of the heroes of Long Sault, and probably thinking that it would be folly to carry on their warfare with a race of whom they judged Daulac and his men to be representatives, they abandoned all further attacks for that season. Thus the heroic sacrifice of these brave soldiers of New France had not been made in vain, and for a long time their praises were sung by the thankful colonists.

Chapter XI

The Heroic Period

La Salle and his Associates—Talon, the First Intendant—Frontenac—The
Great Council with the Iroquois—Laval Restored to the Episcopate—Maids
of Quebec—First Ship upon Lake Erie—Fate of La Salle—Frontenac
Recalled—Treachery of Denonville—Massacre at La Chine—Return of
Frontenac—His "Winter Raids"—Phips's Expedition—Death of Frontenac.

WITH the exit of Champlain from the stage
the curtain falls upon the second act in the
drama of exploration and colonisation in
the valley of the St. Lawrence. When it lifts again it
rises over what has not inappropriately been styled
"the heroic period." The mantle of the explorer falls
upon Marquette, who founded, in April, 1668, the first
mission in Michigan, Sault Ste. Marie, and who reached
the Mississippi in the summer of 1673, and died on the
bank of the little river that bears his name in 1675;
Joliet, his companion; Hennepin, who explored the upper portion of the Mississippi River; and, greater than
either, La Salle, and his faithful friend of the "silver
hand," Tonty; an illustrious group who blazed the path
westward for the coming power which was destined to
be antagonistic to their own. Of these the checkered
fortunes of La Salle will have the most to do with our
work.

GRANDMÈRE ROCK, ST. MAURICE RIVER.

MONSEIGNEUR LAVAL, FIRST CANADIAN BISHOP.

In 1661 a change came over the political and commercial situation in the St. Lawrence valley. Colbert, a clear-headed, fearless financier was chosen by the King to be comptroller of finance and minister of marine. That veteran of two wars, Baron Dubois d'Avaugor, became governor of New France. He immediately saw the possibilities of the country, and declared that the St. Lawrence was the portal to "the grandest empire on earth." At this time (1663) its population, scattered among isolated posts, numbered 2500, one-third of whom lived in Quebec.

The Hundred Associates throwing up their charter, a special council was created by the King to control affairs in Canada, with Quebec its capital. May 24, 1664, under the inspiration of Colbert, the Company of the West was organised, and given the dominion of commerce for the entire territory of New France. This brought murmuring from the people, and to quiet them the company allowed the trade of the Upper St. Lawrence to redound to their profit, but retained the lower and richer section.

Louis XIV., surnamed the Great, was then in the midst of his dazzling career, calling about him some of the ablest men of his time, and making his power in his own kingdom so absolute as to be able to say, without fear of contradiction, *L'état c'est moi* ["I am the state"]. He sent to New France some of the ablest men she had. Among these came Daniel de Rémy, Sieur de Courcelles, who became governor, and Jean Baptiste

Talon, the first Intendant, an office associated in power with the first. These men were thoroughly imbued with the royal spirit of Louis.

In order to help put down the Iroquois raids twelve hundred veteran soldiers of the Turkish campaign and in other wars were sent over. What was of equal importance, two thousand immigrants came to swell the population. With the strong, righteous arm of Talon to fight for them, coupled with the energetic military skill of Courcelles, it looked as if the drooping lilies of France were to be lifted into brighter prospects than ever up and down the great river. It was then the English obtained possession of New Netherlands, and began to move up the valley of that other river, the Hudson, in a way the rival of the St. Lawrence. Charles II. was entering upon his stormy reign in England, and New England, as well as her sister colony in the north, was beginning to feel the iron heel of kingly despotism ; only in her case the master was not as worthy of his subjects.

Talon urged the necessity of establishing posts farther south, and Courcelles invaded the Mohawk country, lost his way, found village after village deserted, and was glad to get out of the wilderness. He was followed by an expedition under the lieutenant-general Marquis de Tracy, who led the largest force, thirteen hundred men, ever seen until then in the Mohawk country, and with competent guides, which his predecessor had lacked, he devastated town after town of the Mohawks. The succeeding spring the humbled red men for the first time sued for peace. Then followed twenty years in the St. Lawrence valley of freedom from the war-whoop. The population increased rapidly, and in 1670 there were 6000 inhabitants.

The colonists pushed out into the wilderness with good courage. Canada began to look like a land of homes. But, at the same time, the *coureurs de bois* received a wider license of freedom than ever, the most serious menace civilisation knew. Now, too, the explorers cross the border line: Marquette, Joliet, Hennepin, Duluth, rise like the sun, and like the sun disappear in the unknown West.

The astute Talon reserved his favours for another adventurer, who in many respects was to outstrip his rivals. His name was René Robert Cavelier, Sieur de la Salle, who was born in 1644 and appeared in Montreal in his 23rd year. His enthusiastic spirit prompted him to begin work at once. The first result was a palisaded town above the rapids, built as a station for the fur-trade. But his restless energy would not allow him a long period of clearing the wilderness here, and upon the 6th of July, 1669, we find him sailing up the St. Lawrence in quest of China. Somewhat derisively the name of La Chine was given to the estate he left when starting upon this chimerical expedition.

Breaking down under the strain upon him, Courcelles asked to be relieved of his position, and his successor appeared upon the scene in 1672. Strong as had been the men who had gone before him, the new

governor-general was one to rise head and shoulders
above them.   His was a character not pleasant to ana-
lyse ; not always friendly to his King, to his fellow-man,
to himself.   But in spite of the vices of his age and associates, in defiance of his imperious temper, his will that
brooked no opposition, his reputation not the best for
honesty, his home life not free from scandal, his intem-
perate habits, his indifference to religious teachings
according to the tenets of the Jesuits and Sulpicians,
his was a rugged, progressive, untrammelled nature.
One word expresses the name by which he is best
known, Frontenac, but he was really Louis de Baude,
Comte de Palluau et de Frontenac.   He has been
styled the "Saviour of New France."   If this honour
belongs to him it was because the country needed such
an iron will and resolute arm to stem the turgid current
of its political and commercial St. Lawrence.

Among the first things that the new governor did
was to strike at the feudal rights so dear to the King of
France, and which Talon and his associates had been
careful to foster, not caring to try the temper of Louis.
Frontenac called about him the leading spirits of the
colony, and planned to establish a structure of the
States somewhat similar to the Estates General once
popular in France, but thrust aside by the reigning
monarch.   For this he was rebuked by the King, who
had no intention of allowing any semblance of power
to spring up that should in the least interfere with his
absolutism, and New France lost her only opportunity

for freedom. This, coming from one who seemed little short of a dictator himself, was something of a surprise.

Again Frontenac looked about him, and saw wrongs that needed righting in the system of trade, and straightway he had the bushrangers arrayed against him. Nor did it stop here. Perrot, the governor, favoured the class, as they had favoured him. Immediately this aggrieved official started for France, to lay his troubles before the King. La Salle also went, with a recommendation from Frontenac for kingly assistance in opening up the west. The Sulpicians were now up in arms against the governor-general, who bent his will to no man. The Jesuits, while not openly denouncing him, placed every obstacle possible in his path.

While encouraging exploration, and La Salle above all other explorers, Frontenac had deemed it advisable to establish a post upon the shore of Lake Ontario, farther up on the St. Lawrence than had yet been done. In order to carry out this purpose to his satisfaction he planned an expedition to be headed by himself, and also sent La Salle ahead to invite the Iroquois to be present at a council. Leaving Quebec June 3, 1673, he sailed up the St. Lawrence, stopping at Montreal, where his forces were considerably increased. He left this place on the 28th, with 400 men, 120 canoes, and two flatboats. This imposing flotilla, with its brightly painted bateaux and long train of birch barques, all moving to strains of martial music, and decked with the striking and mysterious devices of a people coming as strangers into a strange land, must have created a thrilling awe in the breasts of the dusky lookouts of those island retreats.   In the foremost boat the stately figure of Frontenac was the most conspicuous object, his gold-laced uniform looking exceedingly bright, considering the long and toilsome journey he had made against the current of the mighty river, and in face of the perils of the wilderness.

Moving upon the scene with holiday pomp and gaiety, the new-comers disembarked at Cataraqui, near where now stands the city of Kingston, on the 12th of July.   The engineer, Raudin, was set to work laying out a fort, and La Salle was placed in command.   The Iroquois were promptly on hand, and the most import-ant council which had ever been held with these war-riors followed, these astute sons of the war trail finding the new commander of a different stamp to treat with than they had met before.   He both flattered and threat-ened them, and they went away deeply impressed with his presence.

The result of La Salle's visit to France was, in part, a grant to him of the fort at Cataraqui, with the adjoining territory.   Upon the same vessel that brought him back were Hennepin, the Récollet friar, who was to become noted for his western explorations; Laval, restored to the episcopate of Quebec, and Duchesnau, the successor of Talon, who had been unable to get along with Fronte-nac.   The times must have been prolific of independent spirits, for it is seldom four were ever brought together

LA SALLE HOUSE, LOWER LA CHINE ROAD, MONTREAL.

From a photograph by W. Notman & Son, Montreal.

A SUMMER SCENE ON THE SHORE OF LAKE MEMPHREMAGOG.

From a photograph by W. Notman & Son, Montreal.

who were so strong-minded each in his own peculiar
field of work.

Upon this ship came also another element quite as
disturbing to the decorum of the company as either, on
account of their merry ways rather than from any ma-
licious disposition.   This was a bevy of pretty maids
sent over by the King to become the wives of needy
settlers.   From the beginning in New France there had
been a scarcity of women, and Talon, in his endeavour
to increase the number of settlers, called especially for
young ladies to save the country from a matrimonial
famine.   In 1665 one hundred girls arrived in Quebec,
and were quickly supplied with husbands.   The following year twice as many came, and still the demand was
not met.   Another company of over a hundred came in
1667, and from year to year this practice was kept up.
Many of these girls were selected from good families
at home and were intended to supply the seigneurs, and
thus from the beginning were built up two classes in
Canada, the *noblesse* and the habitants ; the first holding
the lands of the King, and the others cultivating it upon
leases.   Upon being separated into the class where the
candidates for matrimonial honours belonged, those who
desired a wife stated their wishes to a person in charge,
usually a woman, gave proof as to his possessions and
ability to support a home, when he was at liberty to
select one most to his fancy from the class in which he
had a right to look.   The maids, on their part, were
given the privilege to reject any man that might not

appear congenial, when he would be obliged to try again. The choice being mutual, the couple sought a priest and notary, and were speedily united for better or worse, and there is no record to show that these impromptu marriages did not prove as satisfactory as weddings made with greater leisure.

In 1676, encouraged by Frontenac and the peace of the country, at the time when the New England colonists were in the midst of King Philip's War, La Salle rebuilt in masonry the walls to Fort Frontenac, as Cataraqui had been renamed, strengthened the palisades, laid the keel of a ship, and brought cattle from Montreal. The settlement grew under his fostering care, and another year he had three vessels plying upon the lake, whose profit to him amounted to 25,000 livres a year.

Still he saw through his ambition a vision of the Mississippi for ever rolling into the mysterious west. So he went to France in 1678 to obtain permission to extend commerce in that direction. He secured from the King, who never seemed to refuse help to the struggling colony, a patent which empowered him to go on with his work. What was of almost equal importance to him, he secured the friendship and companionship of a remarkable man, who was never to falter in his behalf through the trying scenes to follow. This was Henry Tonty, the son of Lorenzo Tonti, the Italian refugee, whose name is connected with the Tontine system of insurance. La Salle and Tonty came with a good force of mechanics and shipbuilders to help along their plans.

We next see them upon Lake Erie, building the first vessel ever sailed upon this inland sea, which he named the *Griffin* for the fabulous monster, half bird, half beast, dwelling in the Rhipæan Mountains and guarding the treasures of the Hyperborean regions. Completed in May, this little vessel, with an armanent of five guns, proudly left her rude dock in August, her crew singing *Te Deum*, as she unfurled her canvas to the virgin breeze. With the prospect gradually unfolding to him like a vision seen in a dream, as he sailed away in the eye of the westering sun, that was probably the happiest moment of La Salle's checkered life. Out of Erie into Huron, by the river between, flew the triumphant *Griffin*, looking indeed like a veritable bird to the wondering eyes that saw her from the distance. A stop was made at the mission of Ignace at Michilimackinac, where the hero in his gold-laced uniform and air of a conqueror attended divine worship, to kneel with becoming grace among the humble and dusky followers of the cross.

La Salle learned here that some of the men he had sent to trade with the Indians had deserted him and become traders on their own account—*coureurs de bois.* Others were only lukewarm in his interest, and he felt that his presence was none too welcome. He arrested a few of the unfaithful, and sent scouts to look after those abroad. Then he broke faith with his patrons by securing at Green Bay, from the Ottawas, a cargo of pelts, though his commission stated that he should not do this. His excuse to himself, if his conscience called for an explanation, must have been that he had got to do something of the kind to satisfy his creditors, for he had been obliged to depend largely upon borrowed capital in order to carry on his undertaking.

On September 18th, her ill-gotten cargo stowed away, the *Griffin* sailed upon her return trip under the charge of a captain, pilot, and three men. That was the last La Salle ever saw or heard of his ship. It was rumoured she was lost in a storm, and all on board perished. It was whispered that her pilot had run her aground upon the nearest point of land, and with his associates undertook to get away with the cargo, only to fall into the hands of hostile Indians who put them to death. Which was correct the owner never knew, and to this day no one has become wiser than he.

Upon parting with his ship laden with its goods, flattering himself that his creditors would be pleased, La Salle then entered upon a career whose account reads like a pathetic romance. He passed up Lake Michigan; he built a fort upon the St. Joseph, now the Illinois, River; with his dream of exploring the Mississippi still uppermost in his mind, he laid the keel here for another vessel; not overpleased with his stern ways, some of his best carpenters deserted him; haunted by the dread of some mishap having befallen the *Griffin*, he left his station, which he had named *Fort Crêvecœur*, in remembrance of a fort by that name in Netherlands, under the command of Tonty, and started for Ontario across the peninsula of Michigan, where he and his companions

encountered perils enough to make the stoutest heart quail. . . . They waded through drowned lands. They were obliged to thaw their stiffened clothes in the morning before they could move. Where they found a path in the opening they burned the grass to destroy their trail, for warring savages invested the country, little discriminating as regarded their human prey.

La Salle reached the shipyard where the *Griffin* had been built, to learn to a certainty that the vessel had been lost. To his further disappointment, he was told that a vessel he had expected to come to Niagara with supplies had been wrecked on the St. Lawrence. To complicate matters still more, a report had been circulated by his enemies that he was dead, and under this pretence his property had been sold under the hammer, and his agents had taken the profits. Fortunately, he had the robust friendship of Frontenac left him. This enabled him to resume his tortuous path of exploration, not the least of his dangers being the jealousies and discouragements of rivals, each anxious to get the credit of what was being done. This chapter of discovery and adventure, in which the names of La Salle, Tonty, Marquette, Hennepin, Duluth, and others are associated, is filled with records of hardships and sufferings, the rewards to the individuals small for the sacrifices they underwent. Out of this stormy conquest came a union of the St. Lawrence with the Mississippi, and by these great rivers was the Gulf of St. Lawrence linked to the Gulf of Mexico.

La Salle perished miserably at the hands of a renegade follower in the midst of his explorations, a victim, perhaps, to his own arrogance. No character among the early voyagers and discoverers has been more variously estimated than his. He was certainly not without his faults, the greatest of which seemed to be his inability to make many friends and never to placate an enemy. He did not a little for the development of the St. Lawrence valley, and he deserved all the praise his memory will ever get.

In the meantime, a storm had set in at Quebec, which threatened the ruin of the colony. Frontenac and the Intendant were at sword's point over matters trivial and serious. Laval, the bishop, and the Jesuits combined against the former ; the Récollet friars and the merchant stoutly maintained that he was right. So fast and furious did this war wage that both were recalled. Unfortunately, this was done in the midst of an uprising on the part of the Iroquois, who had been encouraged to open hostilities again by the Governor of New York, Colonel Dongan. The blow was not aimed directly at the inhabitants of the St. Lawrence valley, but against the Indians of the Illinois River. Frontenac had warned them to take their hands off of this tribe occupying a country he, through La Salle, was trying to open up. They replied insolently at first, but, not daring to try the bluff old soldier too far, finally came to Montreal to treat with him. Now La Barre, an old man sent to do a young man's work, succeeded

Frontenac. He made a sad mess of the warring elements. He evaded, he fought, he implored, he betrayed his allies on the one hand and feebly pleaded for them on the other, until, had not the Iroquois been too far-seeing to carry out such a scheme, there is little doubt but the last Frenchman in the St. Lawrence country would have bade a long farewell to its scenes. The saving grace for La Barre was the fact that the politic Iroquois leaders could realise that with the removal of the French from the field of action they would have a power more to be dreaded in the English. For this reason they suffered them to remain and harass the others.

Then La Barre was recalled and one Denonville sent in his place. James II. was on the throne of England, and between him and Louis XIV. existed amicable relations. The two fixed up terms of peace between their possessions in America, without either entering into the full depth of the problem. This was nothing less than the settlement of the mastery of the west. Dongan's first move was to capture the trade of the St. Lawrence for the Hudson. To obtain this, he sent his men far into the north, where never an Englishman had gone before. His next aim was exactly what the French had been trying to do by the English; that is, confine them to the smallest extent of territory possible. Dongan was favoured in this part of his scheme from the fact of the raids on Acadie by the New Englanders. Denonville, in his eagerness to carry out the policy of his predecessors, Talon, La Salle, Frontenac, ignored the treaty of peace made by his King, and sent troops to rout the posts established by the English in the Hudson Bay region. Then both he and Dongan decided it was for their interest to maintain a fort at Niagara, the best man to win the race. The site considered most desirable was held by the Senecas. They were not an easy occupant to placate, either by the wiles of peace or by the arts of war. But Denonville considered himself equal to the task, and he set himself about it in a manner which has blackened his name with infamy.

In 1687 he gathered his armed forces and moved up the St. Lawrence to Fort Frontenac, where he invited some of the Seneca chiefs to a council. Innocent of the treachery of their host these came, were seized by surprise and sent to France, where they were punished as slaves in the King's galleys. He then pillaged the villages of some neutral Iroquois, who were living quietly and peacefully near by. These shared the fate of poor slaves, though it was claimed the evil of the deed had been mitigated by converting the captive women and children to Christianity. Losing no time lest the news might spread, Denonville moved swiftly over the lake, and, reinforced by friendly Indians from Michilimackinac, he hurled his allied forces upon the surprised Senecas. A short and terrific resistance was made, but the end was inevitable. The towns of the Indians were laid in ruins, their stores of grain were confiscated, and their herds of swine seized. The survivors of that terrible day came forth from their concealment in the forests, when the enemies had left, broken in spirit and desolate.

Denonville had now a clear way to build his fort at Niagara, which he proceeded to do, and then armed it with one hundred men. If triumphant in his bold plans, he had to learn that the viper crushed might rise to sting. The Senecas had their avengers. Maddened by the cowardly onset of Denonville and his followers, the Iroquois to a man rose against the French. This was not done by any organised raid, but, shod with silence, small, eager war-parties haunted the forests of the St. Lawrence, striking where they were the least expected, and never failing to leave behind them the smoke of burning dwellings and the horrors of desolated lives. From Fort Frontenac to Tadousac there was not a home exempt from this deadly scourge ; not a life that was not threatened. Unable to cope with so artful a foe, Denonville was in despair. He sued for peace, but to obtain this he had got to betray his allies, the Indians of the Upper Lakes, who had entered his service under the condition that the war should continue until the Iroquois were exterminated. The latter sent delegates to confer with the French commander at Montreal. While this conference was under way, a Huron chief showed that he was the equal of even Denonville in the strategies of war where the code of honour was a dead letter.

Anticipating the fate in store for his race did the

French carry out their scheme of self-defence, this chief whose name was Kandironk, "the Rat," lay in ambush for the envoys on their way home from their conference with Denonville, when the latter had made so many fair promises. These Kandironk captured, claiming he did it under orders from Denonville, bore them to Michilimackinac, and tortured them as spies. This done, he sent an Iroquois captive to tell his people how fickle the French could be. Scarcely was this accomplished when he gave to the French his exultant declaration : "I have killed the peace !"

The words were prophetic. Nothing that Denonville could say or do cleared him of connection with the affair. His previous conduct was enough to condemn him. To avenge this act of deceit, as the Iroquois considered it, they rallied in great numbers, and on the night of August 4, 1689, dealt the most cruel and deadly blow given during all the years of warfare in the St. Lawrence valley. Fifteen hundred strong, under cover of the darkness they stole down upon the settlement of La Chine situated at the upper end of the island of Montreal, and surprised the inhabitants while they slept in fancied security. More than two hundred men, women, and children were slain in cold blood, or borne away to fates a hundred times more terrible to meet than swift death. The day already breaking upon the terror-stricken colonists was the darkest Canada ever knew.

In addition to these perils and horrors of Indian warfare, from which Quebec suffered her share, this town was visited in the summer of 1682, on the 4th of August, by a fire that swept the Lower Town, leaving only one house standing, and licking up more than half the wealth of New France.

Following the massacre of La Chine, Denonville awoke to the fact that instead of conquering the English and exterminating the Indians, he had got to look to the protection of his own flock. Already it was rumoured that Major Andros, who had succeeded Dongan in New York, was planning to conquer New France. James II. had been succeeded as King of England by William of Orange, who hated Louis, and war was declared between the two nations.

Fortunately for New France Denonville was recalled. He had shown himself too weak to strike a blow against the enemy after the La Chine horror, as well as having proved that he was unable to follow up the advantage gained by La Salle and even then faithfully guarded by Tonty, Duluth, and Perrot. The one man needed at that lonely hour was Frontenac. His faults forgotten, he was prayed for by the Church and the people; his sterling qualities remembered, he was sent by Louis to become the saviour of New France.

It was near the middle of October, 1689, when the ship upon which the grizzled veteran, erect and vigorous in spite of his seventy years, was taken back to Quebec, sailed up the St. Lawrence and dropped anchor under the frowning walls. It was late in the evening, but his arrival had been anticipated, and the expectant citizens had gathered upon the quay, lighting the scene with torches, while fireworks and thousands of coloured lights illuminated the streets of the Upper Town in honour of his coming. There was no murmuring Jesuit protesting against him ; no Intendant chafing at his iron rule ; but one and all gave the glad hand of welcome to the hero, and that night Quebec slept with a hopeful calmness she had not known for years.

While deficient in both money and troops, Frontenac quickly infused new life into the hearts of his people. He restored the Iroquois chiefs, so basely captured by Denonville, to their subjects, and the Iroquois felt the powerful *Onontio*, as they called him, would not hesitate to deal with them as they had dealt with the French people. But Frontenac's first move was against the English in what has passed into history as his "three winter raids." Made up of regulars, *coureurs de bois*, and Indians, these war-parties started in the dead of winter from Montreal, Three Rivers, and Quebec. The first, by following the Richelieu valley, reached the Dutch settlement of Corlaer, now Schenectady, N. Y., which they desolated. The second passed up the valley of the St. Francis, through the deep snow and the "white swamps," to finally reach the settlement of Salmon Falls, on the border of New Hampshire, where the inhabitants were inhumanly butchered. This division then joined the company from Quebec, and moving against the villages in Maine carried on the work of desolation, the Indians, breaking the pledges of the French made to

CHEVALIER DE LA SALLE.

FRONTENAC.

From Hébert's Statue at Quebec.

those who surrendered, adding to the horrors by a shameless slaughter of captives.

News of these successes coming to their ears, the Indians, who had faltered in their allegiance to the French, now came resolutely forward. Light hearts reigned in Quebec, while up and down the valley of the St. Lawrence bonfires were lighted in honour of the brighter prospects of New France. But if Frontenac had invested his followers with renewed courage, by this very act of blood and rapine he had aroused the New England inhabitants to such a feeling of indignation that they became united in a struggle against Canada which did not cease until Quebec fell.

Plans were laid for the capture of the towns on the St. Lawrence by the concerted efforts of the militia of New York against Montreal, and a naval expedition against Quebec commanded by Sir William Phips. The command of the former undertaking was intrusted to Fitz-John Winthrop, under a commission from Governor Leisler dated July 31, 1690. It proved a failure from the outset. Phips, an adventurer of checkered experience, with little military or naval skill, but withal considerable resource of tactics and a large reserve stock of bluff, in command of thirty-two vessels of various sizes, and a little over two thousand men, set forth upon his expedition with entire confidence in his ability to clear the rock of Quebec of every foe. To distract Frontenac's attention, Colonel Church was sent along the Atlantic coast with a land force. He at least accomplished his purpose. Phips had been encouraged by an easy capture of Port Royal a short time before with a smaller force, but he was to find a far different reception at Quebec.

At the time, Frontenac was in Montreal dancing the war-dance with some Indians from Michilimackinac. News had just come to him of Colonel Winthrop's raid on La Prairie, all that came of New York's part in the "conquest of Canada," and he was planning a counter-attack for this assault when a messenger apprised him of the advance of an English fleet up the St. Lawrence. He returned to the capital with all haste possible. Since his arrival from France he had caused the weakened defences to be repaired. A call was made for the rallying of the Canadian militia, then scattered over the country. It was a lively day in Quebec, with her fortifications still incomplete, her guns in bad shape, her stock of ammunition low, her provisions scanty, her troops meagre in number,—but they had Frontenac!

The grim warrior showed no signs of trepidation. Ay, they do say he smiled when, on the morning of October 16th (1690), the English fleet was discovered coming up the river. For some reason Phips, usually so energetic, had dallied on his way, stopping nearly three weeks at Tadousac for no apparent reason, unless he wished to give his enemy so much time to carry on the work of preparation for him. If he lost courage at sight of the embattled heights he did not show it. Dropping anchor not far from where Kertk had done

the same upon the eve of his conquest, Phips coolly
sent a demand for the surrender of the French stronghold. This messenger, according to an order from
Frontenac, was blindfolded and then led by a circuitous way to the great council hall in Château St. Louis,
where the royal governor and his associates awaited
him. Upon having the covering removed from his eyes,
this officer must have been possessed of nerves of iron
not to be, for a moment at least, dumfounded by the
warlike group before him.

He found himself standing before a tall, thin old man of commanding presence, with a nose like an eagle's beak, who looked at
him sternly out of a pair of fierce grey eyes, deep-set under great
tufted brows—a weather-beaten, age-lined face, which, better than
the upright figure and the easy grace of movement, bespoke years of
campaigning on the field. It was Frontenac.

Upon either hand of him were representatives of the
noblesse of the colony, gay courtiers in brilliant dress,
some young in years, but of noble families and destined
to carve for themselves names of renown in the coming struggle of New France ; others already, like their
leader, grown grey in the service of their King. To
these men, but first to the white-haired governor in
their centre, the young English officer delivered his
audacious message. Frontenac's associates would have
burst forth into indignant laughter, but their chief si-
lenced them with a wave of his hand, which also conveyed his answer to Phips, with the added explanation
that the cannon would be his spokesman. So Phips's

boastful campaign ended in bluster. Possibly he might have succeeded had he followed the advice given him to lead his men up the same pathway where, a little less than three-fourths of a century later, Wolfe climbed to immortality, but the obstinate Englishman had a plan of his own that ended in disaster to his hopes. It was a forlorn fleet that straggled into Boston, the ships coming by twos and singly, such as did return ; for several, with those on board, were never heard from. New England must indeed recuperate her strength and replenish her treasury before she again thought of invading New France.

Proud indeed was the moment to Frontenac, when he watched the departing fleet disappearing around the point of the Isle of Orleans, though he was not fitted to attempt any further the conquest of the land of his rivals. He stood higher than ever in the estimation of his followers, and another good stroke of fortune lifted him yet higher in their esteem. This was his success in collecting and running down from the upper country a flotilla of canoes, numbering over a hundred, every one heavily laden with pelts, to gladden the hearts of the traders of Montreal. Nothing like that had been seen for years, and a festival of rejoicing was held, during which it is said the courtly governor, despite his more than seventy years, danced with his dusky *voyageurs* in their merry-making.

If the war between the French and the English abated for a time, the great three-cornered fight was not yet ended. The Iroquois were not vanquished from the vales of the Mohawk; while in the east, the Abnakis were already duplicating their deeds against the French by leaving trails of blood between the New England homes. Everywhere in New France and New England the torch and the scalping-knife were held aloft, and both were crimson. The advantage, if it came to either, fell to the French.

The fur-trade continued to yield a good income, and the people began to prosper as they had never prospered before. To ensure greater glory in this direction, Frontenac planned a campaign against the English trading posts in the region of Hudson Bay. This expedition was commanded by D'Iberville, who had been successful in crowding the English down to the seacoast in the lower districts. He was so far successful in the north that Frontenac felt as if he had but one enemy more to overcome. This was the irrepressible Iroquois, though even these had not rallied as they had at the time of the La Chine massacre. He resolved to strike one more blow in that direction, and heavy enough to be his last.

So, in 1696, in his seventy-sixth year, he assembled at Fort Frontenac over two thousand men, and, crossing the lake with a vast fleet of canoes, entered the Oswego River. Following this stream to the falls, and transporting their boats by portage, the expedition, the largest invading force ever seen in that country, moved majestically up Lake Onondaga. Discovered by

Indian scouts, the news flew like wildfire through the encampment of the Iroquois, and, dismayed at the imposing sight of such an enemy, the red men scattered through the woods, like rabbits driven from the brush. The French force, marching in military array, with drums beating and colours flying, advanced upon a pile of smouldering ruins, where a short time before had stood the proud village of the Long House. A few tardy Indians, hesitating in their flight, were captured and put to tortures that even their own skill could not have outdone. Fields of corn, orchards of apples, and patches of melons had been left undisturbed by the fugitives. These the French ravaged; and despoiling village after village, though securing few prisoners, leaving only when he had completed a scene of desolation, Frontenac returned in triumph to the place of starting. At last the pride and power of the Five Nations had been humbled. Soon after, the Iroquois sued for peace. Then, September 20, 1697, followed the Treaty of Ryswick between the French and the English, which closed at last Frontenac's long series of campaigns.

In truth, the illustrious career of the hero was itself drawing to a close. In his last campaign it had been necessary to carry him in a chair, though his eagle spirit had not been daunted. Now the iron will, unbending still, was broken by the touch of the eternal hand on the 28th of November, 1698, in his seventy-eighth year. Thus passed from the stage of action the strongest,

grandest figure since Champlain, and not to be equalled
until the third of the great trio, Montcalm, should fall
fighting for the glory of the grey old rock upon which
the first had founded and the second had defended so
nobly the honour of New France.

Chapter XII

Bushrangers and *Voyageurs*

The *Coureurs de Bois*—A Unique Canadian Character—Their Dress and Habits—
The *Voyageurs*—Rangers of Romance—Personal Appearance—Their Roving
Natures—Rowing Songs—Story of Cadieux—His "Lament"—Revelry at
the Rendezvous—Homeward Bound.

FREQUENT mention has been made in connection with the fur-trade of a class that gave no
little uneasiness both to the religious teachers
and the Government. As the traffic in beaver pelts increased, this evil grew, until not only the morals but the
very life of the colony was threatened. This element
has since found its rival, though not its equal, in the
sable hunters of Siberia. The nearest approach to it
with the English has been the trappers of the Far West,
who led the way for civilisation beyond the Rocky
Mountains. As gold-seekers, instead of fur-seekers, it
overran Australia for a period, and then vanished as
mysteriously as it came,—as it finally disappeared from
the Canadian wilds.

I come now to speak at closer range, as it were, of
that class of early immigrants to Canada which had the
most to do with its acclaim and the least to do with its
good. These were the *coureurs de bois*, or "runners of

the woods." *Coureurs de risques!* "runners of risks," says the keen-witted Hontan. Unlike the pioneers of New England they were rovers of the wilderness, the fur-trade offering them a ready excuse for their wanderings. But the actual spirit which led them far into the forest fastnesses was that restless nature ever urging them on to find solace for souls that neither compassed restfulness nor longings that were satisfied. This daring of the solitude, voluntary isolation of homes, led the King in the middle of the seventeenth century to order the colonists, for their own safety, which meant the well-being of the colony, "to make no more clearings except one next to another, and to reduce their parishes so as to conform as much as possible to the parishes of France."

In their lives alone Canada offers a great field for the romancer. With a swarthy face, his small head covered with a red woollen cap, made loose, or a head-gear made of the skin of the fox or the wolf, his lithe body clad in blanket-coats, girthed about the waist with stout leathern thongs, his lower limbs encased in deerskin leggins, fringed along the seams, and his feet thrust into moccasins ornamented with porcupine quills, the Canadian ranger looked what he was, the most picturesque character that came to the front in those adventurous times. In the course of his career he was wandering all over the great North-west. Without him New France must have remained a dream in the troubled sleep of the French; with him, she became a nightmare.

Following close upon the heels of the fortune-seeking fur-traders who pushed out into the wilderness along the St. Lawrence and its many tributaries, establishing their posts to carry on their rude commerce, came that class of adventurers styled the Canadian *voyageurs*, whose very name became synonymous of bravery and romance. By this term I am not understood to mean the first sailors and explorers who came to Canada, but rather their descendants, many of whom were half-breeds, all of whom were roving, care-free followers of the wilderness, noted for the skill with which they handled their birchen skiffs, and found wherever these could penetrate with their sharp prows the many streams abounding in a country richly endowed in this respect. Their temperament seems to have been the embodiment of the restless energy for conquest and intense longing for loneliness that pervaded all of the earlier enterprises of New France. It was the controlling spirit of Cartier and his followers ; it was the guiding star of the *coureur de bois*, setting only when the *fleur-de-lis* of France faded from the rock of Quebec ; it was the overruling power of the zealous missionary, sending him far and wide into the savage wilderness ; it even entered into the foundation of the colonial homes, scattering them in a way that greatly enlarged the domains of New France. In Champlain we find a happy combination of the missionary and the *voyageur*, with a leavening of home love.

There was possibly no phase of life in the breaking of the American wilderness which afforded a

VIEW OF THE ST. LAWRENCE RIVER, FROM CITADEL, QUEBEC.
From a photograph by Livernois, Quebec.

ST. PATRICK'S HOLE, ST. FERREOL.

From a photograph by Livernois, Quebec.

larger meed of romance and adventure than that
of the Canadian *voyageur*, in the days when the forest
was pathless and the St. Lawrence bore on its broad
bosom no larger craft than an occasional caravel from
the Old World.   Trained from early boyhood to the
exciting work of propelling their crafts up and down
the streams, now stemming some furious rapid, anon
running the cataracts, at periods compelled to make a
tedious portage where the waters ran too wild to risk
the loss of their freight, apparently calling for more
concern than their lives, they could not have been other
than hardy, reckless, intrepid spirits, whose only relaxation was to be found at the trading station, where too
often their meagre earnings were spent in the jovial
bowl.   At these rendezvous the wine ran freely, so much
the worse for them, as those were days of liberal drinking, when joviality reigned over the flowing bowl and
under the spell of the goddess of song.   Frequently
they were of pure Iroquois or Huron blood; more
often they were a mixture of white and red parentage,
often noticeable in the dark features of some Norman
whose skin was given a deeper bronze by his mother, a
dusky Indian maid.   The majority of the *voyageurs*
were of French extraction.

The garb of this rover of the forest and river was in
poetical harmony with his character and surroundings.   It consisted of a cotton shirt, generally striped
in bright colours, cloth trousers, and leather leggins.
The feet were encased in deerskin moccasins.   Over the

shoulders rested lightly, each passing breeze lifting it in graceful imitation of the movement of the wearer, a *capot* or little cloak. His waist was girthed about with a wide worsted belt with flowing ends, from which were suspended a knife and tobacco pouch. This half-wild dress of the *voyageur* was rendered more picturesque in case the owner was the favourite follower of some brigade leader, when he would have a long black or red feather attached to his close-fitting cap.

In keeping with the supple figure of the man, his canoe was builded of wonderful lightness, considering that no sacrifice of the strength and lasting qualities that were necessary had been allowed. It was made of birch bark cut in sheets of suitable length, and selected by an experienced eye for its thinness and durability. The seams were pitched so as to be water-tight. One of these crafts, capable of carrying great weight, could be easily carried upon the shoulders of a single man. It passed the comprehension of the Indians that these new-comers could outdo them with generations of training in this handicraft, and they believed the Frenchmen had been given special secrets by the Great Spirit.

There were heavier canoes for transporting freight, and these were marvels of lightness, considering their ability to carry from three to four tons' burden. A crew usually consisted of a dozen men, who were capable of moving their boat along at a rapid rate of speed, notwithstanding its heavy freight.

Nothing suited these rowers better than their periodical trips into the river-bound interior of an unexplored country, and yet, like sailors about to embark upon their long voyages, upon the eve of their departure upon a trip which might keep them away for months, they delighted to drown their anxieties in brimming bumpers of wine, until it often became necessary for their leaders to carefully keep them in ignorance of the actual day set for the journey. Otherwise, the day of their departure known, a generous feast was given by their friends and loved ones, when wives, children, and sweethearts gathered around them to bid their husky farewells and hopeful "*bon voyage.*"

No sooner was the ordeal of separation over than the wild natures of the crew asserted themselves, and while the cheers of those who remained behind rang on the air, serving to encourage them, each round growing fainter and more prolonged, the entire party would strike up a *chanson de voyage*, the volume of the song more than making up for its lack of melody.

Not infrequently some old French song of traditional love affair would be started by him at the steering paddle, when his companions would quickly join in, until the welkin would ring with the melody of voices. These were usually selected with a remarkable fitness for the occasion and environment of the situation. Was the canoe gliding over some placid lake, where scarcely a breath of air moved the glassy surface of the water, the song was sure to move in harmony with the calmness of the tranquil scene. Should they be approaching a

waterfall, the foam upon the river was no surer indication of the coming struggle with the elements than the
quickening notes of the singer, the increased volume of
the song, the growing impetuosity of the melody, ringing with the spirit of enthusiasm to do and dare whatever lay in their pathway.   Did the arms of the rower
tire, or his spirits lag for a time, some gay song burning
with new-born activity would revive the faltering energy.
At all times the paddles kept time with the singers.
Among the favourite songs was *À la Claire Fontaine*,
whose opening stanza runs—

> À la claire fontaine,
> M'en allant promener,
> J'ai trouvé l'eau si belle,
> Que je m'y suis baigné.

A free translation in English makes this :

> Unto the crystal fountain,
> For pleasure did I stray ;
> So fair I found the waters,
> In them my limbs I lay.

Another popular rowing song among the *voyageurs*
was *Dans les Prisons de Nantes*, which, unlike most of
the Canadian songs that could be traced back to an origin in the old country, seems to have been composed by
one of this hardy class.   This goes on to describe in
verses of more than ordinary merit how a soldier was
captured and thrown into prison at Nantes to be freed
by the gaoler's pretty daughter the eve before the day
upon which he was to have been shot.   There was still

another of these songs frequently sung, around which clung a pathetic story of heroism unto death.

As far back as the days of Champlain an educated and adventurous Frenchman named Cadieux met, upon one of his trips into the wilderness in quest of furs, the beautiful daughter of a chief of the tribe of Indians living upon the upper Ottawa. Falling in love with this dusky belle of the wilds, he made her his wife, and built him a dwelling in that region within sight and sound of the river. For several years his cabin home was the rendezvous for *voyageurs* ranging the country in that direction, until the hospitality of this couple became widely known. But one day they were surprised by a band of hostile Iroquois just as they were launching their canoes upon the rapid stream. Cut off from reaching their cabin, Cadieux shouted to his companion to keep on down the river while he went up-stream, expecting by this stratagem either to divide the force of their enemies or give his wife an easy way of escape by calling all the Iroquois after him.

Confident of capturing both of them the latter gave pursuit in both directions, expecting to make quick work of overtaking the woman, as her light canoe was plunged into the boiling water where it did not seem possible to escape. But like a feather it was lifted from pool to pool, while in the mist that enveloped the escaping spouse the Iroquois discerned a female figure beckoning her on. The fleeing Christian wife afterwards declared that she was guided to safety by " Bonne

Ste. Anne." At any rate the Iroquois abandoned their
pursuit of her, and she succeeded in getting away without being harmed. Cadieux was less fortunate. After
seeing his wife successfully shoot the rapids, having
killed two of his enemies, and received himself a painful
wound, the brave *voyageur* kept on up the river to a
cave opening upon its bank. Crawling into this retreat
he prepared to defend himself unto the end. So desperately did he do this, that his foes tried in vain for
three days and nights to drive him out or reach him.
But the end was near now. The pangs of hunger, his
lack of sleep, his exhaustion from his unbroken vigilance,
to say nothing of the weakness resulting from his wounds,
all combined to warn him of his fate. Surrender he
never would, and so deliberately planned to die of starvation, if he escaped death otherwise. In the intervals
of his long and painful suspense, he composed his
Lament de Cadieux, writing it down upon scraps of
birch bark in his own blood. This was found beside
his lifeless body, by his faithful wife, who sought to
effect his rescue as soon as she could find succour, and
its touching and beautiful strains became a favourite with
the *voyageurs* as they drew near the foaming currents
of the upper Ottawa, while on the St. Lawrence they
were long popular and are still remembered, as well as
the pathetic fate of their author.

So these half-wild beings of woods and water,
thoughtless of future perils, paddled industriously
against the current of some rapid stream, carrying their

boats and freight around the rifts that were impassable, now making the welkin ring with the melody of their songs, anon gliding like shadows over some sheet of dark water, camping at the close forgetful of the dangers and hardship of their voyage, while they peopled the night with weird creatures of their fanciful tales told under the mystic spell of the pipe and the glowing embers.

Wherever they went, and that was all over Canada, their track was marked at frequent intervals by wooden crosses, where some comrade, worn out with the ceaseless toil of his journey, or meeting a more untimely fate in the swirling eddies of some uncommonly dangerous rift, found his resting-place,

> Where the stalwart oak grew and lived
> Long ages and died among its kind.

The *voyageurs* from each section of the St. Lawrence had their particular rendezvous where they found a hearty greeting at the end of their arduous journey. Those who went up the Saguenay found their destination at the station of Roberval on the headwaters of that river, a place filled with tragic memories. The followers of the Ottawa from Montreal stopped at Fort Nicollet, later renamed Fort William. A large wooden building had been erected here to accommodate the *voyageurs* and *coureurs de bois* who met here to transfer their merchandise and barter news as well as trade. The great council hall, where the whites had been wont to meet the Indians in trying a debate, now became the banquet-room and the scene of ungovernable revelry, when the passions of half-wild men were loosened by the brimming bowl and the merry songs. Especial effort was made to load the tables with the choicest viands from nature's storehouse of game. Among the daintiest morsels served at these banquets were buffalos' tongues and beavers' tails. Then, the cargoes loaded and everything in readiness for departure, a final feast was given, a closing toast drunk, the last handshake over, our *voyageurs* start their canoes homeward, as they glide with the current of the river, singing some favourite song expressive of their freedom from cares :

> The river runs free,
> The west wind is clear,
> And my love is calling to me.
> There is a good wind,
> There is a free tide,
> And my love is waiting for me.

Those who may feel that all this was close to an element of savagery should not forget that it is but a step backward from civilisation to barbarism. If it was a trait to be found in our ancestors that we believe we have not inherited, it was because they lived nearer to nature. But we have not escaped it if we would. In the rapidity and pleasure with which men delight to isolate themselves, break away from the shell of conventionality and wallow in the furrow of indolent imagery, we see ample proof of the truth of this. We see it typified in the hunter lured into the depths of the forest under the pretence of slaying some helpless victim, but really governed by the irresistible impulse to be by himself. There is evidence of it in the naturalist, in the mountaineer, in the friend who frequently breaks away from the social ties of life to roam the open fields, wander in the fastness of the forest, loneliness of the mountain, the sublimity of the seashore. It is not an indication of weakness. Rather it is the vital spark of humanity. So long as its embers last will there be hope for the race.

Chapter XIII

When Quebec Fell

FRONTENAC left New France at the high-water mark of prosperity and power. Never before had its people been favoured with such rare good fortune ; and never would it enjoy such favours. The St. Lawrence bore upon its broad shield more ships of commerce than it had ever known, and every inland stream was the pathway of the hardy *voyageur*, *en route* with his cargo of furs. The population had increased; new towns had sprung up; and now the fickle goddess which had so long coquetted with " Our Lady of the Snow " seemed to surrender without reserve.

Still there were many perplexing problems to be settled. Much as the trade of the St. Lawrence valley had increased, it was not yet sufficient to meet all its obligations without help from the mother-hand. The Iroquois were not yet fully subdued, and from time to time they raided the country, in small parties it is true, but none the less to be dreaded. It cost considerable to maintain the friendship of the Abnakis in the east. The English were drawing from them their trade by the way of the Kennebec, Hudson, Ohio, and the Mississippi. The cabins of English pioneers, as well as the huts of their traders, were springing up where least expected. In order to protect the valley of the west it was necessary to draw from the valley of the St. Lawrence.

The population at this time of New France did not reach higher than thirty thousand souls. Besides these there were not less than five thousand soldiers in the country, comprising some of the best-drilled regiments in the world. To strengthen the military force were the country militia, which consisted of every male citizen able to bear arms, while there was not a seigneur of the villages and fortress-like châteaux that was not capable of leading these men in war. Added to all of these were the scattered bands of savages, trained by the Jesuits, themselves imbued with a martial spirit scarcely inferior to their religious enthusiasm. These were powerful allies in the sanguinary struggle waged so long. In point of military ability New France was far superior to her rival.

But the worst enemies this fair empire knew were those within the fold. If England was accustomed, now and then, to steal a plum from the pudding of her colonists, France was ready to take the pudding. Few of the many who were intrusted with the guardianship of this fair ward of the St. Lawrence were faithful to their charge ; to the pity of the child ; to the shame of the

mother. And each despoiler, regardless of the sufferings he had inflicted, turned from his victim with the
disdain of the libertine, spurning the virtue he had
violated. But the day of reckoning was not so far
removed.

Frontenac was succeeded by Vaudreuil, under whose
long rule the cultivation of flax and hemp and the home
manufacture of clothing was encouraged. Greater
attention was paid to the fisheries, and shipbuilding
flourished. Considerable trade with the West Indies
was opened, while the traffic in furs was not abated.
Continual efforts were made to hold the two great waterways of the continent, the St. Lawrence and the Mississippi, against the encroachments of the English. A
French fort was again planted at Niagara, but the
English counterbalanced this by erecting one at Oswego. Louis XIV. died in 1715, and from this time
on New France felt the loss of his strong arm.
Vaudreuil died in 1725, and was succeeded by Marquis
Beauharnois, who gave more attention to checking the
advance of the English and less to home enterprise.
At the head of the Narrows of Lake Champlain he
built the stronghold known as Crown Point, and which
was to play such an important part in the war to follow.
In 1745 the troops of New England, with the assistance of some British ships, captured Louisbourg. In
1756, what became known as the Seven Years' War was
declared.

No matter what else may be laid to the charge of

THE ST. LAWRENCE RIVER IN WINTER.

MARQUIS DE MONTCALM.

France, she generally sent her best to help fight the battles of the colony on the St. Lawrence, and now she quickly dispatched one of her ablest commanders, the Marquis de Montcalm. With him she sent De Levis, De Bougainville, and De Bourlamaque, and some of the best regiments. In respect to military skill the English soon proved far inferior. But if stronger from the point of the sword, so to speak, New France was in every other way much the weaker of the two. This had come about through a gradual weakening of the parent hand. Canada had, through no fault of her own, become a jest among certain ones high in kingly favour. "Fifteen thousand acres of snow!" said one, "a beautiful inheritance!" Immigration had long since ceased, and the increase in population had not been as great as had been wished. There were about·sixty thousand inhabitants at this time; possibly a few more, probably a few less. Of these, seven thousand lived in Quebec, mostly in the Lower Town. Montreal could claim between three and four thousand, while the balance were scattered up and down the valley. Nor was this sparse population the only weak spot of the country. The political power of the colony was rotten to the core. This had been slowly decaying, until the worst came upon the appearance on the scene of him whose brilliancy was more than sunk by his infamy. More's the the dishonour, he came not as the choice of the weakling with the title of king, but through the wish of his mistress, Madame de la Pompadour. His name

was François Bigot, and he disgraced the high office
created for the noble Talon. One of Canada's historians (Roberts), in describing him and his atrocious
acts, says :

> Offices of profit under his authority he filled with such men as
> would follow his example and act as his tools. The old seigneurial
> families, unable to stem the tide of corruption, for the most part held
> aloof on their estates; though a few yielded to the baneful example.
> The masses suffered in hopeless silence. Montcalm, the military
> chief, had small means of knowing the real state of affairs, and still
> less means of interfering had he known. The governor alone,
> Vaudreuil, might have changed it; but he was either blinded by
> Bigot's cleverness or in sympathy with his crimes. Either directly
> or through his confederates, of whom the most notorious was a con-
> tractor named Cadet, Bigot's thieveries rose to a colossal figure.
> The King's millions sent out for war, the people's millions squeezed
> from them in crushing taxes, alike found their way into these
> rapacious pockets. The enemies of New France within the walls
> were as deadly as those without. As outside perils thickened
> Bigot's thefts grew more daring. Forts fell like ripe fruit into the
> hands of the English, because they were commanded by weak
> favourites of the Intendant, or because the Intendant had kept the
> money which should have supplied them with arms and food.
> . . . It is claimed that in two years alone, 1757 and 1758, the
> Intendant cheated his King and country out of nearly five million
> dollars.

While that fact, as satisfactory as it may be, did not
help the situation then, it is gratifying to know that this
infamous wretch was finally punished for his misde-
meanours by banishment from France, and his estates
confiscated.

Under these adverse circumstances was Montcalm
called upon to defend the honour of this ravaged people. As might have been expected, for a time this

gallant soldier was successful. He was victorious at Ticonderoga, following the capture of Fort William Henry, with its accompanying horrors. But the French lost Louisbourg, and Canada was cut in twain through the capture of Fort Frontenac by a body of colonial militia. In the east and in the west Canada was writhing under the blows of her enemy. Montcalm was driven back to the St. Lawrence, but where he moved there was hope. Now, if ever, New France needed the aid of the King, but Montcalm's earnest request for men and money was met by a firm refusal, and he was told to stand upon the defensive and await the turn of fortune. Under such conditions as these, with the vultures still clutching at her throat, Montcalm prepared for the inevitable at Quebec.

The story of the siege and capture of Quebec by Wolfe has been told so frequently, and so well, that a detailed description is not called for here. Of the commanders, the British general was the junior of his rival by fourteen years. He was of slight frame, and not physically strong. He was the son of industrious but humble parents, educated for war, had seen some hard fighting, and had been the choice of Pitt, then the dominating spirit in England, to command an expedition against the stronghold of New France. He had under him less than nine thousand men, composed of tried and stalwart regulars of the English army, and a company of New England rangers, who had made the success of the English on the lakes of the highlands certain.

Montcalm was the son of a nobleman of the best blood of France. He, too, had been trained from boyhood as a soldier, and had won signal distinction as a military leader. Like Wolfe he had accepted this charge from a sense and love of duty, rather than from his own choice. He had a force of about sixteen thousand men, of whom about four thousand were regulars, and five thousand belonged to the Canadian militia. One of the last-named was considered to be equal to three regulars when it came to bush-fighting, but he was an uncertain factor in open battle. The balance of his troops were undisciplined peasants and Indians. He knew the fate of New France rested with him. Should Wolfe fail another might renew the struggle. Should he fail, and Quebec fall, slight hope would there be for the French in the St. Lawrence valley.

Montcalm closed the mouth of the St. Charles with great booms of timber, and planted upon its banks frowning batteries. At the outlet of the Beauport stream he constructed a floating battery of twelve guns. In fact he ranged defences along the St. Lawrence as far down as the Montmorency. De Ramesay was given two thousand men with which to defend the Lower Town, while a cordon of fire-ships and gunboats lined the water's edge. Behind a hundred cannons bidding defiance to the enemy from the summit of rock, he stationed the main body of his force, ready at a moment's warning to rush to the defence of any position. His situation seemed impregnable,—without a possibility of an attack from the rear; with a front that seemed insurmountable.

Wolfe and his fleet appeared opposite the Isle of Orleans toward the last of June, 1759, and disembarking his troops he intrenched himself on the western point, within four miles of the enemy's guns looking ominously down upon him from the rocky citadel. The French fleet had been sent up the river for safety, and to allow the crews to assist in the defence of the city.

Before Wolfe's eyes was now unfolded the magnitude of his task.[1] On his right was the splendid white cataract of Montmorency leaping out of the dark fir groves on the summit of the ridge. Beyond lay the long, serried lines of intrenchments, swarming with the white uniforms of France. Then the crowded, steep roofs and spires of the Lower Town, with the gunboats and fire-ships on its water-front. And then, soaring over all, the majestic promontory of Cape Diamond; its grim face seamed with batteries, and stairs, and climbing ribbons of streets; its summit crowned with portentous bastions and with the chivalrous banners of France.

Escaping a desperate effort on the part of the French to destroy his ships by the fire-boats, Wolfe fortified himself, and planted batteries on Point Levi, from whence he could bombard the city. He took possession of the height below Montmorency, and tried to get in the rear of Montcalm's line of defence, but failed in his purpose. Under cover of his guns on Point Levi, he did succeed in sending a portion of his fleet up the river, to harass his enemy between Quebec and Cap Rouge. But in spite of his endeavours the summer passed without bringing him any encouragement of ultimate success. He had lost half a thousand men in a vain attack upon Beauport, and nearly as many more from the firing of their foes and sickness. The expected aid from Amherst was not likely to come. Troubled to obtain supplies for his army, and himself ill with a fever, it was little wonder the brave and sanguine commander began to lose courage. Without having gained any vantage after over two months of desultory fighting, was there any prospect that

[1] Roberts.

he could do better for the next sixty days? By the end of that time cold weather would be upon them, and it would not do for them to remain and get ice-locked. Looking the situation squarely in the face, without losing courage or buoying himself up by any dream of success, Wolfe began to consider a new, and bolder, plan of operation.

About the first of September he was apprised of what Phips had been told in his forlorn attack years before. This was the fact of a slight break in the river-bank, where men could scale the ascent to the top. The place was guarded, but a small body of men climbing up to them unawares might easily overpower them, and hold the pass until the main body of the army could ascend to the plains. Wolfe profited where Phips lost. It was a desperate undertaking, and to do it he must recall his force from Montmorency. But even this worked in his favour, for the watchful Montcalm concluded that it was the first step toward withdrawing; and every move Wolfe made was given this substantial colouring. The alertness of the French commander is expressed in his own words:

"Our troops are in their tents, with clothes on, ready for an alarm; I in my boots; my horses saddled. In fact, this is my custom. I wish you were here, for I cannot be everywhere, though I multiply myself, and have not taken off my clothes since the 23rd of June."

Again, on the 11th of September, only two days before the great battle, he wrote to Bourlamaque, probably his last message :

I am oppressed with work, and should often lose my temper, as you do, if I were not paid by Europe not to do it. Nothing new has occurred since I wrote you last. I give the enemy another month, or even less, to stay here.

He had written that a hundred men could hold at bay any force the enemy might try to push up the gully of *Anse du Foulon*, where Wolfe had fixed his gaze. Perhaps he was right. It should so be under proper watchfulness. Even the hawk sleeps sometimes. Fortune favours the bold. In order to replenish their lessening stock of provisions, the French planned to run down, under cover of night, boats from Montreal. While this scheme had really been abandoned, the sentries were in ignorance of the fact, and nightly looked for the coming of the friendly boats.

On the 4th of September, Wolfe's illness again fastened itself upon him, and, though he recovered somewhat by the 7th, it was his opinion the end was not far distant with him, should he escape the bullets of his enemy. But this solemn conviction did not discourage him from carrying out his daring purpose. It rained for two days and nights in succession, making it uncomfortable for all, but affording partial concealment for the work in hand. Wolfe's ships were moving back and forth upon the river, worrying the French by their pretences to effect a landing at different places. On the 12th, the vessels anchored off Cap Rouge. The evening of that day had been selected by Wolfe for his attack. A demand had been made for a squad of men to lead the way up the gully to overpower the guard. Twenty-four brave men volunteered to do whatever duty was asked of them. Though every soldier felt that some momentous undertaking was coming, no one knew just what it was to be.

The night selected was starless, and under its cover the troops, numbering not quite five thousand, were ordered to enter the boats, and there await the ebbing of the tide. It had been the custom for the vessels to move up with the flow of the tide, and back with its

ebb.　This was a part of the plan now.　The boat with
the brave twenty-four was to lead, while Wolfe was to
follow next to it.

During the interval of waiting the young commander, suffering from his illness, but hopeful of victory, took from a chain about his neck a miniature of a
beautiful young woman to whom he was betrothed.
His gaze lingered long and tenderly over the sweet
face looking into his faintly in the dim lamplight of the
rough cabin, and then he handed it to a companion, a
youthful naval officer named Jervis, who was afterwards
to become a great admiral, asking him to return it to
the owner, Miss Lowther, adding that he did not expect to live until another day.　Then he gave a short
message for his mother, and with thoughts of these,
mother and sweetheart, the most tender that sway the
human heart, he descended into his boat, to depart
upon that errand which was to shake an empire founded
upon a rock, but whose structure had become honey-
combed with the follies of weak men.

The darkness and silence of this midnight journey is enlivened by the pretty story of Wolfe's reciting
Gray's Elegy while he was being borne on the tide, re-
marking to his companions that "I would rather be
the author of that piece than take Quebec." This
plausible conceit, to a certain extent illustrates the
peculiar traits of the British commander, his moods
of enthusiasm, his love for good literature, and clear-
cut courage that never faltered under the most trying

THE LOUISBOURG GUN IN THE YARD OF THE CHÂTEAU DE RAMEZAY, MONTREAL.

From a photograph by W. Notman & Son, Montreal.

CAP ROUGE.

situations. No less authority than Sir Walter Scott seems first to have given the legend prominence by relating it as it was told to him by one who overheard the speech. But as nearly three-fourths of a century had elapsed since that eventful night, it is possible that error may have crept in and that the incident which gave the legend substance occurred a few hours, or even a day before. But this does not rob the gem of its lustre.

The foremost boat, or rather boats, for it took two to convey the vanguard of this expedition, was in command of Lieutenant-Colonel Howe, who in later years became a prominent English general during the American Revolution. In this boat was also an officer of the Highlanders who could speak French perfectly. Behind these followed the others, in darkness and in silence, while they were carried swiftly down to *Anse du Foulon*, from that night known as Wolfe's Cove.

As the boat came abreast of the Palisades a sharp-voiced sentry challenged : " *Qui vive ?* " " *France*," replied the Highlander, promptly. " *Quel régiment est ce la ?* " " *De la Reine*," responded the quick-witted officer, naming a French regiment he knew was at Cap Rouge. They were allowed to keep on amid a silence that none dared to break. A little lower down they were hailed again, and as before the shrewd officer made replies that were satisfactory. This time he boldly declared they were French provision boats, and that silence must be maintained.

Upon reaching the cove the troops hastily landed, and the foremost began the ascent of the bank, led by the Highlander.   More frequently than otherwise great victories are the result largely of some blunder upon the part of the loser.   Montcalm may not have blundered, but it so happened that at this very hour, four A.M., while the twenty-four daring climbers were ascending to the Plains of Abraham, the officer in command of this pass at *Anse du Foulon* was one Vergor, who had been once tried for cowardice, and who had escaped only through the influence of Vaudreuil and Bigot.   He may not have been a coward, but he was asleep in his tent! Some say he had been bribed by the English, but a bribed man would never sleep under those circumstances.   Be that as it may, the sentinels were easily surprised, and Vergor was seized as he sprang from his bunk.   The signal was given for the others to follow, and in a minute Wolfe, though weak and faint, stood at last at the top.   The breaking day disclosed his army arrayed along the summit.   With a portion of the French forces above him at Cap Rouge under De Bougainville, and the main body under Montcalm at Quebec, now fairly between the two, there was no alternative save to push forward to victory or death.

Two small pieces of artillery had been dragged up, and with these Wolfe advanced to the edge of the Plains of Abraham, within a mile of Quebec, though this could not be seen on account of an intervening ridge. The Plains, so called for one Maître Abraham, a noted

river pilot in former days who had owned the land,
were covered with tall grass, broken here and there
with patches of corn and clumps of bushes. As Wolfe
drew up his line upon this broad plateau, flanked on the
one side by the high bank of the St. Lawrence, on the
other by the meadows of the sleepy St. Charles, and
fronted by the fortifications of Quebec commanding the
surrounding country, he passed along encouraging his
soldiers with spirited words to strike that day for love
and honour of Old England, and theirs would be the
glory. He had seemed to throw off his recent illness,
though he looked little like the hero, with his tall, emaciated figure, his sloping shoulders, small head, receding forehead, met by red hair cut short, a long, pointed
nose, and pallid skin, but there was the fire of a martial
spirit in the flashing eyes, and the inspiration of unbounded courage in his voice.

At this moment a breathless courier was informing
Montcalm of his peril, and immediately there was lively
effort put forth to prepare for the enemy. The regiments were ordered up from the trenches at Beauport.
Help was summoned from the garrisons of the Lower
Town, but these refused to leave their post. Other
regiments, owing, it is said, to Vaudreuil's influence,
were not on hand. But with about 4500 men Montcalm formed a line of battle, and leading them in person, mounted upon his magnificent black horse, he went
forth to meet his conqueror, knowing that the fate of
Canada was to be decided within that half-hour. It

may be he ought to have waited, as some say, until he could have had a better understanding with the governor; until De Ramesay at the city could have been persuaded to have sent him a dozen pieces instead of only three; until De Bougainville could have come to his aid; until many things possible and impossible might have happened, but his destiny and Canada's had willed it nay. Every inch a commander born to gain victories did he look, while he addressed a few words to his followers. "As he brandished his sword in gesticulating to them, the wide sleeves of his coat fell away so as to disclose the white linen of his wristband," said one of his soldiers in after years.

With greater calmness the British commander and his soldiers in their red uniforms awaited this desperate charge. When the French were within forty yards they suddenly found themselves confronted by a human wall thrown across their pathway. The sharp command, the rattle of musketry, a sheet of flame, and the ranks of the oncoming army were riven. The French fought bravely, answering volley for volley, but while they strove they staggered back, enveloped in smoke. Swift to follow up his advantage, Wolfe gave the command to charge, himself leading his men. Amid wild cheering the British regulars, the Highlanders, and the New England Rangers under Captain Stark sprang forward, and the tide of battle was stemmed if not turned. Wolfe's wrist was shattered by a bullet. Binding it with a handkerchief, he kept on, only to receive a second,

and then a third shot. The last entered his breast, and
he sank to the ground, unable to go farther. A lieutenant of the grenadiers named Brown and a volunteer
by the name of Henderson, assisted by two others,[1]
seeing him fall, carried him in their arms to the rear.

"Run for a surgeon!" cried one. "There is no need
of that," he answered. "Lay me down. It's all over
with me." Glancing from the sufferer toward the scene
of action, Lieutenant Brown exclaimed: "They run!
look, how they run!" "Who run?" asked Wolfe, starting up from the lethargy stealing over him. "The
enemy, sir. Egad, they are giving away everywhere!"
Rallying somewhat at this welcome announcement, he
said: "Go, one of you, and tell Colonel Burton to order
Webb's regiment down to the Charles River, to cut off
their retreat from the bridge." Then the dying victor,
moving slightly, murmured: "God be praised! I will die
in peace." A moment later and the hero lived in name
only.

It was in vain Montcalm tried to stem the tide of
retreat, and on horseback he was fairly swept toward the
town. The bullets were still flying thick about them as
they reached the St. Louis gate, and one pierced his
body. He would have fallen from his horse, but two
soldiers held him in position until he had passed through
into the town, where an excited crowd was anxiously
awaiting the result of the ominous firing. One of the

[1] I have reason to believe that one of these was Captain William Stark, of
the New England Rangers. See Turnbull's painting of *The Death of Wolfe.*
—AUTHOR.

spectators, a woman, who recognised him, discovered the blood upon his white shirt-front, and cried : " *O mon Dieu ! mon Dieu ! le Marquis est tué !* " " It's nothing," he replied, rallying somewhat ; " do not be grieved for me, my good friends." He was taken to a house to be treated by a surgeon. But the great French leader was beyond mortal aid. When he was told of this, he said : " I shall die happy not to live to see the surrender of Quebec." Refusing to confer with De Ramesay and others, he gave his attention to arranging some business matters. He did not forget to look after the welfare of those who had been intrusted to his care, and almost his last act was to send the following appeal to the British commander :

Monsieur, the humanity of the English sets my mind at peace concerning the fate of the French and Canadian prisoners. Feel toward them as they have caused me to feel. Do not let them perceive that they have changed masters. Be their protector as I have been their father.

He lived until morning, quietly breathing his last at four o'clock. He was buried in a coffin made of rough boards by an old servitor, on the morning of the 14th, his grave a hollow scooped out of the earth under the floor of the Ursuline Convent by a bursting shell, —a sepulture grand in its very simplicity, and befitting the hero. In far-away Candiac, the stately home of the Montcalms, one of the most beautiful women in France had awakened from a night's troubled sleep a widow ; and three fair children, hopefully looking forward to his

home-coming, listened in vain for the sound of his step
and the music of a father's voice.

The body of Wolfe was embalmed, and conveyed to
England upon the gun-ship *Royal William*, the rejoicings over his great victory saddened by the sorrow of his
death. He was given sepulture in the vault of the
parish church at Greenwich, where his aged father had
been borne only a few months before, and where his
mother followed six years later.

Five days after the battle De Ramesay formally surrendered Quebec to General Townshend, who had become the successor of Wolfe. While the English felt
jubilant over their conquest, the French were still hopeful, but even they could not realise how near they were
to come in their efforts to recapture Quebec.

Chapter XIV

Under the New Régime

Second Battle of the Plains—Surrender of Montreal—Conquest Closes at Pont-chartrain—Result—Campaign of 1775-76—Fall of Montgomery—Arnold's Retreat—The "Hungry Year"—Heroism of the Canadians at Chateauguay—Naval Fight on Lake Champlain—Victory of McDonough—Hard Blow to the English—End of War of 1812-15—Result of this War to Canada—Important Periods in History—Final Union of the Provinces.

THE fall of Montcalm left the French at Quebec without a commander able to rally the demoralised forces. Oh, then for one hour of Frontenac! or that up from the dust of her streets might rise the shade of Champlain! The weak Vaudreuil, though he had a larger force than the English could muster, beat a hasty retreat up the St. Lawrence. De Levis, who was alone worthy to succeed Montcalm, was in Montreal. Fearful that he might appear upon the scene with superior forces, Townshend, who was now in command of the British army, pushed the campaign so vigorously the terrified citizens demanded that De Ramesay surrender. This he for a time refused to do. Finally he consented, and the flag of truce was run up. Some one pulled it down. A second time it was raised, and that time it remained until the hands of the conquerors removed it. Townshend proved a magnani-

MAJOR-GENERAL JAMES WOLFE.

MONTMORENCY FALLS.
From a photograph by Livernois, Quebec.

mous captor. The garrison marched out with full honours of war, and were sent away to France at the expense of England. The citizens and Indians were promised all the protection that could be given English subjects, providing they should prove loyal to their pledge. Then the lilied standard of France, the *fleur-de-lis* of Champlain, the founder of the city, the proud emblem under which Frontenac had conquered, came down from its lofty position, and in its stead was flung to the breeze the red cross of St. George.

While the result proved a decided victory, there was a following interval filled with unrest and uncertainty. During the succeeding winter the English commander found himself placed in greatly straitened circumstances. The British fleet sailed away to England, the command being left to General Murray. First the rigour of the climate, and then the scarcity of provisions, made the situation desperate. To add to this, with the return of spring it was found that a determined effort was to be made to recover the city and its fortifications. At this time famine, climate, and disease, the outcome of the two former, had reduced the British forces from seven to three thousand men fit for duty. Toward the last of April the only vessel that Murray could get to perform the errand, the *Lawrence*, was sent down the river to look for the expected fleet from the homeland, and to hasten its coming, while a small band of New England Rangers, who had served under Wolfe, were sent with a lieutenant to convey to General Amherst, then stationed

at Lake Ontario, information of the critical condition of
the garrison. Unknown to them, at that time over nine
thousand regulars and volunteers were on their way
down the river from Montreal under the leadership of
De Levis, who had sworn to recapture Quebec.

There are conflicting accounts as to the manner in
which the British were apprised of the coming of the
enemy. One of these was that the sentry on duty was
warned of the coming of De Levis by one of the latter's
officers whom he rescued from drowning in the river
through the capsizing of his boat, when all his men
were lost. The other, and better authenticated explanation, shows how the advancing French were discovered
by one of Murray's men stationed at the outpost at
Ste. Foye. It was about three o'clock on the morning
of April 27th, when General Murray was aroused, and
the order " To arms !" was immediately given. Marching out through the St. Louis and St. John gates he
hastened to the outpost at Ste. Foye. De Levis at that
moment was advancing through the growth covering the
lowlands at the foot of Ste. Foye, and upon receiving a
sharp cannonade, when he had expected to make the
surprise, without knowing the weakness of the British
he quickly fell back, deciding to outflank the enemy he
had failed to take unawares, still in ignorance of the fact
that he had encountered more than the regular force
stationed here.

Realising that he would be unable to cope successfully with so large a force, Murray destroyed his works

here, and retreated to the city. But having done this he quickly decided that the condition of the fortifications was such that it would be folly for him to stake his fortune upon a single chance, and he resolved to muster every man he could and meet the enemy at the most favourable spot. This he considered to be the gentle swell upon the Plains known as *Les Buttes-à-Neveu*, where he ordered his troops to be formed, while he rode ahead to reconnoitre. The foremost brigades of De Levis were then swinging around toward Sillery, while the main body was coming along the Ste. Foye road in marching order. Without waiting for the enemy to open the fight, the ambitious Murray, brave to rashness, ordered his troops forward, and, regardless of the fact that he was outnumbered two to one by some of the best troops of Canada, led by one of the most skilful strategists of the times, opened fire upon the French columns. Then ensued one of the most desperate battles, while it lasted, ever fought on Canadian soil. Every man proved himself a hero, but when Murray had seen each third man under him go down, he found that he could save the others only by falling back, which was defined to mean by his grisly veterans "retreat." De Levis did not deem it wise to follow, and thus the golden opportunity to recover New France to the French was lost. It is true, anxious months of siege followed, and De Levis played a losing game with credit. All depended upon the arrival of succour from the old countries. Should that of France come first, the *fleur-de-lis* would

again float above the walls of Quebec. In the midst of
this suspense a vessel was sighted coming up the St.
Lawrence, but she carried no flag at her masthead.
Was she French, or English, or did she come from another port? While friends and foes alike watched with
feverish interest the mysterious stranger, realising that
the destiny of a nation hung upon the character of the
approach, in the midst of the suspense the flag of England was run up the mast! Quebec was saved to the
English! While the cheers of his enemies rang on the
air De Levis prudently withdrew his fleet. Nothing remained for the French but a forlorn hope at Montreal.

De Levis was followed up the St. Lawrence, in due
time, by Murray, who stationed himself a few miles
below Montreal. At the same time Lord Amherst,
General Jeffrey, in answer to the summons sent him,
started down the river from Lake Ontario, as described
elsewhere. Down the Richelieu came Colonel Haviland, who speedily joined Murray, when the united
forces moved forward, the latter to take up a position
just below the French, while the former chose his
nearly opposite. About this time Amherst appeared
before the western walls of the city. The Canadian
militia, foreseeing the ultimate outcome, upon receiving
promise of protection from the British deserted De
Levis and returned to their scattered homes, thankful
to escape the toils of war. This left the gallant De
Levis with barely two thousand regulars under him, and
he had no other alternative than to surrender, which he

did on the 8th of September, 1760, within six days of a year from the memorable morning that Wolfe led the way to victory upon the Plains of Abraham. The same generous terms as those given at Quebec were made here. General Murray was appointed as the first governor under the new government.

The closing act in this drama of conquest was yet to be played. The leader intrusted with the work was Major Robert Rogers, with his Rangers, sent by Amherst to take possession of Fort Pontchartrain on the Detroit. It was in November, 1760, and in ignorance of the capitulation at Montreal the French commander here saw with wonder the presence of English troops where they had not dared to venture before. The first summons to surrender he treated with disdain, but the second, given in *facsimile* of the capitulation at Montreal, with an order from Marquis de Vaudreuil directing the surrender of the fort, put a different phase upon the situation. Nothing else could be done. The flagstaff was soon bereft of its *fleur-de-lis*, and made to swing to the breeze the flag of the incoming power. New France was only a memory.

Never was conquest more fortunate. What the outcome might have been in the valley of the St. Lawrence had this been delayed awhile longer is vain to speculate. Let it be said to her honour that seldom has fairer treatment been accorded a vanquished party than that England allowed her new subjects here in Canada. In the words of one of her historians:

Previous history affords no example of such forbearance and generosity on the part of the conquerors toward the conquered— forming such a new era in civilised warfare, that an admiring world admitted the claim of Great Britain to the glory of conquering a people less from views of ambition and the security of her colonies than from the hope of improving their situation, and endowing them with the privileges of freedom.

Upon the other hand, it was shown that the people who had borne with fidelity the duties pertaining to them as French citizens during the protracted struggle between the colonies, of border warfare and its attendant evils, were capable of bearing with a spirit of resignation the humiliation of defeat as well as the *éclat* of victory. The Quebec Act of 1774, which recognised the French civil laws, allowed free religious and civil rights, and, granting the official use of the language of their race, made them faithful, loyal, and loving subjects. The real wellspring of history is the homes of the common people. It is here, rather than in the stormy scenes of battle, that we must look for the true source of their success. Here we find Canada especially fortunate. Her peasant population, which have ever been the filling in the fabric of national greatness, has not only been of a firm texture, but of lasting, durable qualities.

Despite this fact, upon the conquest of the British a large percentage of the old seigneurial families, unable to face the necessity of owing allegiance to the flag which they, their fathers, and their fathers' fathers had spent their lives in fighting, quietly slipped away to

France. The St. Lawrence country was greatly the loser on this account. To take their places, if not to fill them, came the English immigrant, the Scotch and the Irish, with later a goodly lot of New Englanders who had remained true to the King during the American Revolution.

The Treaty of Paris of February 10, 1763, had marked a notable change in the situation in America. By it France relinquished her claim to more than half of the continent. Besides this she yielded the territory of Louisiana to Spain, which in turn had given up Florida. All that the descendent power of Louis XIV. could now claim across the ocean was a few small islands of New Foundland, which had been reserved for fishing stations. Not a pleasant ending to the dream of Champlain, though into such hands had his heritage fallen 't were better so.

England was now mistress of America, and inflated with the prowess of her arms. But no greater statesman than Montcalm had predicted that the success of England in the St. Lawrence valley would prove disastrous to her power over the colonies in the provinces she had fostered. Here was an aggressive element of a different stamina from that she had subdued in the north. If they had sufficient cause for the course they pursued is not a matter for consideration here. When they rebelled it was natural they should look for allies among the French in the valley of the "great river," who they took for granted must be still smarting under the

pains of their recent defeat. Their overtures proving
failures, as described elsewhere, they resolved to accomplish by force of arms what they could not secure
by peaceful means. This resulted in the famous attack
upon the citadel of Quebec under General Montgomery
upon the morning of December 31, 1775, aided by
Arnold and his contingent.

This unfortunate campaign, unfortunate both from its
conception and the death of General Montgomery, was
one of the most heroic and arduous that American history
records. Arnold, the first upon the scene, and to whom
has been credited the daring scheme, though some say
it originated with Washington, reached the valley of the
St. Lawrence with decimated ranks and forlorn appearance after his memorable journey up the Kennebec
through the wilds of Maine, over "the terrible carrying-
place," and down the Chaudière. Having less than
half the men he had started with, but a gallant five
hundred, he climbed the same steep path to the Plains
of Abraham that Wolfe had followed a little over sixteen years before. The audacious Arnold, parading
his troops, then demanded the surrender of the city.
But the commander at this time, Lieutenant-Governor
Cramache, not to be caught as Montcalm had been,
by running into the enemy's power in ignorance of
their numbers, replied with the voice of the cannon, and
remained in his stronghold. Arnold wisely retreated
to *Pointe aux Trembles*, and sent for Montgomery to
come to his assistance. By this move the Americans

commanded the river above Quebec, and Quebec only remained to be taken.

Montgomery, who had recently been promoted to the position of Major-General, than whom no more valiant officer ever commanded an army, lost no time in starting to the assistance of Colonel Arnold. He had fought under Wolfe at the battle of the Plains of Abraham in 1759, and looked eagerly forward to another conquest of the "Gibraltar of America," with himself as leader. He had good reason to feel hopeful, for he had not only pushed his way successfully down the Richelieu, seizing the forts of St John's and Chambly on his way, but had found Montreal an easy prize. Leaving sufficient of his troops here under General Wooster to meet any uprising that might take place, he hastened down the St. Lawrence with three hundred men.

With the English the situation was less hopeful. The command had devolved upon Sir Guy Carleton, also a comrade under Wolfe at Quebec sixteen years before. The regulars under him had been but a small force, and the French peasants, claiming a desire to remain neutral, had defied the orders of the seigneurs and the expostulations of the priests to rally to the defence of the Government. In this plight he had been unable to cope with Montgomery at Montreal, and had barely escaped by flight in the disguise of a habitant. Upon the very day that Arnold withdrew his troops, Carleton appeared in Quebec, to the joy of its loyal inhabitants. Here he decided to make a desperate stand, and after sifting out the disaffected " neutrals " he had about four hundred regulars and a few more French Canadian volunteers, upon whom he could count under all circumstances. Besides these, the citizens of Quebec stood ready to assist with all their power.

Immediately upon reaching Arnold at *Pointe aux Trembles*, General Montgomery resolved upon moving against Quebec at once, though their combined forces did not quite reach one thousand men. He had increased his little company at Sorel with Captain Lamb's company of artillery, who had taken along several mortars. Colonel Arnold, more perhaps than he, had been greatly disappointed in finding the Canadian peasants unwilling to join in the undertaking. He had counted with confidence upon being strongly reinforced from this direction, and now he did not find a man disposed to lift a gun. In the face of difficulties which must have daunted less sanguine leaders, they besieged the stronghold. Though they held tenaciously to their purpose for over a month nothing was gained.

Toward the last of the year General Montgomery decided upon an attack by night, hoping to surprise the enemy. Into this undertaking Arnold entered heartily, and, as he was well acquainted with the situation of the defences, the plan was largely his. But the intentions of the Americans became known to the British through a traitor, and Carleton resolved that he would not be

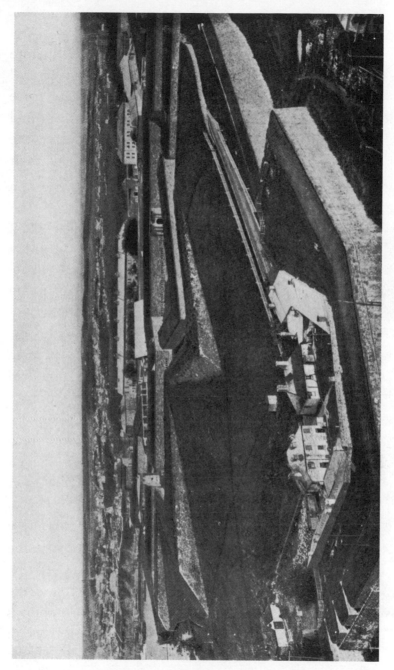

THE CITADEL, QUEBEC, FROM PARLIAMENT BUILDING.

From a photograph by Livernois, Quebec.

IN THE DAYS OF THE PIONEERS.
From a drawing by W. H. Bartlett.

taken by surprise. The night selected for the desperate assault was the last of the year, and it was on the early morning of December 31, 1775, when the assaulting columns moved upon their stern purpose. A bitter snow-storm was raging with Canadian fury, a fitting night for such a wild venture. One column was led along the St. Charles through the suburb of St. Roch. A terrific fight ensued, during which Arnold was wounded, and, the British getting in the rear of his troops, he was driven back, and about four hundred men were captured.

General Montgomery was even less fortunate. He sought to gain the city by a narrow defile known as *Pres-de-ville*, near what is now Champlain Street. Here, with a precipice running down to the river upon one hand, and on the other the scarped rock reaching above, he was confronted by a battery of three-pounders manned by a squad of Canadians and British militiamen. Still believing he was going to effect a surprise, the American commander urged his men forward in the face of the pelting storm, and the yet more deadly hail of grape that instantly swept the pass. Montgomery fell, with two officers and ten of his brave men, while the rest beat a precipitous retreat. Over the body of the unfortunate officer, worthy of a nobler end, the falling snow quickly threw a white shroud as if in compassion for his fate.

In the morning the bodies of the fallen Americans were taken into the city and given burial. The body of the leader was buried with special honours, and his grave in the St. Louis bastion was marked with a cut stone. In 1818, upon the desire of Mrs. Montgomery, the widow, the remains of General Montgomery were removed from their resting-place in Quebec to New York, and there re-interred. Over the spot where this brave American fell in the service of his country, a tablet has been placed bearing this inscription :

HERE MONTGOMERY FELL,

December 31st, 1775.

The command now devolved upon Arnold, who maintained the siege, or, more strictly speaking, blockade, until spring. The Americans had been reinforced, but no sooner was the river beginning to clear of ice than a British ship was seen coming up the St. Lawrence with troops to assist the besieged garrison. Arnold hastily retired. This retreat was soon turned into a rout, for Carleton gave pursuit, capturing the artillery. Later an attack by the Indians upon the Americans at "The Cedars," on the St. Lawrence, resulted in the capture by them of about four hundred of the American troops, in May, 1776. A month later the Americans undertook the capture of Three Rivers, but after a fierce battle they were repulsed. Realising by this time the hopelessness of their attempt to conquer Canada, the Americans withdrew to Lake Champlain, where they commanded the inland gate to the valley of the St. Lawrence until the following autumn. Both sides knowing the importance of holding this waterway, each prepared to battle for it. The American fleet, consisting of fifteen vessels carrying eighty-eight guns and defended by eight hundred and eleven men, of whom over a hundred were unfit to do duty, was placed under the command of Arnold. The English squadron, commanded by Carleton, was greatly the superior both in number of men and the quality of its ships, and Arnold was forced, after a gallant resistance, to abandon the lake to the English, when for over a third of a century the St. Lawrence valley was free from the invading foot.

Following the close of the American Revolution, which gave to the Thirteen States their independence, the population of Canada was greatly increased by the Loyalists. They found here refuge and new homes, though only after severe hardships and such trying experiences as those of the "Hungry Year" of 1787, when even Mother Earth forgot her children and left them to find meagre sustenance upon the roots and buds of the wild land. If there was plenty of game in the forest, and an abundance of fish in the waters, the men had neither powder and bullet to slay the one nor tackle to catch the other.

Gaunt men crept about with poles, striving to knock down the wild pigeons; or they angled all day with awkward, home-made hooks for a few chub or perch to keep their families from starvation. In one settlement a beef-bone was passed from house to house that each household might boil it a little while and so get a flavour in the pot of unsalted bran soup.   A few of the weak and aged actually died of starvation during these famine months; and others were poisoned by eating noxious roots which they grubbed up in the woods.   As the summer wore on, however, the kernels of wheat, oats, and barley began to grow plump.   People gathered hungrily to the fields, to pluck and devour the green heads. Boiled, these were a luxury ; and hope stole back to the starving settlements.

With those who came from the States to swell the population of the St. Lawrence valley, and prove her faithful defenders in wars to follow, were those old-time enemies, the Mohawks, among whom rises the grand figure of Brant.   A little later, from farther west came other tribes of Amerinds, led by the heroic chief of the Shawnees, Tecumseh, who fell fighting bravely her battles.

Whatever other reasons may be assigned, and there were several of more or less significance, the underlying purpose of the declaration of the War of 1812 was the sentiment: "Europe for France; the New World for America."   This meant the annexation of Canada to the United States.   At this time the former had a population of little over three hundred thousand, while the latter had nearly eight millions.   The valley of the St. Lawrence, which included the region of the Great Lakes, from its geographic position became the battle-ground between the Provinces and the States.   During the period when Napoleon was leading his great armies upon Spain and Russia, Great Britain had all she could attend to on the continent of Europe, and so Canada was left this time to fight the war of defence mainly through her own efforts.

Following their success at Moravian Town, where their dusky allies under the ill-fated Tecumseh put to shame the English troops, the Americans designed to carry out a plan which should place the whole of Upper Canada in their possession. Two divisions of the army were expected to co-operate in this ominous campaign. A body of troops comprising about six thousand men, under Major-General Hampton, was to move from Lake Champlain into the valley of the St. Lawrence, while a larger force of over eight thousand, under Major-General Wilkinson, was to move down the St. Lawrence from Lake Ontario, and together the armies were to capture Montreal. The first division moved promptly to the Chateauguay River, which finds its way into the St. Lawrence from the mountain range of the same name in northern New York. To check this, the English had a force of about fifteen hundred, so scattered as not to be available at once. In this plight De Salaberry, a veteran in England's cause, while belonging to the old Canadian *noblesse*, with less than four hundred French Canadians and a few Highlanders, intrenched himself in the path of Hampton and his troops. The result was a signal triumph for the valiant De Salaberry and his brave followers, who were specially honoured in consequence by England. In the meantime, General Wilkinson got down as far as Cornwall, where he learned that Hampton had retreated. Without his co-operation he did not deem it wise to push down to Montreal. Accordingly he went into winter quarters on Salmon

River, thinking to make up in part for his disappointment by capturing Prescott and Kingston. But a lack of provisions obliged him to fall back to Plattsburg, the entire campaign simply giving the Canadians opportunity to concentrate their forces on the Niagara frontier. Early in the spring General Wilkinson, with a little over four thousand men, undertook to capture the British post on the Richelieu River, held by Lieutenant-Colonel Williams, at the head of fifteen hundred men, but he failed in this. Losing courage over his defeats General Wilkinson soon after resigned his commission.

The campaign about Niagara, which brought some hot fighting on both sides, and heavy losses of men, particularly at Lundy's Lane, where every fifth man on both sides was slain, was practically a series of drawn battles. Having defeated the Americans in their invasion of the St. Lawrence valley, the English now turned their attention to invading the country of the enemy. Triumphant in Europe over the powers of France, England could now assist in the cause of her colony. She sent over reinforcements to the troops, so that on the 3rd of September, Sir George Prevost, in command of fourteen thousand veterans, moved up the Saranac toward Plattsburg. The militia from New York and Vermont rallied under General Macomb to contest this advance, but, though they fought nobly, they could not stem the tide of invasion by so formidable a body.

At the same time Admiral Downie, with a force of a

thousand men and ninety-five guns, was moving up the Richelieu with his fleet.   This squadron was met by Commodore McDonough, with a force of a little over eight hundred men and eighty-six guns.   Then followed one of the most sanguinary battles of the war, resulting in victory for the gallant McDonough.   The brave Englishman, Admiral Downie, was killed, and all of his ships were sunk or captured.   Dismayed by this defeat of the English fleet, Prevost retreated precipitately from the scene, greatly to the chagrin of his army, and thus the English invasion ended even more disastrously than that of the Americans.   The fighting was now turned toward the south, resulting in Jackson's victory at New Orleans, and it could be said at last that the revolution of the colonists was fully consummated.

The result of this war was particularly beneficial to Canada in one respect at least.   It had tended to solidify the elements composing its population as no term of peace, for many times that number of years, could have done.   The French militia had fought nobly in defence of their homeland, and no English or Scotch had shown greater valour within her gates.   If paid for dearly, the prize was worth the sacrifice, and from this time the doubt of sincerity and loyalty was lifted from the colonists of the St. Lawrence valley.

The history of Canada from this period has been chequered with a few disturbing incidents, one or two of which have threatened serious results, but her statesmen have usually shaped her course in peaceful waters, and on the whole she has progressed steadily and with credit. One of the most important periods since the conquest was during the division of the country into two provinces in 1791. The population at this time was 120,000 in Lower Canada, and only 10,000 in Upper Canada. In 1826, the "Company of Canada" was incorporated with a capital of one million pounds sterling, for the express purpose of peopling the Canadian wilds. In four years, 1828–1831, it is claimed that over 150,000 settlers founded homes within her borders. This time has been called the "Period of the Great Immigration." With its great good to Canada, the limits of whose benefit cannot be placed, this movement brought a grievous misfortune in the form of the Asiatic cholera, which came with a ship-load of immigrants from Dublin in the summer of 1832. Started at one of the islands below Quebec, this dread scourge could not be held within bounds, and it swept with horrible devastation up the valley of the St. Lawrence, until checked by cold weather. Again the following summer it broke out, though with less loss of life.

In 1828 there was to be seen evidence of the uneasiness of the people over the political situation, when a petition was signed in Lower Canada by 87,000 persons, remonstrating against the distribution of public patronage and the illegal application of the money, and of the Trade Act of the Imperial Parliament. The sequel to this came ten years later, in 1840, when the British inhabitants, angered by Lord Elgin's sanction of the Rebellion Losses Bill, burned the Parliament building and made a demand for a peaceful separation from the old country. The outcome of this animated struggle was the triumph of reform, and the union of the two provinces, which had been estranged for half a century.

Chapter XV

The Mysterious Saguenay

IF Gaspé can lay an uncertain claim to being the older settlement, Tadousac has the positive honour of being the first French station established upon the St. Lawrence from which evolved a permanent town, where trading posts were maintained in the early stages of exploration. The link which connects it to those trying days, with a deep feeling of veneration, is a little church, still standing, the first that was built in Canada.

The natural features have changed so little since Champlain's visit, in 1603, that his description can be quoted :

Le dict port de Tadoussac est petit, où il ne pourroit que dix ou douze vaisseaux ; mais il y a l'eau assés à de l'Est, à l'abry de la ditte Rivière de Saguenay, le long d'une petite Montaigne qui est presque coupée de la mer. Le reste ce sont Montaignes haultes elevées où il y a peu de terre, sinon rochers et sables remplis de bois de pins, cyprez, sapins et quelques manières d'arbres de peu. Il y a un petit estang, proche du dit port, renfermé de Montaignes couvertes de bois.

The said port of Tadoussac is small, and could hold only ten or twelve vessels ; but there is water enough to the east, sheltered by the said River of Saguenay, along a little mountain which is very nearly cut in two by the sea.   For the rest there are mountains of high elevation, where there is little soil, except rocks and sands filled with wood of pines, cypresses, spruces and some species of undergrowth.   There is a pond near the said port, inclosed by mountains covered with wood.

As we enter the realm of sombre attractiveness, the inky hue of the water of the dark Saguenay is seen in marked contrast to the clear flood of the St. Lawrence. Tadousac, its warder for a period older than history, has played an important part in the development of Canada as well as this vicinity, since that distant day when Cartier was first lured hither by the wonder stories of his dusky pilots.   From its very position it became the original post for trade with the aboriginal hunters, who found the river their way of entrance from the solitude beyond the surrounding mountains.   To-day, only the remnants of the Montagnais roam the interior, gaining a precarious existence where their ancestors, with a sprinkling of French, went in search of furs and pelts, often falling victims to privations and hardships which made their earnings dear.   As has been shown, all through the old *régime* this region figured conspicuously in the output of pelts and the fisheries.

Tadousac has also another phase of history, if less profitable.   As early as 1615, only four years after the coming of the pioneer of his faith, a little band of Récollets landed here for the avowed pious purpose of overcoming the baneful influences of the evil spirits that were supposed to have their abode on that forbidding point of rock Champlain aptly christened *La Pointe de Tours des Diables*.

This attempt proving unsuccessful in more ways than one, it was repeated in 1647 by the brave Jesuit Père Duquen, and still a third and more satisfactory trial was made by Father Albanel in 1679, when he and young De St. Simon actually penetrated the unexplored regions, going as far north as Hudson Bay. To the heroic Pierre Chauvin, an associate with Pontgravé, as we have seen, belongs the credit of first trying to establish the Catholic faith among the natives, he and some of his brave followers spending the winter of 1599–1600 here, suffering terribly from cold and hunger.

By this time it had dawned upon the active French mind that the true source of wealth from the Saguenay lay not in mines of gold and diamonds, which had been such potent factors in guiding the earlier explorers, but in the abundance of fur-bearing animals existing in the interior. So, just as Yermak, the discoverer of Siberia, and his followers, discovered in the sable and kindred animals a profitable revenue in that inhospitable clime, so Pontgravé and his successors found the beaver and its associate animals the true source of income from the broken wilds of Canada. Straightway huge companies were formed, and with remarkable indifference to the exact boundary of their domains, seventy thousand miles of area, reaching from Les Éboulements to the Moisic River, three thousand miles distant, and

THE OLD TADOUSAC CHURCH.

A GROUP OF MONTAGNAIS INDIANS.
From a photograph by Livernois, Quebec.

northward to the highlands of Hudson Bay district, was leased for twenty-one years. A little over forty years later we find this tract of country given over to a body of leading *bourgeois* then in the country. This generous act did not seem to be more lasting than many of the other gifts and counter-gifts of that changeful period, for sixteen years later, 1658, Sieur Demaure obtained from the French Government the first regular lease, and a survey was soon after ordered, though this was not carried into effect until 1732.

While the Saguenay district was looked upon during the French dominion with a greater degree of professed knowledge than the unexplored country lying to the north of the great river between Quebec and Montreal, in reality this conception was based upon the most vague hearsay evidence. Under the command of those who were reaping a rich harvest from its wilderness of ignorance, it was business policy to guard well its secrets, to throw over its solitude a shield of silence as impenetrable and unbroken as the primeval shadows, drawn like a curtain over its rugged features. This was the more easily done through the assistance of Nature herself, who, in one of her wildest moods, had flung at the gateway rapids that only the bravest dared enter, and reared over them rocky bulwarks that gave an air of gloom and oppression which few cared to meet.

Thus a few hundred pounds of revenue to the Government, and no one outside of the pale of this secret dreamed of the great resources lying beyond the barriers until in 1820 an investigation disclosed the facts in the situation.   Suddenly the abundance of the forest, the fertility of the soil, the stores of the mines, the loaf leavened with a climate hitherto believed to have been impossible, awakened the people to its possibilities. In 1837, upon the expiration of the lease of the Hudson Bay Company, a swift transformation began.   Energetic colonists swarmed into the territory; hundreds of homes were formed in the wilderness.   In an incredibly short time the isolated trading posts of the fur-traders became thriving, bustling centres of population.   In this way, the ancient prophecy was solved, and the Saguenay became in truth the stone gateway to an Eden lying within.

An episode that never fades from the memory is one's first ascent of the Saguenay,—the cavern river, the Styx,—as dark and dreary to-day as it was when the imperious Roberval tried to penetrate its mysterious realm, remaining so long to solve its secret.   The frown that greets him at the gate; the air of mystery that invests the distance; the solitude that overhangs the way: these rival powers combat with each other to stop his entrance and to lure him ahead.   The result is a disappointment, or is it perplexity?   You may have ascended the Hudson, and gazed with rapt admiration upon its palisades, upon its rocky northern banks, upon its constant charms; and here you meet—what?   You may have passed the castled banks of Europe's grand old river; you find yourself comparing this to the ancient Rhine as a block of stone in the sculptor's hand in the first stage of his chiselling.   You may have come fresh from the dazzling streams of old Norland, whose short rivers run brief but glorious careers; you find your attention here repelled rather than held.   It is so with some scenes.   The beholder is overawed by his environments, and he reels back with his senses dazed. Then, as he appreciates better the masterful display of Nature, he feels gradually stealing over him the unseen forces which chain him and imprison his very soul.   It is this feeling the tourist experiences upon entering the templed hills of Nikko, Japan, but before he leaves the sacred mountain he finds its grandeur indelibly fixed upon his mind.   It is so with the Saguenay, and he wonders that he had not felt this before.   Then he begins to feel that there is an infinity and grandeur, a reach of distance, a solemnity of height he had not realised.   Allow me to improve upon my narrative by quoting the vivid description of another, who declares that

by degrees the immensity and majesty assert themselves.   As an abrupt turn brings the steamer close in ashore, you realise that the other bank is a mile away, aye, two miles distant, and that the black band at the base of the mountains, which roll away one beyond the other, is in truth the shadowed face of a mighty cliff, rising sheer from the water's edge, like that which now towers nearly two thousand feet above you.   There is an indescribable grandeur in the very monotony of the interminable succession of precipice and gorge, of lofty bluff and deep-hewn bay ; no mere monotony of outline, for every bend of the river changes the pictures in the majestic panorama of hills, water, and sky, and every rock has its individuality ; but the overwhelming reiteration of the same grand

theme with infinite variety of detail, till the senses are overpowered
by the evidences of the mighty force—force which you know, as
soon as you see those grim masses of syenite split and rent by
upheaval, seamed and scarred by icebergs, was once suddenly,
irresistibly active, but has now lain dormant for ages of ages.
There is the inevitable sternness of the manifestation of great
power, and this effect is heightened by the transparency of the
atmosphere, which allows no softening of the clear-cut lines, and
heightens their bold sweep by intense shadows sharply defined.
There is no rich foliage ; forest fires have swept and blackened
the hill-tops ; a scanty growth of sombre firs and slender birches
replaces the lordly pines that once crowned the heights, and struggles for a foothold along the sides of the ravines and on the ledges of
the cliffs, where the naked rock shows through the tops of the trees.
The rare signs of life only accentuate the lonely stillness. A few
log-houses on an opportune ledge that overhangs a niche-like cove,
a shoal of white porpoises gambolling in the current, a sea-gull
circling overhead, a white sail in the distance, and a wary loon,
whose mocking call echoes from the rocks,—what are they in the
face of these hills, that are the children of the mighty landsmith
whose forge fires have not yet burned out and the stroke of whose
hammer is still heard at intervals among the hills of the north !

We follow sixty miles of this awe-inspiring passage—sixty miles of majesty, calm bays, rippling
currents, giant cliffs cut in solid rock, solitude and
loneliness, waterfalls veiled in mists that hang over
them like silver threads, through mountain walls that
are fit portals to the scenes that lie beyond, vista upon
vista of country dotted with hamlets, and we are told
that the bay whose fame we had heard sung before we
started lies before us. We laugh in our feeling of
relief from the solitude we have left behind, as the first
explorers did, and in the echo that comes back from
the rocky hills, we find its name, " Ha Ha Bay." It

is nine miles long and six miles wide, in reality an un-
filled waterway leading from the interior. We see
ample evidence of this in the rich alluvial deposits.
Another relic of the past, Lake Kinogama, we are told
lies about twenty miles to the west, a sullen depth of
black water extending for fifteen miles, with a width of
only half a mile and a depth of a thousand feet.

Ha Ha Bay, quite as appropriately called Grand
Bay, is really a breathing-place in this vast amphi-
theatre of mountains, though the gloom of the lower
regions is not wholly shaken off. As we resume our
course we realise that the land is made up from
the deposits of some mighty stream in the past, that
which we are following being a shadow of its departed
greatness. The end of steamboat navigation is Chicoutimi, which, unlike Tadousac, does not conceal its light
under a bushel. It stands upon a prominent summit,
and the tall spire of its church is the first sight to greet
the eye, as the steamer glides along the smooth river
above the narrows, where those stern sentinels of the
waterway, Cap Ouest and Cap Est, look down with
searching grimness. The name of the town is said to
be derived from the Cree expression, "*Ishkotimew*,"
which means "up to here the water is deep."

Chicoutimi is the great lumber-yard of the north.
This timber has been brought down chiefly by the
rapid upper Saguenay, portage roads connecting its
source, Lake St. John, with the trading posts of the
Hudson Bay Company. The town presents a pictur-

esque appearance. Its cottages are conspicuous for their gabled roofs, often covered with birch bark, which gives them at a distance a resemblance to stucco-work. The yards—and every one has a small plot—are made cheerful by several varieties of annuals, asters, larkspurs, marigolds, and zinnias, all in their brightest hues, while the doors are framed in with climbing bean vines, in their flowering season radiant with crimson blossoms.

It was here that an adventurous Jesuit missionary established a pioneer mission that afterwards became a trading post for the Hudson Bay Company, building as early as 1670 his chapel of cedar-wood noted for its perfume and durability. Fifty years later another was built. Both are now covered by mounds of earth, and surrounded by a fence to protect them from relic hunters.

The Chicoutimi River turns over its flood to the Saguenay, after a descent of nearly five hundred feet in seventeen miles. It is the outlet of Lake Kinogama, already mentioned. Among the carrying-places at the rapids of this turbulent stream is one known as *Portage de l'Enfant*, so called in commemoration of the miraculous escape of an Indian child that was carried over the falls of fifty feet in a canoe without being injured.

Chicoutimi has its rival in the village of Ste. Anne, perched recklessly on an opposite bluff, where it commands on one hand a long, beautiful view of the descending river, on the other looks upward toward its source thirty-five miles distant. The rapid stream is

THE LITTLE SAGUENAY.

From a photograph by Livernois, Quebec.

OUIATCHOUAN FALLS.

as large at its starting-point as it is here. Possibly it has lost something of its volume in its fretful passage.

Once the rocky barriers of the Saguenay are passed the new-comer finds himself in a country which he had not expected, where many prosperous hamlets have sprung up, and where there is room for many more—a country drained by a network of rivers. Among the gems of inland seas, Lake St. John, about forty miles in diameter and nearly round in shape, is the natural reservoir of one of the grandest water systems to be found on the continent. This lake is the magnet sought from the north-east by the stately Pribonca, the outlet of three great ponds; from the southland, reaching away toward Quebec, comes Metabetchouan, with its offerings from a silvery chain of lakelets; on the north-west winds the Ashuapmouchouan; from the north, the Mistassini draws down its stony descents the great volume of Lake Mistassini, as large as Ontario. Until recently Lake St. John was embowered in the heart of a great wilderness, composed of pines, oaks, and other hardy woods forming a band of forest across the continent in the same parallel of latitude that strikes the upper portion of the State of Washington. If robbed of its forest mantle, its forty rivers that feed it, three of them as large as its outlet, remain, showing the plainer upon the broad plateaux of country for their undress. The blue fringe of mountains still lingers in the distance, and on its rolling flood repose its purple islands. As long as waters run, the dazzling whirlpools

that toss milk-white foam high in the air will continue
to glorify the "grand discharge" at the narrow outlet,
while over all will float the white veil of Ouiatchouan,
as this mad stream takes at one leap a fall of three
hundred feet.

There are really two Saguenays: the one seen
under the northern moon and the stars being cold, dark,
and forbidding; but the same rocks and clefts, seen
under the breaking light of a new day, present a milder
aspect. The crimson of early morning or the gold of
sunset lights up like oriflambs of grandeur the mighty
pillars of the square, massive walls, and send down to
the water's edge legions of dancing sprites in bright
and orange hues. The unseemly feature to him who
looks for the sunlight and the glory are the burnt forests, whose naked yeomanry rattle their skeleton arms,
while they hover grimly above him like hosts of departed
greatness, lingering for a time to mourn over nature's
loss, fit warders of such a region of solitude.

The climax of this awe-inspiring scenery is reached
at Trinity Bay, where the stupendous height of Cape
Trinity frowns down upon the intruder, a bare wall of
limestone that towers nearly two thousand feet into
mid-air. Its frowning brows thrust out three hundred
feet over the water, give the beholder a dread lest it
tumble upon him. Rent asunder by some far-distant
glacial power, the great column is really made up of
three sections so placed that at first sight they look
like huge steps leading to a mighty flight of stairs,

such a ladder as the ancient Titan, warring here against the elements, might be expected to climb in his ascent to strive with the gods for a supremacy.

In marked contrast to this gloomy giant of three in one—a Trinity—stands Cape Eternity, within a hundred feet as high as its sombre brother, but clothed in a warm vesture from foot to crown, and looking calm and peaceful. Wrapped in never-fading vestments drawn closely about its huge body, well may it defy the storms of this wintry region for all time.

With what feelings of emotion, and yet something akin to relief, the visitor turns from that "region of primeval grandeur, where art has done nothing and nature everything." In defiance of all training his mind will linger over the impressive scene, where the massive cliffs have tipped a river upon edge, and where solitude reigns supreme. For many days he will not be able to rise above the illusion that he is again among the rocks and dark waters, a mile and a half deep—reaching far below the bed of the St. Lawrence—while the steamer sweeps majestically into the Bay of Eternity for ever guarded by her twin sentinels of rock.

Chapter XVI

Up from Tadousac

The Mission of the Montagnais—Story of the Last Missionary—*Rivière du Loup*
—Murray Bay—Giant of Cap aux Corbeaux—Earthquake of 1663—A Vivid
Scene—Isle of Hazels—A Legion of Mountains—First Mass in Canada—
Baie St. Paul—Gouffre—Nature Asleep and Awake.

TADOUSAC is situated on the lower terrace left
at the base of the hills when the mighty floods,
held long in leash above, first opened the gateway for the great inland sea that must have existed
there. The most conspicuous object is the great hotel,
that seems to overflow with its summer tourists, made
more distinct, perhaps, by the setting of dark spruces
that cover the second bench, with the hills above forming an oval frame. From the plateau one looks across
the St. Lawrence, twenty-five miles wide, and as unruffled as it is possible for a plain of water to be.
From this, with its distant bank dimly seen through
the summer haze, dotted faintly with its clustered
homes, he sees with marked contrast the dark waters of
the Saguenay reluctantly leaving their deep bed for the
blue shallows of the greater river. The historic mind
turns from this pretty picture, pervaded with the wildness of nature, to the little church standing on the

site of the bark-roofed hut which served as the mission chapel until 1648, when the original church was built, and what may be termed one of the most extended fields of missionary work in New France was definitely entered. Beginning with the romance of thrilling adventures, this mission of the Montagnais closed in 1674, under circumstances as picturesque as the most vivid imagination could conceive. Of course it is repeated now as a legend, but no historic incident has stronger testimony in regard to its actual occurrence. Père La Brosse is the Jesuit around whose memory clings this charming tradition, which the swarthy Montagnais, as well as the devout follower of the faith, still love to cherish:

The Father had been working hard all day, as usual, among his converts and in the services of the church, and had spent the evening in pleasant converse with some of the officers of the post. Their amazement and incredulity may be imagined when, as he got up to go, he bade them good-bye for eternity, and announced that at midnight he would be a corpse, adding that the bell of his chapel would toll for his passing soul at that hour. He told them that if they did not believe him they could go and see for themselves, but begged them not to touch his body. He bade them fetch Messire Compain, who would be waiting for them the next day at the lower end of Isle aux Coudres, to wrap him in his shroud and bury him ; and this they were to do without heeding what the weather should be, for he would answer for the safety of those who undertook the voyage. The little party, astounded, sat, watch in hand, marking the hours pass, till at the first stroke of midnight the chapel bell began to toll, and trembling with fear, they rushed into the church. There, prostrate before the altar, hands joined in prayer, shrouding his face alike from the first glimpse of the valley of the shadow of death, and from the dazzling glory of the waiting angels, lay Père La Brosse, dead. What fear and sorrow must have mingled with the pious hopes and tender prayers of those rough traders and rougher Indians as, awe-stricken, they kept vigil that April night. With sunrise came a violent storm; but mindful of his command and promise, four brave men risked their lives on the water. The lashing waves parted to form a calm path for their canoe, and wondrously soon they were at Isle aux Coudres. There, as had been foretold by Père La Brosse, was M. Compain waiting on the rocks, breviary in hand, and as soon as they were in hearing, his shout told them he knew their strange errand. For the night before he had been mysteriously warned: the bell of his church was tolled at midnight by invisible hands, and a voice had told him what had happened and was yet to happen, and had bid him to be ready to do his office. In all the missions that Père La Brosse had served, the church bells, it is said, marked that night his dying moment.

On the north shore of the St. Lawrence nobody goes beyond Tadousac, unless he is a salmon-fisher, and accounts from the interior of the country come in the strain of traditions, vague and visionary. The southern shore has more attractions below this point, as has been shown, but from Tadousac to Quebec the north bank can claim the prize for picturesque wildness, though the French annalist, Boucher, in his *Histoire du Canada*, wrote in 1663:

The country is quite uninhabitable, being too high and all rocky, and quite precipitous. I have remarked only one place, that is Baie St. Paul, about half way and opposite to Isle aux Coudres, which seems very pretty as one passes by, as well as all the islands between Tadousac and Quebec, which are fit to be inhabited.

In a marked degree what this veracious historian said of the shore nearly two hundred and fifty years ago will apply to it now, with the added presence, here and there, of a small hamlet clinging to the foot of the precipitous bluffs, rather forcibly proving that the exception to the rule does not affect the grand result. The boldness of the rocky ramparts thrusting themselves down to the water's edge with a front that cannot be scaled could scarcely have presented a wilder aspect to the early voyager than it does to the modern tourist passing on one of the palatial steamers that ply on the river.

Leaving Tadousac on our upward trip, with L'Anse St. Jean on our right, following nearly in the track of Cartier, we cross the St. Lawrence to what was then the unpeopled site of the present-day lumber port, *Rivière du Loup.* It is sufficient, perhaps, for the reputation of this bustling place that it possesses the most magnificent view of the opposite bank to be found along the river. The distance lending a beautiful effect to the rare colouring of the atmosphere, the combination is especially happy at the setting of the sun, when the soft radiance of its beams falls aslant the background of dark-green hills touched with the variegated hues of the maple and birch of the lowlands.

The first place of importance to mention is that popular resort for tourists, Murray Bay, the Newport of the St. Lawrence, nearly encircled by the beautiful Canadian scenery, with the salt breeze fanning its brow and the briny surf displaced by the blue tide of the inlet at its foot. This place is eighty miles below Quebec. From the east of the bay rises into the clouds the lofty Cap aux Corbeaux, a name given this

peak in the days of the early explorers from the dismal croakings of the ravens, as they hovered over the
jagged cliffs and rock-shelves beyond the reach of the
most nimble climber.   Nor are they all gone yet by
any means, for great numbers still build their nests
in the inaccessible crags, unfearing the molestation
of man ; while, finding a precarious existence in the
stunted growth, browses the caribou, and the bear
fattens upon the berries afforded by the dwarfed bushes
clinging to the crevices of rock.

Like other wild spots, this is the source of many
legends, such as hang over Blomidon of Nova Scotia.
Here, as the susceptible habitan believes to this day,
is the abode of demons, and there is a tradition that in
the misty years of yore a giant, in some respects like
Glooscap of Blomidon, held sway until the cross drove
him farther into the solitude of the land of Ungava.
He is still angry over his forced abdication of a throne
he had held so long, and frequently he stamps his great
foot in his wrath and peals forth his voice in thunder-
tones, so the entire northern shore is shaken with such
violence as to terrify the people.   This thrilling narrative is given a touch of truth by the fact that the
region is subject to periodical shocks of earthquake,
the worst of which was felt in 1663, when the shaking
lasted for over six months, and was felt as far south as
New England.   The last shock was in 1870.   According to contemporary accounts, at this time the air was
dark with smoke and cinders, illuminated ever and

anon with meteors. Vegetation dried up, and nothing grew that year. Ferland, in describing this, says in part :

New lakes were formed, hills were lowered, falls were levelled, small streams disappeared, great forests were overturned. From Cap Tourmente to Tadousac the appearance of the shore was greatly altered in several localities. Near Baie St. Paul an isolated hill, about a quarter of a league in circumference, descended below the waters, and emerged to form an island. Towards Pointe aux Alouettes a great wood was detached from the solid ground, and slipped over the rocks into the river, where for some time the trees remained upright, raising their verdant crests above the water.

As many as ten severe shocks have been recorded since the first voyager came up the river. In the fastness of the broken interior at the upper end of the valley is pointed out the place where the inhabitants living toward Quebec found concealment from the soldiers of Wolfe's army at the time of his campaign in 1759. Many of these came from the Isle aux Coudres, which name was given it by Cartier from the abundance of hazel trees growing there at the time of his voyage. This is one of the oldest French settlements, and it was here that Admiral Durell's squadron waited two months for the coming of the rest of Wolfe's army, the inhabitants fleeing to the mountains, as described. It is said two of Montcalm's scouts swam the river at night, captured two English officers, one a grandson of the admiral, and took them to Quebec.

The Breton, upon arriving at the island of hazels, found the natives busy catching porpoises, and this industry of the simple natives was taken up by the

Seminarists of Quebec one hundred and fifty years later, and from that time has become the permanent employment of the *seigneurs* during the season. It is recorded that as many as three hundred and twenty have been captured at the incoming of a tide. When it is considered that each porpoise yields over a barrel of oil, and that its skin is valuable for leather, it can be seen that this occupation was decidedly lucrative. Soon individuals and companies contended for exclusive rights to carry on the fishery. The method employed was exceedingly simple and effective. It was simply to drive rows of saplings long enough to reach above high water into the shelving beach from the extremes of high and low water, each end stopping with a spiral curve so as to form a half circle. The porpoises coming with the tide in pursuit of shoals of small fishes, smelts and herrings, that keep close to the shore, unwittingly passed within the trap set for them. Upon seeking to return they found themselves confronted by this curved line of poles, and frightened in their efforts to find an escape, swam along the swaying barrier, which served to add to their frenzy, until, coming to the twist at its end, they were turned back over their course. Repeated attempts of this kind finally so distracted them that they gave up in despair, to be left high and dry by the ebbing tide. Then they became easy victims to the murderous assaults of the fishermen. The hapless victims died without defence, the female sacrificing her own life in a vain effort to save her young, displaying most pathetic examples of maternal devotion unto death.

This isle, with a population of between seven and eight hundred, two persons out of three being church communicants, has the distinction of being the place on the St. Lawrence where mass was first celebrated.

With a legion of mountains in the background, we are overlooked by the frowning Les Éboulements, here marshalling, as of yore, the rocky host and bidding defiance to the combined forces of nature and man. It is not difficult to picture to the mind's eye something of the terrific battle waged in the days when the earth was young between these giants, whose broken and scarred veterans remain as eternal warders of the battlefield. From the summit one looks down upon fertile valleys set with white villages, and buttressed by the mountains. The placid river is unrolled like an endless ribbon from a mighty spool, the distant shore mirrored in transparent clouds, jewelled with stars as the sun-rays play upon the pointed spires of its churches. In the centre of this beautiful vista lies Isle aux Coudres, fairer, brighter, younger, than it appeared on that auspicious September morning, in 1535, when

> *De Saint Malo, beau port de Mer,*
> *Trois grands navires sont arrivés,*

and the *Grande Hermine*, the *Petite Hermine*, and the *Emerillon* swung to their anchors in the bay behind the little promontories that jut out near the western end of the island. One can almost imagine that the sweet and solemn strains of the Mass which Dom Antoine and Dom Guillaume le Breton offered for the first time on

Canadian soil, and the fervent responses of Jacques Cartier and his men are borne across the water. But it is evening, and the soft sounds we hear are the chimes of the Angelus from the churches in the valleys.

Boucher, whom I have already quoted, in writing twenty years later says that two settlements have been founded in this wild district, "that of Baie St. Paul being the first inhabited land to be met with on the north shore as you come from France." It contained only three brave families then, and a population of only thirty-one souls. If it has grown slowly since, the river more rapidly has been robbing it of its fertile soil, year by year, until to-day it is little more than a cleft in the rocks through which a furious mountain torrent dashes over rocky shoals where stood the dwellings of the earliest inhabitants mentioned by the historian. As if one spite was not sufficient for nature to have against a place, Baie St. Paul was the scene, some years since, of severe earthquake shocks. This parish suffered at the hands of Captain Gorham's soldiers during the raid of 1759, when all the villages as far down as Murray Bay on the north bank were ravaged.

In juxtaposition to Baie St. Paul is the delightful retreat of Gouffre, with its groves of birch, maple, and hazel, and arbours of spruce and cedar, its pebbly shores, its clusters of bright cottages; the whole sanctified by the little church, whose spire mingles with the tree-tops like a golden star upon a field of green. A marked tranquillity of peacefulness and contentment rests upon all, as if here was one spot where troubles cease from vexing and the soul is free from doubt. As it is with man so it is with nature. The rugged heights melt in the distance into a soft liquid blue and grey mingling, while the nearer cliffs, seamed and scarred by many fissures and jagged points, are relieved by silvery bands of crystal water hanging like tremulous drapery over the brink of the precipice. Anon, plunging desperately down the descent, a subdued cry of triumph comes up from below, as if the tumbling waters would proclaim to the world the daring feat they had performed. Disappearing then with a parting shout of glee, apparently lost to sight for ever, they as suddenly and merrily reappear upon the vision, brighter than before if that were possible, ready to leap another chasm as fearless as if it had not taken a hundred just such plunges in its wild journey to the great river that seems to linger here to catch in its arms these runaway naiads of ravine and forest. The murmur of many of these streams falls upon the ear like the subdued strains of sacred music, while the sweet aroma of field and forest perfumes with an indescribable sweetness the miles of entrancing land‧ scape and sympathetic river. But those who have braved its wintry fastness tell me it is not always so calm and peaceful at Gouffre. There comes a time when

melting ice and heavy rains swell these mountain streams chafing at the long restraint the mountains have imposed upon them, until they fret and tear at the flanks of the hills, and uncover the secrets of the prehistoric world. Rocks, trees, and bridges are swept into the turbid flood of the Gouffre, which, raging like a demon un‑ chained, destroys everything that impedes its headlong course.

Chapter XVII

Between Cap Tourmente and Beauport

Where Art and Nature Meet—a Climax in Mountains—the Island of Sorrow—
Legend of Crane Island—Château Le Grande—Prisoner of the Jealous
Wife—Cartier's Isle of Bacchus—Ancient Petit Cap—Divine Ste. Anne
—Canadian Mecca—Story of the Saint—A Bird's-Eye View of Beauport—
Falls of Montmorency.

ABOVE Tadousac the northern shore is bounded
by a rocky ridge that comes so close to the
water's edge for miles at a stretch as to rise a
sheer precipice into the air. Something of the impressive wildness and majesty of the Ichang Gorge of
China's great river is recalled. Only one thing is lacking to remind us of the Highlands of the Hudson, and
that is the fact that everything here is on a mightier
scale—the great breadth of water-scene robbing the
banks of their impressiveness. Bring these walls into
closer companionship and the result would amaze the
beholder. At Cap Tourmente a climax in the mountain range is reached. The rounded summit of the
Laurentides come into plainer view, and Mont Ste.
Anne stands out in bold relief, deserted, it would seem,
by her sister heights, who slowly retreat to make room
for the surprise they have planned a little farther up
the broken way.

POINTE-À-PIC, MURRAY BAY.

CAP TOURMENTE (ST. JOACHIM.)

Where the river begins to narrow, among the many island gems that repose upon its peaceful bosom, is a jewel known as *Île de Grosse*, with no apparent evidence in sight of the grewsome history thrust upon it by a stern necessity that knows no sentiment in its devotion to duty.   When the accommodations upon the ships during their long passage over from the Old World were such as to advance disease and death, this island was made a quarantine station for the immigrants.   Here, in the year 1847 alone, as many as seven thousand, through fever and cholera, found an end to their bright dreams of homes in a new country.   But when we come to think of it, others have scarcely less happy records, for among all of the fair isles of the lower St. Lawrence, so fragrant with innocence, not one but has its dark tale of human misery, some story of treachery and massacre, wherein is preserved the memory of life's unfortunate sons and daughters.

About thirty miles below Quebec lies a little group of islands in mid-river, the largest of which is known as Crane's Island.   Over this lingers a goodly share of romantic memories of that day now fruitful of legends. The very atmosphere seems to breathe this, and the shimmer of the sunlight, as it quivers over rock and grassy slope, until it finally rests upon the highest point of land, pictures it upon the imagination of the beholder.

"Looking upon the ruins of Château Le Grande?" breaks upon our meditation a voice at our elbow.

"That has gone the way of mortals," the speaker, an old river-man, continues, "though it was only in the eighteenth century it was raised as the monument of a woman's whim." Of course it was a love romance, and if short it compassed the happiness of two rivals. The hero, for I suppose he must be considered such, was a gay courtier of the social circles of Old France. His wife was handsome, pure, and true, but of a temperament that brooked no oppositon to her slightest wish, and secured little happiness to her lover or to herself. Up-braiding him one day for his freeness in the presence of Court beauties, he proposed a compact with her, which she quickly accepted. This was nothing less than for them to build a home near the capital of the then famous New France, and there live exclusively in each other's society. In such a place there could be no anticipation of jealousy or family discord.

The site chosen was Crane's Island. The feathered denizens, which had held here their right of domain for ages, were frightened from their old rendezvous by the sound of the hammer of civilisation, and they speedily retreated before the aggressor. On yon summit rose directly a fine residence of the provincial architecture of the times, and to this wild, lonely retreat in the heart of the island Le Grande transported his young and beautiful wife. Happy months followed, winging themselves all too swiftly into years, the self-exiled couple finding delight in the picturesque surroundings. Both loved nature, and they saw here much to admire, for no more lovely and entrancing scene was to be found in the New World. Nor was there the monotony one might have expected in this isolation. The scene seemed to change day by day. Now the landscape looked fresh and innocent as some coy maid in its mantle of spring newness; anon it blossomed as the rose; grew grey and brown under the autumn sun; took on a brightness given it by the brush of the frost-king; and then fell asleep under the virgin robes of winter, looking fairer, purer than ever before. There were no two days alike, and each was unto them a poem written in the sweet language of love and filled with the inspiration of immortality. The birds, finding here kindred spirits of affinity, returned slyly to their old-time haunts, singing merrier than ever before. At intervals, some weather-beaten vessel, a messenger from the outside world, would come up the river, flying in the ambient breeze the beloved *fleur-de-lis* of their homeland.

The fairest sky must some time become flecked by a cloud. Even into the sweet contentment of this life came a shadow, and it was the shadow of a smile. While their lives had flowed on silently, quietly, happily, Madame Le Grande had become aware of the painful fact that a gay life had sprung up close by them, transforming, as it seemed to her vivid mind, this wilderness into Paris. Not alone at Quebec had this free spirit of gaiety entered into the every-day conduct of her inhabitants, but into the lives of the smaller towns and Indian villages something of this freeness and

indifference to decorum had also come.   Le Grande was
now often away from the company of his suspicious wife.
It is true he made liberal and plausible excuses for being absent so much, but it dawned upon her that these
were more profuse than an honest purpose demanded.
Affairs went on in this manner, until frequently his
boat did not return from over the river till an early
hour of morning.   She said nothing, but bided her
time.   This came but too soon for her peace of mind
and his happiness.   It usually does when a woman
waits.

Making some trivial excuse to her as the reason for
being away for the evening, Le Grande left the château
one summer day just as the westering sun was kissing
the mountains on the farther view good-night, and
rowed over the water to the opposite shore.   She had
been told by one of her secret spies that the Indians,
a few miles above, were holding a dance that would last
until late into the night.   Throwing over her shapely
shoulders a thick dark cloak, though the weather was
warm, she followed in his course, until she reached one
of those hamlets where a mixed population of French
and Indian prevailed.   She soon found her informant
had not been mistaken.   One of those wild, pantomimic
dances, for which the Indians were famous, was in the
midst of its dizzy, bewildering pleasure.   Ay, at the
moment she paused by the edge of the timber bordering
the sequestered spot, Le Grande, her husband, who had
sworn upon his sword and the crucifix to be ever faith-

ful to her, was then leading forward to the dance a beautiful dusky belle! She did not stop to listen to the music, or dwell upon the surprise she was to create. Like a shadow her tall and regal figure glided forward and stood beside her faithless husband.

What she said to him no one ever knew. In fact, the poor Indians fled at sight of her supernatural figure, thinking it was some evil spirit angry with them for their sport. Le Grande dropped the arm of the dark-hued beauty hanging upon him for support, and followed his wife. The return to the château was made in silence, so far as is known. Once there, she is reported to have turned upon him with a steely glitter in her dark eyes, saying:

"Is this proof of your fidelity to me? Was it for this you brought me to this lonely spot? You made a vow then to grant me any demand I might ask if you proved recreant to your pledge. Are you ready to fulfil your promise?"

"Name it," he said simply.

"You are never to leave this island again while you live."

He bowed his head in silence, and from that day Seigneur Le Grande was never seen away from the château, which suddenly lost its erstwhile cheerfulness, while silence reigned where formerly was life and vivacity. At last there came a day when Madame Le Grande engaged passage to France on a homeward-bound ship, when it was known that her doubly unfortunate husband had been released from his imprisonment and the tyranny of a woman's love by that grim freeman, Death. She was never heard of afterwards in Quebec, though it was rumoured that she had taken the veil. The château long since crumbled to dust, there being no one to preserve its glory.

Another island to claim our interest is the Isle of Bacchus, as Cartier christened it in 1535, on account of its great profusion of vines and grapes. Later, in honour of the Duke of Orleans, the son of Francis I., it received its modern name of Isle of Orleans. Between the two, for a long period, it was known among the pioneers as "Wizards' Isle," under the belief that the Indians who inhabited the place were in such close touch with nature as to be able to predict with certainty the coming of a storm or high tide. For a long time it was claimed that during the nights phantom lights played over the land and water, and the white inhabitants became alarmed, until it was found that the "spirit lights" were torches in the hands of dusky fishermen moving swiftly and silently to and fro in their canoes. Even then, so strong a hold had the spell thrown over the island by the uncanny stories that had been told, there were many who still whispered by the fireside of grotesque midnight dances by lamps that no mortal hands lighted. Very peaceful and innocent of supernatural deeds rests the beautiful island to-day under the benign influence of modern civilisation.

Coming up the river and approaching the Isle of

Orleans our gaze becomes attracted by a bluff that is the site of the ancient church of St. François. In the distance the Laurentian hills fretwork the horizon, from among whose pinnacled tops stands out in bold relief one at the base of which stood the little stone chapel that was the centre of attraction for one of the oldest settlements in Canada, *Petit Cap*. Hither fled the remnant of Christian Indians in the days of the missionaries and warfare with the Iroquois. It was here they listened with the devout priests to the sweet-toned sacred vespers, whose soft music floated swiftly, sadly, across the rolling river on the wings of the wind to the dusky warriors skulking in the depths of the forest, but with enough of their native stamina left to refuse to sell their birthright for a bumper of French rum, or a few gaudy trinkets, if less harmful, quite as worthless. What a panorama of wilderness overhung the scene upon that day!

A hundred years later, and this was the scene of the attack of the brawny Highlanders upon the allied French and Hurons. The village then known under the more divine name of Sainte Anne, suffered sorely on this occasion. Every other building in the hamlet was burned, save the little church, which defied the invaders' torch, and remained a sacred shrine to many pilgrims in the years to come. When war's red flame had burned out, the town was rebuilt, and to-day the picturesque little community exists as a living example of the Roman Catholics' faith and work in Canada, one of the oldest, if not the oldest, altar of worship in the St. Lawrence valley. What stories cluster about the venerated place! What memories cling to its shrines! What voices come in subdued whispers of that far-away past in which it was founded! What changes it has outlived! That pagan race, to whom it was originally consecrated, and in whose welfare so many of the faithful brotherhood laboured, loved, and lost during the long years of missionary work, have passed away, until only a handful remain to fan the embers of departed lordship. The far-reaching forests have also disappeared, and on the hill-tops and on the plains have risen the homes of a prosperous people. This has not been the fulfilment of the old dream of French colonisation, but the upbuilding of a rival race. The scheme of the ambitious Richelieu to found a French empire in America proved a delusion under his system of development. It has been truthfully said that

when he excluded the Huguenots from France and her colonies, he was doing as much as possible to add to the wealth of the Protestants of Europe and to the prosperity of the Puritans of New England, and one of the results of his policy was to be the perpetuation of the very heresy he hated.

The old church built in 1660 at Ste. Anne de Beaupré was taken down some years since, it having been declared unsafe. On its site was erected a modern and more pretentious building, but one that lacks the ancient interest of the other. It is true you will be told that the interior is of the same finish, and

ST. JOHN'S CHURCH, ISLE OF ORLEANS.

From a photograph by Livernois, Quebec.

BONNE STE. ANNE—OLD CHURCH.

From a photograph by Livernois, Quebec.

the double bell-tower that surmounts it is the same
that did service for the original ; but the rose window,
the plain façade, the Norman door, the air of a generation long-since departed are missing, and we find
ourselves entering what seems to us a commonplace
structure, lacking that air of deep sanctity which belongs
to the old.

Through all the changes of the years, the subor-
dination of the native race, and the ascendency of the
English over the French, the shrine of Ste. Anne was
left in peace and repose, until it was suddenly revealed
in the nineteenth century, under the revivified belief of
an old creed, that the relics of a dead saint were more
powerful to save the living than all other powers. The
incredible is always the swiftest of wing, and it was
only a brief time before pious pilgrimages were begun
to this early outpost of Quebec, which under the old
régime was the soul of New France, just as Kyoto was
the soul of Old Japan. And to-day, in fewer numbers,
which increase year by year, there are made to this
Canadian Mecca pious pilgrimages like those once made
to a Saviour's grave in the Holy Land, and those which
are now annually performed in Japan, when thousands
wend their way along the noble old road under the
lofty cryptomerias leading to the templed hills of
Nikko.

Ste. Anne is the patron saint of Canada. Where-
ever one goes he is pretty sure to stumble upon a
shrine in which tapers are kept burning, and which is

dedicated to the memory of this virtuous person. A question naturally arises in regard to the history of this omnipresent patron more often appealed to by the ancient *voyageurs* than all others, and whose influence is so marked at this day as to call for comment. Tradition, which is ever bold where history is shy, says she was the mother of the Virgin Mary, and a daughter of the house of David. Her sepulchre is in Jerusalem, but you will be shown in a little glass case what are claimed to be her bones. Are you curious to know how they reached this little niche of the world? Tradition never yet builded a structure it was not able to clothe in proper attire. It does not fail in this case. When the infidels destroyed the monuments of the Holy Land, one casket was found that would neither burn nor open. In their rage the despoilers flung it into the sea, upon the bosom of which it was carried to the shores of Provence. There it was washed ashore, and lay, it is supposed, for a long period embedded in the sand. Finally, a big fish struggling in the captivity of some fishermen scooped out a deep hole in the sand, at the bottom of which this casket was disclosed. But the reverent men of Apt could succeed no better than the infidels of Jerusalem in opening the coffin, and believing it was not to be done by mortals they placed it in a vault, and had the walls hermetically sealed. Here the casket rested undisturbed for over seven hundred years. Then Charlemagne had his attention attracted to it by a boy, blind, deaf, and dumb.

How he came by his information the conqueror did not stop to ask, but upon removing the wall he discovered the casket. From this place, for some unknown reason, it was taken to the little town of Carnac, in Brittany, where it was entombed, and the place became famous as the shrine of Ste. Anne d'Auray. Once more the sacred bones were removed, this time by an over-zealous believer, who started with them to America. After a stormy passage over the Atlantic they found repose here at Ste. Anne de Beaupré.

This church dates its origin from 1658, in which a *habitan* gave the land for its site, and the French governor laid its foundation-stone. On that very day its miracles began. A peasant afflicted with a severe pain in his loins, while in the midst of assisting in the good work, was suddenly relieved of his suffering. Another with a lame limb recovered its use immediately. A blind man was restored to his sight when he turned his sightless orbs on the sacred place. Another who had not been able to speak aloud for years found his speech, and it is needless to say, perhaps, spent much of his time afterwards in sounding the praises of this saint. A pious woman, upon hearing of the remarkable cures of those who had visited the shrine, invoked the blessing of the saint, when she was cured of the disease which had bent her nearly double.

Then miracle after miracle followed, until the sleepy little hollow was the talk of all New France. Soldiers, as they paced their beat on the fort, looked down the river as if they expected to

see a vision.   The peasantry grouped together in large family
circles, just as they love to do to-day, and as the big logs crackled
in the great fireplace, some one who had been to the shrine re-
counted his experiences and gave free rein to his imagination, while
all piously crossed themselves when he had concluded.   Pilgrims
flocked to the New World wonder on the St. Lawrence, and during
the seventeenth century there were never less than a thousand on
the feast day of Ste. Anne.   At all seasons of the year, individual
pilgrims were seen going afoot along the *Côte de Beaupré*, and in
winter in their sleighs on the frozen river.   The Micmac Indians
came regularly from New Brunswick for trade, and before feast
days their canoes were seen coming up the stream to the shrine,
where they built birch-bark huts to shelter the pilgrims.   In fact,
the whole country was excited by the mystery, and many churches
were built in honour of the saint.   It was a regular custom of vessels
ascending the St. Lawrence to fire a broadside salute when passing
the place.   .   .   .   We, who live in this age of electricity, and who
affect to be beyond astonishment, but gape at every new sensation as
if the world was yet in its teens, may imagine the thrill of wonder
which would run through the minds of the simple peasantry, and
the superstitious *voyageurs*, when the miracles were told.

For a time the virtues of this Canadian Mecca
seemed to wane, but the pendulum that swings out
must return, and again Ste. Anne is enjoying her
sacred rights with an ever-increasing following, as witnessed in the silent but eloquent tokens heaped high
at her door by those who have come crippled and gone
away with light steps and lighter hearts; as witnessed
by the constant praise sung in her name and the long
train who come and go with believing minds.

Leaving this dreamy picture behind the village of
Beauport, with its historical memories rising vividly
before us, there flashes on our sight a cluster of picturesque cottages, above which rises the ever-present

companion of these rural hamlets, a church with twin spires.   In the distance, set in a frame of pine and hemlocks, with white birches peeping out between, the background is veiled by the yellow curtain of Montmorency Falls.   Resting on pillars of fragile buoyancy that forever tremble but never tumble, the bended sheet of river, fifty feet in width, drops a sheer descent of 220 feet, and without ado, as if it had done nothing uncommon, glides down to meet the St. Lawrence. The charm of this delightful waterfall does not lie in the depth or the volume of the cataract, but rather in the transparency of its flood which looks like a silver foil laid lightly over the grey rock, and worn so thin by constant friction that its delicate tissues seem about to break asunder.   It is not less beautiful in winter than in summer, and after flinging its mists over tree and shrub, it glistens in the sunbeams like a mine of diamonds.

Chapter XVIII

Picturesque Quebec

A Peopled Cliff—The Lower Town—A Spiral Street—Cape Diamond—The Citadel—A Relic of Bunker Hill—Rare Panorama of Country—Memorable Trip
of Major Fitzgerald—His Unhappy Love Romance—"Ribbon Farms"—
Scene of Cartier's "White Winter"—Two Acres of Clover, Daisies, and
Buttercups—Road to Charlesbourg—Château de Beaumanoir—Ruins, Flowers,
and Vines—Historic Names—Story of the Acadian Maid—Old Fortress—Its
Secret Passage—Plains of Abraham.

THE scenes briefly sketched, with many more as deserving of mention, pass successively in review, and then Quebec, the soul of " Our Lady of the Snow," breaks upon the vision. Gone in a moment are the pictures, but not the memories, of the lower river. Now the grand and beautiful blend in a harmony that is never forgotten. Above the river rises a massive wall of rock over three hundred feet in height, and bidding defiance to the world. " *Que bec !* " (" What a beak ! ") exclaimed one of Cartier's followers, and the name has clung to it ever since. That alone has remained unchanged. It is now a cliff populated ; an unassorted mass of rocks, roofs, ramparts, fortified walls, pointed spires, and ominous muzzles of guns more curious than dangerous. Gone are the ancient walnuts ; varnished are the shades that peopled them. Yet to-day the scene is picturesque—Canadian—yesterday

framed in the present. The keen-sighted Thoreau exclaimed, in describing the scenery about Quebec:

The fortifications of Cape Diamond are omnipresent. They
preside, they frown over the river and the surrounding country.
You travel ten, twenty, thirty miles up or down the river's banks,
you ramble fifteen miles amid the hills on either side, and then,
when you have long since forgotten them, perchance slept on them
by the way, at a turn of the road or of your body, there they are
still, with their geometry against the sky.

Cape Diamond, which, by the way, somewhat re-
minds us of another promontory by that name in mid-
Pacific, is a rock-wedge, composed of grey granite
mixed with quartz and a species of dark-coloured slate,
thrust down between the St. Lawrence and St. Charles
rivers. Something of its rugged grimness is softened
by patches of shrubs that somehow find sustenance
on its Roman features, giving it the appearance of a
bearded Titan.

At the base of this huge bulwark, forming the
"Gibraltar of America," lies the "Lower Town," with
its narrow streets, its weather-stained dwellings, its
warehouses, breathless life, bustle, and confusion, flanked
by the stone stairways leading to sunlight and the rare-
fied atmosphere above, and fronted by the river piers,
harbour, and a mixed collection of water-craft. Here
exist the bone and sinew of the city. This lower section
has been compared to some parts of Edinburgh. It is
connected with the "Upper Town" by *Côte de la
Montagne*, or Mountain Street, which, until within thirty
or forty years, has not been passable for carriages.

Leaving this spiral street, up which have climbed so
many in the past, not a few of whom were burdened
with cares and responsibilities greater than the fate of
their own lives, to the teams and the pedestrians, we
follow along the narrow street running under the frowning cliff.   What if the way is narrow, and the houses
claim so much !   Every foot of this earth has been a
gift from the river—a precious gift, with that crouching
rock looking jealously down upon it.   It must have
been just below this spot where Donnacona and his
dusky followers pushed out in their canoes to greet
Cartier on his first visit.   It was somewhere close
by that weather-beaten building that Champlain, with
his own hand, felled the first walnut tree preparatory to
founding his capital of New France.   Up that zigzag
pathway climbed Montgomery, with the snow blinding
his eyes, to his inevitable fate.

We ascend to the summit of the rocky bulwark by
the wooden stairway, counting one hundred and sixty-
four steps, and are glad there is not another.

The bold promontory upon which we now stand em-
braces an area of about forty acres.   The most striking feature is naturally the citadel, with its continuous
granite wall running along the very brow of the height,
flanked with towers and bastions commanding both the
St. Lawrence and the St. Charles rivers.   The new-
comer cannot be other than impressed with the solid
appearance of this wall, built before the independence
of America was won.

CAPE DIAMOND, SHOWING TABLET TO THE MEMORY OF MONTGOMERY.
From a photograph by Livernois, Quebec.

THE BREAK-NECK STEPS, QUEBEC.

The citadel has been so often described that another detailed account would seem superfluous. But its lofty situation, if nothing else, demands attention, and gives to the visitor one of the finest prospects to be found in any land. The "boys" about the barracks are light-hearted and care-free, though life here, with its steady round of duty, has its monotony. Among the objects of curiosity pointed out to the sight-seer, is a brass piece the British captured from the New England troops at Bunker Hill. It does not look very formidable, and a strong man might carry it off under his arm.

The view from this historic lookout is one of impressive interest, varied in its diversity of scenery and grand in its effect. The St. Lawrence, majestic and magnificent as ever, unfolds its broad band of glistening water, over which craft of every kind, from the birch skiff of the dusky native to the palace steamer of tourist travel, lend motion and vivacity to the picture, and speak not only of the present but of the past when the aborigines were lords of the wilderness. Midway, in the stream below, lies the Isle of Orleans in plain view, while across the river rises Point Levis, rivalling but not equalling Cape Diamond in its bold front, breasting the water like a lion crouching at bay. Beyond this height, which is the site of a populous community, stretches a country noted for its beauty and tranquillity of surface. Unconsciously the mind is carried back to the day when this was an unpeopled wilderness, and to that wintry journey made on snow-shoes through its trackless depths from Frederickton to Quebec, a distance of 175 miles, by Major Fitzgerald, soon after the closing act of the American Revolution.   He had been an officer under Lord Rawdon, and served with distinction at Eutaw Springs, where he was wounded. Upon reaching Quebec with his message, without stopping to recuperate he continued into the western country, guided now by his staunch friend, Brant.   Proceeding to Michilimackinac, and then reaching the Mississippi, he followed down the river to New Orleans. From there he hastened home to greet the loved one who he fondly believed was awaiting anxiously his return.   Alas ! for man's dreams and woman's forgetfulness, he was met at her father's door by the faithless sweetheart and—her husband !   Crushed by the blow, he rejoined the army, to fall a martyr to the cause of Ireland a few years later.   He was more fortunate in having the eloquent Tom Moore for his biographer, the latter himself visiting, in 1804, a portion of the country traversed by his friend, giving a memorial of his trip in his immortal *Canadian Boat-Song* and other poems of the St. Lawrence.

Slowly the eye continues to follow the great river winding sluggishly through the valley, bounded on the south by the distant backbone of the Appalachian Mountains whose far slopes reach down to the shores of ancient Vinland, and on the north by the Laurentides, the oldest mountains known to geologists, looming peak beyond peak, until lost to shape and sight in the distance, and where the vision stops the imagination carries the fancy forward to the vast wilderness sweeping on in majestic silence to the frozen pole.

Looking over the gabled roofs and dormer windows, the minarets of the naval academy, and the spires of the churches, with here and there a glimpse of some narrow street winding upward until, as if tired of the attempt to reach the top, it had tumbled back to lie crumbled and distorted amid the debris of streets and buildings and rocks, a vivid picture is gained of the Lower Town. Quebec, as it is the only walled city in America, is possibly less American than any city north of Mexico. It certainly appeals to the new-comer as no other American city does, and he goes away with that impression strengthened. While it may not be able to boast the ancient castles of a Hamburg or a Heidelberg, with the moss upon its grey walls, the lichens upon its battlements, the slimy moats around its citadel, the legends of a day that may never have been, it has a suggestion of mediævalism older than the Middle Ages and rendered more attractive on account of its modern setting. It requires no imagination to be made to believe that the town at your feet is a corner of Old France, and that the rock beneath them is older than Europe !

As the gaze roams northward from the rounded shoulder of the Isle of Orleans, beautiful and filled with memories, it rests upon the long street of Beauport, where the landscape is adorned with metal-covered

cottages, whose heavy roofs, like bats' wings, reach down
to shelter the unrailed verandas, Old-World features
of some Swiss village or corner in Brittany. The simple dress of the people, their quaint speech, their picturesque manner, each help to complete the suggestion.
The roads around Quebec are well kept, while the
plank sidewalks add to the pleasure of the tourist who
chooses to go amid these scenes on foot. Down on
the flat, within sight and sound of the Falls of Montmorency, the combined French and Indian forces rallied to beat back that adventure-mad New Englander,
Phips, who thought to surprise the northern eagle in
his eyrie. And there, too, was fought the prelude
to Wolfe's far-reaching victory upon the Plains of
Abraham.

Farther away, edged by the rounded horizon, lies
what looks like a fine agricultural country, with its
" ribbon farms," low-walled cottages, and green fields
white-starred with daisies. To the west of these winds
down from the interior the St. Charles, the river of romance. At its mouth Cartier moored his briny caravels, and a little higher up he went into camp for that
long, tedious "white winter." A monument to his
memory now marks the place. Just across the river,
upon the intervale farms that lie between the stream
and the road running northward, leading to the ruins
of Beaumanoir, we saw, only a few days since, one of
nature's most beautiful flower-gardens, two acres of
crimson clover, star-eyed daisies, and yellow buttercups,

the three standing evenly shoulder to shoulder.   Never
did colours blend more happily, and never was sweeter
fragrance wafted on the amorous breeze of June.   Here
was a flower for each conquest of Canada, and the
brightest was the last.

Following up this delightful road bordered with
white dasies and that *fleur-de-lis* of Canadian flowers,
the buttercup, some five miles from the Dorchester
bridge spanning the St. Charles, reposes to-day, under
the shadows of Charlesbourg Mountain, a pile of ruins called by the English " The Hermitage"; by the
French, " The Mansion of the Mountain."   In the days
of its glory it was more poetically known as Beaumanoir, and it was here that the infamous Bigot, with
his boon companions, held his secret councils and car-
ousals to the shame of New France, and which more
than all else led to her downfall.   In those days noble
old forests composed of giant oaks, whose seamed and
weather-beaten bodies showed ample proof of long
lives; lofty elms, with wide-spreading tops that tipped
their tapering branches with becoming grace ; dark pines
that wore for ever a frown, as if bidding defiance to the
axe of the woodsman who had already turned his gaze
hitherward, surrounded the gay palace, which, with its
adjacent buildings, covered an area as large as a small
town, the collection forming a square, illuminated by
beautiful gardens.

The Château of Beaumanoir was built of stone
like most of the buildings of its time, gabled and

pointed in the style of architecture then prevailing. It had been erected by the first Intendant of New France, Jean Talon, the patron of the gallant explorer, La Salle, as a retreat for him to flee to when worried with the cares of his high office that afforded him so small a meed of satisfaction, owing to the indifference the mother country paid to her offspring. Among the famous persons who made historic this old hall were Sieur Joliet, who came here to relate his wonderful exploits in the untrodden West; here, also, came Father Marquette to recount to his wondering listeners his stories, that sounded like fables, of that majestic river styled "The Father of Waters"; while from here the intrepid La Salle, the most chivalrous of them all, set forth on his romantic mission to explore the mysterious stream and claim it in the name of his King. Then, when its illustrious company, of which these were only a trio among a score, had gone the way of shadows, the ancient edifice became dishonoured by the ignoble presence of those who boasted of the ruin and not of the glory of the fair empire intrusted to their keeping. Could their language have been interpreted, what tales of infamous scenes these walls would have told!

The château was entered by a wide gate set at the end of a broad avenue, overhung by a lofty hedge, trimmed into fantastic figures after the manner of the gates of Luxembourg. The main building, as has been said, was set in the midst of gardens of luxurious growth, squares, circles, and polygons radiant through the summer months with flowers of varied beauty and fragrance. The hedges were filled with fruit trees that might well have graced the orchards of the old country, all of which, indeed, had been brought from France by the thoughtful Talon. In their season were cherries, red and luscious as those that thrived in the gardens of Brittany; plums that vied with the rare sweetness of their sisters in Gascony; pears from the famous fruitage of the Rhone valley; and apples rivalling in their soft tints the rosy cheeks of the fair maids of Normandy. But if environed by a prodigal display of beauty and sunshine, the château stood the very image of gloom. Its massive doors were ever kept bolted and barred; its mullioned windows close-shut, as if it were a dungeon holding within its walls unhappy victims denied their freedom.

If there is any truth in local tradition this was, in fact, the case concerning one fair life, too pure, too beautiful to mingle with the wicked world. She was the child of De Castin, that high and noble founder of the name in Acadia. Her mother was the daughter of an Abnaki chief, and, like a true forest princess, was every way worthy of her liege lord. This daughter possessed all of the comeliness of person belonging to her mother, and the dignity of her proud father. As she grew to womanhood, her personal charms and manner more than fulfilling the promise of girlhood, the Castin mansion became the popular resort of persons of distinction connected with the affairs of the colony. Among others came François Bigot, Chief Commissary of the Army, then looked upon as an honoured officer of his King. An attachment quickly sprang up between this couple, sincere and lifelong with the one, a passing whim with the other, but sufficiently sincere to afford amusement for a time that might otherwise have been wearisome. Leaving his post here in disgrace, Chevalier Bigot no doubt thought that his little love romance was over. But he had not come to realise the depth of a woman's love and the sacrifice she was willing to make for him who had enthralled her very soul. He left her, as he supposed, to languish in silence and inactivity ; but it was not long after he had come to Quebec, in 1748, in spite of his infamy elsewhere, to defame the already smirched name of New France, that he learned that a very beautiful woman had been seen about the city. He gave no thought to her, however, until one day, while hunting in the vicinity of Beaumanoir, he met her in the forest and recognised her who was entitled to be his wife. It chanced that he was alone at the time, and, not caring to have his companions learn of his intrigue, unable to induce her to go away, he escorted her to the château. There she remained practically a prisoner during the troublesome times that followed, and until it was rumoured that she had been murdered by one of his agents. Let that be as it may, Bigot has been charged with quite enough for one man to meet at the judgment.

Slightly removed from the château, but according to

story connected by an underground passage, stood a tower of stone masonry, its walls filled with loopholes and crowned with a crenelated crest. This had been built as a place of refuge and defence during the Indian attacks in the days of the Iroquois invasions. The little fortress had proved invulnerable to them ; but the suns and the storms of the passing years proved more destructive than the primitive armament of the dusky warriors, so that long since it crumbled and fell. Little remains now of Beaumanoir—a ruined corner of wall here, a gable there, a few unsightly mounds, the red alders creeping over fallen buildings, the ugliness of the crumbling masonry relieved by the innocent faces of Canadian violets and illuminated by star-flowers, or half concealed by thick moss and tall grass, where the birds build their nests and the winds sigh a frequent requiem over the loss of an empire standing upon corruption and depotism. There are those who claim that the desolation of the unhappy place is made more pathetic by the haunting presence of the most innocent and beautiful life that perished amid the downfall of human hopes.

Chapter XIX

Sights and Shrines of Quebec

Monuments to Wolfe, Montcalm, and "*Aux Braves*"—Ste. Foye Road—Mount Hermon—Château St. Louis—Portraits of Celebrities—Château Frontenac—"The Golden Dog"—Story of M. Phillibert—University of Laval—"Notre Dame des Victoires"—Graves of Richelieu and Laval—A Winter Night—Laughter and Good Cheer.

THE gaze reluctantly turning away from the direction of Charlesbourg, with its ruins and memories, naturally seeks that battlefield where the course of infamy ended in disaster. The Plains of Abraham are a fitting resting-place for heroes, and it needs no modern historian to tell the glory of those who fill them. Recent research has, however, done much toward correcting the errors perpetuated by careless chroniclers contemporaneous with the scenes which they attempted to describe. A plain shaft marks the spot where, according to late-day investigations, the victor did not fall. But the matter of a few hundred yards, more or less, from the exact spot does not matter. Wolfe does not need such a monument. Behind Dufferin Terrace, in the governor's garden, another granite column adds the part of a monument to keep green the story, with the simple inscription : " In memory of Wolfe and Montcalm." Not often is the name of the van-

NATURAL STEPS, MONTMORENCY RIVER.

Frcm a photograph by Livernois, Quebec.

THE RUINS OF CHÂTEAU BIGOT.

quished linked so harmoniously with that of his conqueror, until at this not very distant day it is not worth
weighing the difference to find whose fame is the
greater.   Two miles above the Lower Town a break in
the massive wall affords room for that convenient pathway where both Wolfe and Arnold climbed to dare the
enemy intrenched upon the height.   Had the action of
the foe in each case been reversed—Montcalm remaining
behind his defences and Cramaché seeking battle on the
open plain—who can say that Canada would not now
be a part of the United States instead of Great Britain,
and Arnold, not Wolfe, the great figure in its history?
Possibly this historic and momentous pathway, which
seems to have been designed as the key to Cape Diamond's fortified heights, is not so abrupt and difficult
of ascent as your historian, aided by your imagination,
has pictured it to you.   Such places become, upon close
inspection, wanting in some of the wilder and more im-
practicable parts.   Putnam's ride at Breakneck Stairs
was really a tame affair compared to what it has been
described.   But a hero's fame rises above such minor
facts.   Like the rhyme and rhythm of great poets, their
deeds are entitled to certain licenses of description.
Then it must be remembered that nearly one hundred
and fifty years have softened the rugged trail.   May
the day be hastened when the Plains of Abraham shall
be reserved for a public park !

Beyond the scene of this overshadowing victory is
the battlefield of Ste. Foye, where De Levis won his

victory over Murray in 1760, and which was an interesting outcome of Wolfe's campaign. It is sometimes
called "the second battle of the plains." This place is
marked by a monument " To the Brave," erected by
Prince Napoleon Bonaparte in 1854. It is a tall pillar
of iron, surmounted by a figure of Bellona, the Roman
goddess of war, and with the fraternal feelings which
mark so many of the Canadian memorials it is generously inscribed to the memory of both sides, the inscription reading simply :

AUX BRAVES.

Quebec has many pretty walks, but none prettier
than that which leads through the gate of St. John and
follows along the Ste. Foye road, beneath a leafy avenue bordered with neat villas, until a slight eminence is
reached where Murray made his reckless charge, with
the slush and April snow knee-deep, quickly crimsoned
with the blood of the heroes who fell on every hand.
Near by are the Martello towers.

A visit to a battlefield seems to be fitly followed by
one to a " City of Silence." There can be no more
beautiful cemetery than " Mount Hermon," planned by
an American gentleman, Major Douglas, and almost
equal in area to the Plains of Abraham. It commands
a fine view, and among the noted persons who have
found resting-places here may be mentioned the famous
Scottish vocalist, John Wilson, and the Reverend Daniel
Wilkie, LL.D., the celebrated preceptor of youth.

But leaving the city of the dead and the monuments of heroes, the eye falls upon Quebec's famous terrace, which was laid out by the Earl of Durham, to be enlarged and improved by Lord Dufferin, whose name it now bears.   Under this terrace are yet to be seen the foundations of that ancient Château St. Louis, built by Champlain and destroyed by fire in 1834.   This notable building was for about two centuries the seat of government, and within its walls transpired some of the most momentous scenes in the history of New France.   Its great hall has been described as palatial in its dimensions and adornments.   Its high walls, set with deep panels of wainscoting, and hung with paintings of historic interest, were relieved by huge pillars of polished oak, lifting high overhead the lofty ceiling, tinted a deep blue, and ornamented by delicate carvings of ebony-wood.   Among the richly coloured portraits were the searching features of Cartier, with his pointed beard, sharp nose, and flashing eyes, as if still peering up the rapids of the mighty river he had discovered; there was Champlain, his handsome countenance touched softly with the radiance of clear, dark eyes, and framed in with a profusion of long, waving hair, giving slight token of the fire that burned in his restless brain; Louis Baude de Frontenac, keen of feature and as gallant of look as in life, while beside him was the beautiful woman whom he acknowledged as his wife but whose company he ignored; the unselfish Talon, noblest of the Intendants; the courtly La Salle, to whom New France owed

so much in the West; Laval, the first bishop, the father
of education in the colony; and not far away that faithful founder of schools and the first superior of the Ursulines in Quebec, Mère Marie de l'Incarnation; the
stern, resolute, all-ambitious Louis the Great of France,
with many other men of note,—kings, governors, intendants, explorers, and builders of New France.

Of all this and much more that has never been told
exists only a shade. Near its site stands a modern
structure, the Château Frontenac, one of the finest
hotels in the world. In the yard in front of this, looking calmly down upon the beholder, stands a massive
memorial to Champlain. Just below, at this writing,
another fitting tribute is being raised to the memory of
that truly great and good man, Laval. Near by stands
the post-office, a modern enough building of stone, yet
holding within its walls a block of granite from that
ancient building once standing on its site and known by
the unpoetical name of *Le Chien d'Or*, or "The Golden
Dog." This legend-haunted house was made the scene
of one of Quebec's most famous books, and everything
relating to it is redolent with romance. It was built by
a M. Phillibert, a merchant coming to Quebec from
Bordeaux in the unhappy days of Bigot, the infamous
Intendant. M. Phillibert, with the cause of the common people at heart, undertook to break down the
power of the dishonest ring which was ruining New
France. Over the door to the entrance of his great
store, where was to be found every commodity needed

A DISTANT VIEW OF THE JACQUES CARTIER MONUMENT.

THE GOLDEN DOG.

From a photograph by Livernois, Quebec.

by the people on sale at reasonable prices, he caused to
be represented in relief the figure of a dog gnawing
a bone, under which were the following lines :

> *Je svis vn chien qvi ronge mon os*
> *En le rongeant, je prends mon repos,*
> *Vn jovr viendra qvi n'est pas encore venv,*
> *Ov je mordrai celvi qvi m'avra mordv.*

So stoutly did M. Phillibert fight Intendant Bigot that
the latter finally turned against him, and, according to
story, hired him assassinated, a brother of his beautiful
but unscrupulous wife performing the dastardly deed.

Standing near the brink of rock where the brave
Montgomery fell is the University of Laval, with its
triple towers and a cupola of cross-crowns. This is
Quebec's treasure-house of books, relics, and pictures.
It was founded by M. de Laval de Montmorenci, in
1636, during whose lifetime the buildings were twice
burned. It was originally intended for the education
of Catholic clergymen, but eventually to educate all
who came. Queen Victoria, in 1854, raised the institu-
tion to the status of a university.

Quebec might well be called the city of churches, to
mention all of which would require too much space.
Near the market in the Lower Town stands one of the
finest buildings of worship erected in America. This
church, while services were being held all over the
city in praise of the escape from the attack of the
New England forces under Phips, was dedicated to
Notre Dame de la Victoire. Twenty years later, when

another scheme of conquest was undertaken, and Sir
Hoveden Walker's fleet of fifteen warships was wrecked
at the mouth of the St. Lawrence, while on its way to
capture Quebec, the building was re-dedicated, and its
name made to take a plural form, *Notre Dame des
Victoires.* The gladdened people now built a porch
over its door.

Near where this stands was the house Champlain
built in 1608, and just back of it the plot where he
formed the first garden in Canada. Another fine edifice claiming more than passing attention is the Ba-
silica, built on the site of the ancient church of *Notre
Dame de la Recouvrance*, raised by Champlain to commemorate the restoration of New France by Great
Britain following its conquest by Kertk. Here taught
those missionary martyrs Brébeuf, Lalemant, and Marquette. The remains of Richelieu and Laval repose
within its sacred inclosure. On Garden Street is the
Ursuline convent, in whose chapel rests all that is mortal of Montcalm. What memories cluster round these
Meccas of the mind ! Quebec has done well in marking
these hallowed spots, though it may be not so well as
Montreal. There are outside of these cities many
noted places throughout the provinces which deserve to
be marked, and the coming generation will wonder why
it is not done. It is already too late to act in some
cases, but others can yet be saved.

Having seen Quebec by daylight and lamplight, its
sunshine and shadow, one other phase remains to be

met.   If last with us, it is not least.   With the plains transformed into whitened deserts, the forests tufted with the crown of the northern goddess, the villages asleep under their spotless robes, the majestic St. Lawrence grinding into powder its vast fields of ice, the whir of mills the only sound that comes from an erstwhile busy port, defying the siege of the North King, this Queen of the Northland appears in royal grandeur. Her subjects now light their home fires ; the sleigh-bells jingle merrily in the streets ; and old winter is braved and dared with jest and good cheer.   The street life is, in fact, a merry-go-round, in which the riders are fur-coated giants, as cheery as warm hearts can make them. It is now the heyday for the young people, who can find plenty to occupy their attention, snow-shoeing, skating, tobogganing, and coasting.

No hour is more sacred than that which falls upon a wintry sunset like a winding-sheet over the departing day.   The view obstructed by banks of snow, by the white plumes of the forest, by the grey dimness growing deeper and deeper, the unseen hand of Twilight closes softly the portals of day.   The whole city lies in a huge muffler reaching to its throat, but, like so many big, blinking eyes, the dormer windows of the cottages peep out above it.   Let the wild wind brush you with its long, hoary beard ; let the solitude, which is never so near as then, settle upon you and yours ; in the west are streamers of gold, and you know the god of day is banking his fire for the night.   The low, sweet melody of the Angelus is wafted on the air from the chapel of the nuns, and all feelings of loneliness instantly leave you. Let the street become deserted; let the sun cloak with darkness his light; so long as the bells of humanity ring there is hope and gladness in the old city. Their notes are the heart-throbs of the brave and the hopeful. Soon the darkness is scintillated with the beams of the rising moon; the sky takes on a deeper blue than by day; the snow-crystals of the city walls, the whitened roofs, the frosted eaves, one and all sparkle with the pure radiance of the new-born queen, until it is easy to fancy that this city, wrapped in its winter mantle, is a diamond set in a white stone.

So, when and whither we turn, the picturesque, grand, and beautiful, hallowed with sublime memories, greet our vision: cliff stairs climbing to houses in midair; winding streets shadowed by quaint roofs; gay market-places, ringing with their babel of voices in foreign tongues; mounted guns, thundering forth their challenge to the outside world at sunrise; bands in bright uniforms playing the march of the setting sun; bells ringing solemnly at the close of day; churches and convents; walled gardens and lilac-bordered terraces; monuments to dead heroes; laughter and good cheer for the living; grand, far-reaching environments that are not equalled by any other American city;—all of these and many more sights and shrines make Quebec the Empress of the peerless St. Lawrence.

SILLERY COVE.

A FRENCH CANADIAN FARMER.

From a photograph by Livernois, Quebec.

Chapter XX

From Quebec to Montreal

North Bank—Sillery—Indian Settlements in the St. Lawrence Valley—St. Francis —St. Regis—Three Rivers—Poetical Names—An Atmosphere of Age—Peasant Population—Three Types—Early Farmhouses—The Harvest Festival— Christmas-tide—A True Son of Old Normandy.

THE high bank of the St. Lawrence from Cape Diamond to Cap Rouge is composed of "clay-slate," of a dark brown or a dull red colour, from whence comes the name of the last point of spurious earth. The bed of the river is laid with the same species of stone, the friction of the waters constantly raising fine particles of dust to the surface and laying these in thin sheets upon the shore. As barren of true soil as this long frontage of steep cliff appears to be, a healthy growth of shrubs and trees relieves with verdure what must otherwise be a dreary embankment.

About a mile above Wolfe's Cove is situated the little historic village of Sillery, where, in the stormy days of that Christian conquest of Canada made memorable by its numerous examples of a faith that was not bounded by human suffering, the zealous Jesuits called about them the wondering Hurons, who listened, with a patience beyond comprehension, to exhortations that they could not understand. In later years, when the noted Huron village standing about two-thirds of the way up the St. Charles River, could muster as a remnant of the once powerful confederacy less than two hundred persons, Sillery became debatable ground. The surviving red men then appealed to the British courts for a fief, upon the claim that it belonged to them as heirs of a grant made to their ancestors in 1651. But the courts held that the grant had been made to the Jesuits without specific designations, and simply for the purpose of assembling the wandering natives of New France and instructing them in the Christian religion. It was also claimed that fifty years after conceding this right, upon representing that it had been deserted by the Indians, it was regranted to the Jesuits themselves. Then it remained in their hands until the dissolution of their order in 1800, when it had reverted to the British Government. So the attempt to recover that fine tract of country along the river near Quebec was denied the poor descendants of the original owners. It appears that the grant to the Jesuits was made soon after the overthrow of the Hurons by the Iroquois, and that the fathers were given this in trust. In justice to the English it should be said that in order to compensate their loss here the Indians were offered grants of Crown lands in other sections. But the Hurons replied that any movement which would compel them to separate or change their mode of living would be of no benefit.

Another Indian settlement of pathetic interest about

fifty years ago was that of a remnant of Algonquins near Three Rivers, and numbering about eighty. Near St. Francis River, on the opposite bank of the St. Lawrence, dwelt, in a village constructed of bark huts a little better than primitive wigwams, about 350 Abnakis and kindred red men, descendants of the warlike tribes that inhabited northern New England before the long and sanguinary wars between the races. Higher up on the St. Lawrence, at this time, were three settlements of Iroquois; the first at Sault St. Louis, numbering almost a thousand persons; a second at St. Regis, numbering 350; and a smaller number living at the Lake of Two Mountains. At the latter place also lived about six hundred Algonquins and Nipissings. All of these settlements were then in a wretched condition. A favourable change, in most cases, has taken place, since then; the inhabitants have to a considerable extent taken on civilised ways. Each hamlet now has its little church, and in most cases a native preacher; the people are industrious and apparently content with their lot, all of which goes to show that the native races of New France and New England were not only willing to receive the gospel of enlightenment, but that they were capable of becoming good citizens.

About midway between Quebec and Montreal, noted as a half-way station of these outposts of civilisation through the early struggles of settlement and conquest, its very situation retarding its growth, is to-day the most important town upon the north bank, standing at the triple outlet of the St. Maurice River, from which fact it gets its name of Three Rivers. Thoreau has most aptly remarked that

the Greeks, with all their wood and river gods, were not so qualified to name the natural features of a country, as these French Canadians, and if any people had a right to substitute their own for Indian names it was they. When translated into our language these names lose much of their original beauty and poetry. While a peculiar fitness belongs to the nomenclature of its natural features the utterance of these names cannot other than suggest the lingering touches of romance. What associations are revivified by the mention of *La Rivière de la Rose*, "the River of the Rose," *La Rivière de la Friponne*, "the Wanton River," *La Rivière du Nord*, "the River of the North," and others more or less romantic. Why our own "river" sounds prosaic and commonplace beside that *la rivière*, which fairly ripples with the murmur of running water as it falls from the tongue.

Among the carrying-places, second only in importance to the rivers, were such fanciful designations as *Portage des Roses*, speaking in unmistakable terms of a profusion of wild roses overhanging the place, possibly to the annoyance of the infrequent passer-by; and then, on the Ottawa, that still more picturesque name, *Portage de la Musique*, the tumultuous waters, for ever tumbling over the rocks, sending up their endless song.

Three Rivers early became a trading post, and then to strengthen and give stability to the frontier a mission was founded here in 1617 by Pacifique du Plessis. With all its advantages, however, it failed to receive the attention it deserved. Champlain, in his efforts to advance westward, caused a fort to be erected here in

1634 upon the same site where the Iroquois had destroyed a primitive defence built by the Algonquins in their futile attempts to beat back their powerful foes. It was from here that Father Brébeuf bade his farewell to his associates when he set forth in company with a party of trading Hurons to carry the tidings of the Christian faith farther into the wilderness. This earnest Jesuit soon proved that he was not devoid of the military spirit the Indians strongly preferred to that of religious zeal, and he won their friendship by teaching them how to build a palisaded square with flanking towers at the angles, which enabled them to make a better defence against the enemy than they could from their round inclosures. As has already been said, Champlain made his last visit here in the summer before his death in December. But Montreal became the magnet to draw the tide of settlement, and so Three Rivers, with her many natural advantages, her great iron and lumber industries, lives in her past as well as her present. Besides her rich supply of iron, which the French began to smelt as early as 1737, this picturesque town has proved a rich mine of historical lore, as worked by her local poet and historian. The town is also noted for its noble cathedral, one of the most imposing in the St. Lawrence valley. This is the head of tide-water.

Here, as elsewhere in the St. Lawrence valley, there is something in the atmosphere—or is it more substantial?—which constantly impresses us that we are in

a country older than New England.   The explanation
lies in the fact that the original comers, the old chevaliers, began by setting up a feudal system of colonisation which was a hundred years behind the latter, and
progress yoked to this made an ill-matched pair, so they
have never succeeded in catching up.   It was not until
the beginning of the eighteenth century that the French
could truly claim to have gained a foothold in New
France.   Fifty years of building upon this foundation
did not succeed in erecting a structure that could resist
the British force, but it did leave imprints that three
times that period have not effaced.

Of the States it is frequently declared that the inhabitants are a mixed race composed of various elements.   In Canada this is different.   New France had
many types of colonists, and, to a remarkable extent,
these types have remained pure and unmixed to this
day.   Nowhere, too, is the record of a race more clearly
defined at its different periods than here.   First, there
came the hardy peasants from Brittany and Normandy,
small, muscular men, with bodies toughened by an inhospitable climate, and skins weather-stained through
ages of exposure.   They had heads round and small,
eyes intensely black, an air of unaffected honesty, and,
what seemed stranger than all else, considering their
features, a sluggish manner.   The face was written over
with courage, intrepidity, and power of endurance.
Like father, like son, and these traits live to-day in the
inhabitants of the Lower St. Lawrence.

While many of the early colonists, that helped to form another class, were the sweepings of the gaols and the poorhouses, fortunately not many of these became the founders of families. The women who came belonged to a purer class. But there were not women enough for wives to the colonists, so many of the men married Indian maids, and thus formed legitimate families, whose descendants became no small factors in the development of the country. The small black eyes, the high cheek-bones, the swarthy skin, the scanty growth of beard, the keen, alert manner, these were traits that generations have not lost. The most strongly marked of this class are known as *petit brules*, and are dark, gnarled, and tough. Occasionally we find one whose dusky features have been lightened, and whose cold, phlegmatic nature has been warmed by the fire of another race.

Another phase of the population is the Gaul, who can trace his ancestry back to some soldier in the army under Wolfe and other English commanders, who took unto his bosom a Norman maid, and whose descendants bear English names but cannot speak a word of that language. Then there is the descendant of the loyalist, driven from New England to found a new home in the wilds of the St. Lawrence valley, who speedily secured him a helpmeet in some dark-haired, dark-eyed Canadian lass, unable to speak a word of English, but who understood the universal language of love.

Perhaps the finest specimens of the Canadian peasant, now rare, are the descendants of those pioneer nobles whose fortunes sent them from affluent homes in the old country to help conduct affairs in the new, but who were left after the conquest too poor to return to their native land. They fell back upon agriculture, that form of industry which has received so many, unable to rise to the station their talents and breeding entitled them to take, marrying, if not already united to some fair daughter of Old France, a buxom maid of New France. Their circumstances not permitting greater benefits of education, their children grew up under the limited advantages of the lower class. Each succeeding generation falling a scale lower, they sank to the level of the common peasantry, but without losing that native grace and courteousness which is to-day the wonder and the admiration of those who meet them. In this we see how strongly the traditions of a race follow the tide of fortunes and make courtiers out of plebeians.

Thus we see three distinct races of men, not yet completely amalgamated, composing the leading elements of population: the original French whose descendants are called *habitans;* the British immigrant; and, first in the order of his coming, the Amerind. The first, and third of these formed at the time of the conquest almost the entire population. They held the fertile meadows along the St. Lawrence between Quebec and Montreal, while they had pushed up the banks of the Richelieu, Chaudière, Yamaska, and the St. Maurice, besides having made some minor settlements on the other tributaries of the great river. The tracts held by them were all under the feudal system once prevalent in Canada; that is, the entire country had been first granted to persons of note and prestige, usually in large blocks or districts. This class, not being disposed to improve their broad acres in order to receive any benefit from them, made over small parcels to those who would undertake to clear the forest and build them homes, upon the payment of small yearly rentals, with the stipulation that the land should be theirs after certain amounts had been paid. These sums were usually very moderate, sometimes running as low as ten shillings a year, with some other consideration allowed, such as a small bounty on fish caught, mill-dues, a bushel of wheat, and a fowl or two thrown in. Under such easy conditions the occupants of these fiefs or farms were able to own them in a few years.

These *habitans* proved an industrious, provident, but not an energetic or progressive people. Few added to their early acres, though plenty of opportunity was given them in the extensive tracts of wild lands within their reach. Over all hung that air of contentment which is antagonistic to the improvement and the rapid advance of the American farmer. Here the old way lingered in the path of progress. An air of Confucianism reigned. If the crops grew fairly well, and they got raw material enough to manufacture the plain cloth to clothe them, they enjoyed a sort of idyllic happiness. This modest peasant worked with due deliberation, worrying little, fretting little, and in that way became master of himself, plain, comfortable, courteous, virtuous, without seeking after knowledge or reaching for power.   Perhaps they were better off than their brothers over the line. Who can say? The spirit of the nineteenth century awakened them somewhat, and upon the dawn of the twentieth century we see this restlessness increasing.   What the outcome will be remains to be seen.

The early French farmhouse was built of rough stones, the crevices filled with mortar, and the sharp-peaked roof projecting above the gable, with dormer windows and eaves that threatened to crush the whole structure.   With slight modifications this style of architecture remains, though wood has generally succeeded stone as building material.   The walls are usually whitewashed from sill to ridge-pole. The huge chimney, with its plastered sides, remains; so do the wide eaves projecting over the railless piazza; so does the feeling that winter still lingers in spirit if not in substance over the dwelling.   Shade trees are not so common as in the States, but the stately Lombardy poplar that came with the earliest inhabitants has never lost favour with the peasantry.   There is no display of fruit in the little garden, while there is a dearth of flowers and shrubbery around the yard.   The barn, with its thatched roof, stands a short distance away, as lonely as the house.

Following a rail fence for about two hundred yards —the regulation distance is three arpents (equivalent to an acre) in width, and sixty arpents in depth—we come to an exact counterpart of this. Beyond is another, and yet another, until we have continued on a road that seems endless and a type of dwelling that mocks the love for variety. There is certainly a painful sameness in the rows of farmhouses in the Lower Province, not to mention the Eastern Townships.

The interior of these houses presents a busy aspect. The rough walls hold many high-coloured pictures of a religious nature, a likeness of Jesus, of Mary, or of St. Cecilia and others. Overhead, in the living-room, hang from pegs long strings of onions, dried fruit, and it may be two or three pairs of snow-shoes and the firearms of the men. Passing into the adjoining apartment,—these houses usually contain only two rooms,— the most prominent article of furniture is the ancient bed, with its massive posts and quilt of patchwork laid and sewed by the deft fingers of the good housewife. Over the bed hangs a cross, associated with which are numerous images and relics, all rendered holy objects by the blessing of the parish priest. Altogether the interior of the dwelling is a cheerful scene, and if grimed with smoke and filled with the odours of the kitchen, it is quaint and home-like, where a happy family gather at eventide.

This race, from time almost memorial, has professed the religion of the Catholic Church. This teaches them not to miss the Sunday morning service, but it does not hold them strictly accountable for their actions during the balance of the day.　So Sunday becomes, in a measure, a holiday.　Decked out in their best, certain of the families set forth to visit friends, the male portion to discuss matters that have a decidedly worldly character, while the gentler portion repeat with a kindred spirit the village gossip.　The young men, habited in their finest, improve this time to pay their court to the charming damsels that may favour them with their good graces. And these maidens, clothed in their best, their becoming attire set out with many bright colours in which they take especial pride, wait and watch for their chevaliers with undisguised anticipation of delight.

Not long since the harvest was followed by a festival which seemed at one time to have a national hold upon the people.　It was given during the harvest moon, when the last load of grain was garnered.　A sheaf of huge dimensions, emblematical of an abundant harvest, was placed on top, and beside this loaded wain walked on each side four young men and as many young women, their heads decorated with the heads of the grain.　As they kept measured step with the slow-moving oxen that drew the load, they sang snatches of national songs.

While this load of grain, with its escorts, moved leisurely in the direction of the home of the particular farmer who thus proposed to offer his homage to the goddess Ceres, within the house the good husbandman and his faithful spouse patiently awaited its approach. Says an old account:

The master of the house sits in a large arm-chair at the head of the room, and awaits with a joyful and contented air the arrival of his people. These soon come trooping in, led by the eldest son, who carries in one hand a fine sheaf of wheat all decorated with ribbons, and in the other hand a decanter and a glass. He advances to the master of the house, gives him the sheaf, wishes him as good a harvest every year of his life, and pours him out a glass of brandy. The old gentleman thanks him and drinks off the glass. Then the son goes round the room and serves the company, after which they pass to the next room for supper, composed of mutton, milk, and pancakes with maple sugar. After supper the decanter and glass go their rounds again, and then the young man who presented the sheaf asks his father to sing a song.

The song finished, the young people begin to dance, while a musician plays; others sing, the older members tell stories, the children play games until the festival is brought to an end in the small hours of night.

While this practice, as has been remarked, was some time since abandoned, its spirit still pervades not only the harvest, but the sowing and the cultivation of the crop. Instead of preparing for this festivity of the Big Sheaf, the farmer pays the priest a certain sum to say a mass and offer up prayers of thankfulness for his harvest.

The grain does not grow without the touch of holy water; when harvested it is brought to the altar; the leaven rises under the invocation of Divine aid; and the loaf is not cut till the sign of the cross is made upon it by the devout habitan. The loaf is, indeed, an epitome of their life.

The short, fleeting summer being necessarily spent in constant toil, cutting short the hours of relaxation, the winter becomes the season when light-hearted joy reigns triumphant. Then, in their *carioles*, or little chaises on steel runners, they flit from neighbour to neighbour, spending the long evenings in games and social intercourse, throwing dull care to the wintry blasts waging their bitter battles without, while peace and contentedness vie with each other for supremacy within the little house.

At Christmas-tide the believing peasant will tell you that the stars penetrate to the heart of the earth, often disclosing valuable treasures to him who is fortunate enough to be on hand.   It is then the last *curé* of the parish of the Saguenay awakens his sleeping flock, and recites the litany, his shadowy followers repeating after him the responses.   As soon as this exercise is over, all return to their tombs, where they remain until another Christmas shall call them forth upon their ghostly errand.   In later years we find Christmas observed by its midnight mass, its consecrated bread, and the singing of anthems.   At eleven o'clock the first bell is rung, and half an hour later it is repeated, the chorister at this time beginning to chant the *Venez, mon Dieu*, and *Chansons Noël.* A few minutes before twelve o'clock the *Te Deum* is sung, during which the cannon announces that the divine hour has come, and the mass is to begin.

Perhaps in the history of no people has the love for fatherland been more pronounced or of longer duration than in Canada,—a British body with a French heart. The meaning of this statement cannot be better illustrated than in the advice of the old soldier under

Montcalm, pictured in the romance of *Les Anciens Canadiens*, who, suffering from the bloodless wounds given by the conquerors of Quebec, said to his son, as he handed him his sword, " Serve your English sovereign with the same zeal, devotion, and loyalty with which I have served the French King, and accept my blessing."

With this spirit of allegiance it is not singular that here are " the true French, the successors of the great race that once dominated Europe." It is true their manners have been modified somewhat by the change of government and environment, but centuries of life have failed to eradicate the racial features or change their nature. So we find the sturdy *habitan* of the Canada of to-day an almost identical reproduction of his ancestor who came to New France from Old Normandy in the days of Champlain and Frontenac. One of his historians aptly says :

He is the same cheerful, optimistic, pleasure-loving being that they were. In many respects he is as simple as a child; in others he is as cunning and as guileful as any small trader on earth. The French Canadian cannot live in solitude; he must have society. . . . When the evening comes he leaves his plough in the furrow and greets the stars with a song that his forefathers, who fought with Frontenac, brought over from the land their descendants still call " *la belle France.*" Their tired women are never too tired to dance in the midst of cares and labours so heavy and severe that their like has driven thousands of the *habitans* into the United States. . . . By the light of the blazing logs in the humble cottage they are happy and cheerful to a degree that would seem to the grave New Englander wicked levity and mad irresponsibility.

Thus to-day the environments of Quebec are mainly remnants of that cloak thrown around it by the sons of

Normandy who flocked hither ere that fateful morn when Montcalm rallied his troops in an ineffectual attempt to turn back the tide of British conquest on the Plains of Abraham. If the immigration ceased then with an abruptness quite remarkable, those in whose hands was placed the seal of destiny have proved themselves true to the love and traditions of that France which the *immigrés* of the seventeenth century left to try their fortunes in the forests of a New France.

A FRENCH CANADIAN HOMESTEAD (ST. PRIME.)

CHAUDIÈRE RIVER.

CHAPTER XXI

The Region of Rivers

The Chaudière Valley—Watershed of Northern New England—Falls of the
Chaudière—Eastern Townships—As seen by the Early Voyagers—A Primeval
Picture—Feathered Denizens of the Woods—Noble Old Trees—Memory of
Cartier's Men—Lake St. Peter—Town of St. Francis—St. Francis River—An
Old-Time War-Trail—Rogers's Raid—The Loyalists—Yamaska—A Vista of
Mountains—The Richelieu Valley—Extract from an Old Journal—Saintly
Names—A Ghostly Bivouac.

FOLLOWING the southern shore, soon after
leaving Quebec we reach the mouth of its
most important tributary from this direction
since leaving the gulf. It was up this river, over the
portages crossing the highlands, and then down the
Kennebec that the Indian tribes of the valley of
the St. Lawrence entered the Province of Main, now
the State of Maine.

In its hues, from the blossoms and foliage, it is a
valley of rainbows; in its shape, from the old seigniory
farm-grants cut into small parcels through the laws of
inheritance, each running back from the river's bank,
it is a huge landscape checker-board. Each parcel is
divided from its neighbour by lines of fence as straight
as runs the eye, one distinguished by a distinct shade
of green, another by a deeper hue; one starred with
the bright-red blossoms of the Canadian elderberry;

another splashed with a profusion of yellow buttercups on its ground of meadow-green ; and still another gemmed with the poet's ox-eye daisies.

Here, as elsewhere, we see vivid evidence of wealth and poverty in varying degrees. Now a dwelling that shows comfort and ease from unreasonable toil ; just beyond, within a stone's throw, a poorer abode, where several poverty-pinched faces peer out from small windows, saying in unmistakable language that the day is not far distant when all but one, son or daughter, must go forth to seek a fortune—most likely in the States— while the exception must remain at home and eke out a precarious existence as his or her parents have done. Unfortunate home-stayer ! Happily, perhaps, it is the rule here, that a man at fifty retires from active work, and lives, and smokes, and gossips until the end. I have not been able to learn if this rule applies in part or entirely to the woman who took up early the burden of the home with him. But no doubt the rule applies with forcible truth here, that "woman's work is never done."

Tradition—good old soul !—says the bed of the Chaudière is inlaid with gold. If that be true or not, no man has taken the trouble to ascertain. For nearly two centuries the simple people have been content to follow the pace set by their ancestors, and, if they did not choose to look for gold, why should they ? In the distance a windmill lifts its stationary arm against a rising background, like a sentinel on duty to warn away the intruder from this peaceful land with a grimness that is a part of its long service. What is man, after all, but a pointing finger on the dial of time?

Only the most modest demands are made upon the land here in the valley of the Chaudière, where, at most, the farmer expects a little hay, a little fruit, a few vegetables, some wheat, and rest from toil. Fortunate old earth; happy man!

The Chaudière, which word means a "kettle" or caldron, has its source in Lake Megantic, situated on the dividing ridge between the Atlantic slope and the valley of the St. Lawrence. Upon the one hand the rivers flow toward the Atlantic Ocean, and on the other seek the great river of Canada. This watershed, extending for hundreds of miles between the slopes running down on the east to the Gulf of St. Lawrence, and on the west to the Great Lakes, had to be crossed by the native inhabitants and the early pioneers by the painful process of portage. Of these places, that connecting the Chaudière with the head waters of the Kennebec was second in importance. It was over this "terrible carrying-place," from the Dead River to the Chaudière, that Arnold passed with his weary men in the winter of 1775–76, when making his arduous march to meet Montgomery at Quebec in a joint assault upon that stronghold, the most famous campaign in American history, and one of the most trying in the history of the world.

The Falls of the Chaudière are among the most

attractive in America, though they do not exceed 130
feet in height.   Their beauty and majesty, however, is
trebled by a division of the stream into three channels,
which unite below.   Much of the sublimity of this fall
has passed with the coming of the woodsman, though
he could rob the jewel of only its setting.   It was described three-fourths of a century ago by the eloquent
Willis in the following words :

> Nothing is on the same great scale of its two rivals (Niagara
> and Montmorency), yet it surpasses both in the magnificent
> forests by which it is overhung, whose dark foliage, varied and
> contrasted by the white foam of the cataracts, produces the most
> striking effects.   These are heightened by the deep and hollow
> sound of the waters, and the clouds of spray, which, when illumined
> by the sun, exhibit the most brilliant variety of prismatic colours.   A
> succession of rapids for some space upwards displays a continuation
> of the same bold and beautiful scenery.

Here, as elsewhere, the impressive sublimity of the
ancient forest has given way to the sunny slope and
the pastoral vale.   Where the blockhouse that once
bid defiance to an enemy that neither knew pity nor
compassed fear, the great warehouse of a prosperous
community stands ; and the labyrinthine château of a
Vansittart would now be sadly out of harmony environed by an apple orchard, the bower of some modern
Rosamond.

To get the best effect of the Chaudière Falls, visit
them by moonlight, when the great wilderness of night
has bound the scene in a solitude born of the distant
past.   It is then the naiads of the foaming waters,

daughters of the mist, don their whitest raiment, dance in their wildest glee, and sing their merriest songs. No sound more discordant than the plaintive cry of a belated thrush, or the distant baying of a hound that has, peradventure, run its game to earth, breaks upon the steady roar of the rolling river, while the sympathetic moon glides overhead in her slippers of silence. When we finally break away from the invisible arms that would draw us with a mysterious power into their fatal embrace, and the deep thunder of the impassioned waters becomes fainter and fainter as we recede, it seems as if the magnificent machinery of Nature had ceased its revolutions, while a deep, impressive calm settles upon the earth. The breeze sweeping down from the distant mountain dies away before it enters here. The trees, like tired children, suddenly fall asleep, and stand with heads bowed in repose.

Lying to the south of the St. Lawrence, between the Chaudière and the Richelieu rivers, with the watershed between the States and Canada forming the interior boundary, is a region of rivers, lakes, plains, and valleys, punctuated here and there with some mountain peak, and known as the Eastern Townships. At a time when only a few squatters had settled upon it, in 1833, the British-American Land Company made the great block purchase of that territory later divided into the towns of Garthby, Strafford, Whitton, Adstock, Chesham, Emberton, Hampden, Bury, with portions of Weedon, Singwick, Ditton, Auckland, and Hereford.

The company decided to begin their settlement upon
that fertile section watered by the Salmon River, and
named "The Meadows." Just below the falls they
built a village called Victoria, and, in 1836, cut a road
through to Sherbrooke.

Nature reigns with a free hand in the Eastern
Townships. Nowhere have the mountains a deeper
gloom ; the sunlight, that gilds their summits, a brighter
halo. The spirit of wild life everywhere abounds.
Clothed in their evergreen vesture from base to crest,
the mountains half reveal, half conceal their wealth of
ravines and crags, gentle slopes and precipitous cliffs ;
the silvery streams that rush downward with frenzied
haste to the plains ; the meadows and the valleys,
scarcely one of which is not jewelled with some sheet of
glistening water. Added to these charms are the
numerous villas and home-like cottages scattered by
man over the fair prospect. What a picture of primeval completeness this country must have presented to
Cartier, as he boldly advanced up the St. Lawrence in
his smallest vessel, most appropriately named the *Emerillon*, which means in English *Merlin*, the designation of a small falcon common in Great Britain.

Allured hither by the attractions, some of the voyagers went ashore, and they came back laden with luscious
grapes and filled with glowing accounts of the beauties
of this New World Eden. Among the sweet singers
of the forest they declared they heard linnets, thrushes,
blackbirds, and the *rossignol*, as sweet and as charm-

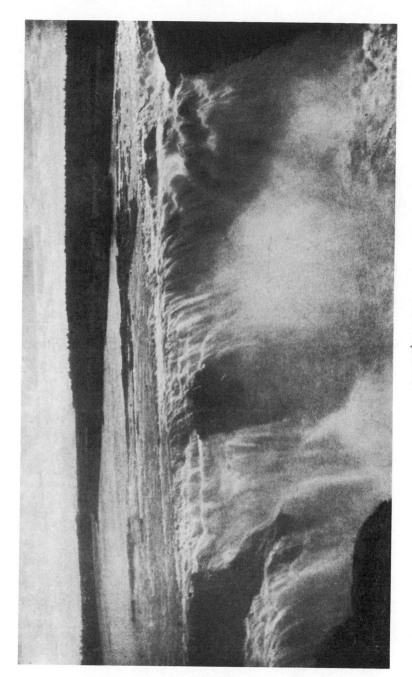

CHAUDIÈRE FALLS.

From a photograph by Livernois, Quebec.

A TOSS-UP.   A FORM OF CANADIAN SPORT.

From a photograph by W. Notman & Son, Montreal.

ing as they had ever sung in the native parks of Fontainebleau. Little did it matter if they had mistaken the Canadian sparrow for the nightingale, as they would never know the difference, or hear the loved strains again of their favourite singers, for did not Cartier write, with a tear in his words : "*les principaulx et bons compaignons que nous eussions*"?

Cartier was pleased to christen the water into which they soon after glided *Lac d'Angouleme*, in honour of an ancestral earldom of his patron. Sixty-eight years later, June 29, 1603, Champlain upon arriving here renamed it Lake St. Peter, after a habit these early explorers had of remembering the day upon which a certain spot was first seen.

Cartier and his followers were now opposite the present city of Three Rivers, where they first began to find the odd-shaped dwellings of the natives, who were to be seen along the banks, some of them fishing, others repairing their rude nets or mending their simple tackle. Several thriving towns have since sprung up along the stretch of shore running westward, the most conspicuous of which is Berthier, situated on the North Channel, so called, and about midway between Three Rivers and Montreal.

Lake St. Peter receives the waters of two historic tributaries to the St. Lawrence. The first of these, as we move up the great river, is the St. Francis, a name given to it in a baptism of blood long after the coming of Cartier. In this vicinity were springs of great

medicinal virtue, known to the Indians, and as far
back as tradition reaches, the red men, one tribe after
another, had sought the locality, and maintained their
lodgments. Here the missionary established his outpost of religion, and here collected the remnants of the
Indian families inhabiting the lower provinces as fast as
the New Englanders, in the long and bitter frontier
wars, routed their tribes, one after another. Here came
the last of the Pennacooks, the Ameriscoggins, the
Wavenocks, the Canibas, and last, but not least, the
Sokokis, to say nothing of several minor bodies. The
scenery in this vicinity is delightful, and it is eminently
fitting that the descendants of the warriors named
above should exist here to-day, living in a prosperous
community without a suggestion of the cruel struggles
which once dyed the budding foliage crimson, and
reddened the current of the broken waters. It is well
Nature does not cherish the memory of the outrages
committed against her, and that the old earth seeks
immediately to heal scars received in mortal combats, her forests nodding to each other in forgetful
glee, and her fields and pastures yielding, in their seasons, an abundant harvest as lightly as if never written
over with the story of human tragedies, and furrowed
with the graves of innocent victims.

From time immemorial the St. Francis River was
the middle pathway between the debatable valley of the
St. Lawrence and the hillsides of the Atlantic. Up and
down its rugged course, through the gateway of the

highland lakes, and thence along the Connecticut or the Merrimac on the south, passed and repassed the rival races of ancient Canada and New England. Over this war-course were taken, perhaps, more English captives to Canada than on all other routes combined, and there is not a bend in its winding waters, a rapid in its race-ways, which has not known the wail of human distress. Over this war trail was Mrs. Rowlandson borne to her years of captivity among the Indians; over this route was John Stark, afterwards of Bennington battle fame, taken in the spring of 1752; over this trail followed, in his pursuit of vengeance, that half human, half demon, the wolf-stalker; somewhere, within sight and sound of its murmuring waters, but unmarked and unknown, is the double grave of the beautiful sisters of the Pilgrim Church; and in 1759, a fitting climax to all of these and many other trying scenes, over this same course sped those Nemeses of the forest, Rogers and his Rangers, stealing down upon the sleeping red men. The sleep of death it proved indeed to over two hundred, who awoke only to fall into the slumber of eternity. The handful that escaped this tardy reply to Frontenac's "winter raids" were too few and weak ever to rally at the call of the war-cry.

The St. Francis River is really the combined flood of seven streams, the most prominent of which are the Magog, outlet for Lakes Magog and Memphremagog, and the Massawippi, which brings the tribute of the Coaticook.

On the hill-slopes of the main river stands the city
of fairs, Sherbrooke, whose glittering spires are conspicuous objects for miles around.   In 1834, Sherbrooke
was selected as the headquarters of the British-American Land Company, which had much to do with opening up the promising country comprising the Eastern
Townships.   With its manufactures, as well as farming
interests, this district owes considerable of its development to the loyalists, those robust men who upon the
ascendency of the American colonies found themselves
without resources, and, driven from New England, settled, many of them, in this region.

Picking up the disused axe with a sigh—often with a secret tear
—they once more hewed out for themselves homes in the forest.
They brought across the frontier, with their old Hebrew names, the
pith and industry and intense earnestness of the Puritan.   They
transplanted to Canadian soil that old farm-life of New England,
which, by its quaint ways, has stirred so many delightful fancies in
American novelists and poets.   Such fire-light pictures and winter-
idylls as Hawthorne and Whittier love to paint, were here to be seen
of a winter evening in every snow-bound farmstead.   Among the
dusty heirlooms of these Township homesteads may still be found
andirons that stood on the early New England hearths.   Burned out
and fallen to ashes are the last forestick and backlog ; and so are
that brave old couple who, in their grey hairs wandered into the
Canadian wilderness, and, with trembling hands, hung the old crane
over a new hearth.

Romance and legend cluster thickly about those
days and the trying experiences of the brave hearts who
sacrificed their all of earthly comfort in love for their
king.   He only partially paid this debt by the grants of
land made in 1784.   Canada owes more to this incom-

ing of the loyalists than she has ever fully acknowledged. But for this immigration, enforced, if it pleases
you to say it, the development of the country must have
been retarded for a long time, while it is doubtful if an
element to equal it could ever have been attracted hither.

Now it is the Yamaska, which meant in the Indian
tongue " the rush-floored river." In order to stem the
tide of Iroquois invasion, Frontenac undertook to establish here a cordon of dusky regiments composed of the
hereditary enemies of the former. Along the Yamaska
have since sprung up many pretty towns. Not the least
among these is St. Hyacinthe, where the deep-toned
cathedral bell falls on the evening air somewhat as the
swelling anthems of the forest songs were brought out
by the wild winds as they shook the roofs of the giant
pines forming great natural cathedrals when the Genius
of the Solitude reigned supreme. Climbing this river
we pass under the shadow of Mount Yamaska, and
finally enter a narrow valley shut in by the lofty twins,
Mount Brome on the north and Shefford on the south,
to stumble upon that gem of waters which is the fount
of Yamaska. From the summit of one of these we can
look down upon the noble country hastily sketched, a
landscape lifted into prominence by the scattered mountains dotting the view from the Richelieu to the Chaudière, the Canadian children of the White Mountains in
New Hampshire and the Green Mountains in Vermont,
the highest of which is Mount Orford, rising 4500 feet
into the air. If the day is clear the dreamy outlines of

Mount Royal on the bank of the St. Lawrence lend grace and beauty to the panorama of scenery. The largest of its many water-jewels are Lakes Memphremagog and her sister, Massawippi.

A still more important pathway over the dividing ridge between the rival powers was that by the Richelieu River, which has been partially described in narrating Champlain's journey of discovery and invasion against the Iroquois. Following up this river to Lake Champlain, and thence by Otter Creek and Black River to the Connecticut, made entrance into central New England easy. On the west from Lake George, the Hudson was reached by a short portage and an almost complete waterway effected into the country of the "Long House," now New York.

This great main war trail, upon the advent of the French and English on the stage of warfare, became speedily protected by armed garrisons. As early as 1664 Jacques de Chambly erected a fort at the foot of the rapids on the Richelieu, which could also be reached by a thirteen-mile portage from La Prairie on the St. Lawrence, three miles above Montreal. The passage of the French and their allies was also defended by three other forts, St. Louis at the mouth of the river, afterwards renamed Fort Sorel, Forts St. Therese and Richelieu, the latter at the head of the river. The French, ascending Lake Champlain and improving the strategic position of the country at the end of the portage from Lake George, erected Fort Crown Point in

1727, and four years later Fort Frederick, afterwards known as Ticonderoga. Meanwhile the English, coming up the Hudson above Albany, built at Stillwater, in 1709, Forts Ingoldsby and Nicholson, following these with Fort Schuyler, since called Fort Anne, Forts Edward and William Henry, the last two built in 1755. Thus a cordon of forts, French and English, guarded this important waterway, with its portages, from New York to Montreal, and it was known as the " Grand Pass."

A contemporary idea of the condition of the settlements at this time can be best obtained from the narrative of James Johnson, who was captured at old Fort Number Four on the Connecticut in 1757, and taken over this route to Montreal. The following is an extract from his journal, which has never been published :

From Crown Point I went to St. Johns fort (Richelieu) at the end of ye lake, and from there to Champlain River (Richelieu) & that from St. Johns fort to St. Francis is about fifty miles near north & from St. Francis to St. Lawrence is about five miles & that ye Rout between St. Johns and St. Francis there are two Rows of houses one on each side of ye River (Richelieu) in the whole about two hundred in some places pretty thick & a fort at Chamblain as Strong as Crown Point & the whole village of St. Francis stands on an rise of Ground Mountains nearly forty buildings of all sorts that there is no fort in it but some stone buildings no considerable settlement within fifteen miles of S. Francis and that there is St. Francis and Shatacooks (an Indian settlement below St. Francis) about one hundred and twenty fighting men that St. Francis Lyes on ye north side of ye River of that Name.

The valley of the Richelieu is the land of the butter-

cup. It is of its towns that the thoughtful Thoreau,
who has been quoted before, says :

> The names of humble Canadian villages affected me as if they
> had been those of the renowned cities of antiquity. To be told by
> a *habitan*, when I asked the name of a village in sight, that it was
> *St. Fereole* or *Ste. Anne*, the *Guardian Angel* or the *Holy Joseph's*;
> or of a mountain, that it was *Belange* or *St. Hyacinthe!* As soon
> as you leave the States, these saintly names begin—and thence
> forward, the names of mountains, and streams, and villages reel, if
> I may so speak, with the intoxication of poetry—*Chambly, Longueil,
> Pointe aux Trembles, Bartholomy*, &c., &c., as if it needed only a
> little foreign accent, a few more liquids and vowels, perchance, in
> the language, to make us locate our ideals at once. I began to
> dream of Provence and the Troubadours, and of places and things
> which have no existence on earth. They veiled the Indian and the
> primitive forest; and the woods toward Hudson Bay, were only as
> the forests of France and Germany. I could not at once bring my-
> self to believe that the inhabitants who pronounced daily those
> beautiful and, to me, significant names, lead as prosaic lives as we
> of New England.

Another shade, however, rises above these clustered
memories of saints and divines, a wraith of war with its
mail-clad legions :

> Through this cassock gleamed a steel cuirass. Though the splen-
> did illusions of the Old Régime have long since faded, the haughty
> names of that epoch still kindle with an afterglow. By the mere
> names of these villages, towns, and seigniories, you may conjure
> back Louis Quatorze and Versailles ; the statecraft of Colbert ;
> the soldiers of Turenne and Vauban. Picketed around the ancient
> rendezvous at the confluence of the Richelieu and St. Lawrence
> are the officers of the Carignan-Salières, as though still guarding
> the Iroquois River-Gate and the approaches to Montreal:—Captain
> Berthier, Lieutenant Lavaltrie ; Boucher, Varennes, Verchères,
> Contrecœur. Twilight in these ancient woodlands awakens sleep-
> ing echoes and dead centuries ; with the rising night-wind the whole
> place seems
>
> Filled as with shadow of sound, with the pulse of invisible feet.

Through the forest-aisles ring out elfin trumpet calls ; we hear the *réveillé* of ghostly drum-beating ; the prancing of phantom horses ; the clinking of sabres ; the measured tread of Louis the Fourteenth's battalions. At roll-call we hear officers answer to familiar names :—" Captain Sorel ? "—" Here ! "—" Captain St. Ours ? "—" Here ! "—" Captain Chambly ? "—" Here ! "—And in good truth most of them are still here. In the soft grass of God's Acre they are resting, surrounded by those faithful soldiers who in death, as in life, have not deserted them. Together these veterans fought the Turk in Hungary and drove them into the Raab ; together they chased the Iroquois up the Richelieu, and down the Mohawk Valley ; and, after van and rear had passed a darker valley and an icier flood, they mustered here at last in ghostly bivouac together.

Ay, the historic Grand Pass of the Richelieu was the pathway of illustrious trains, led by Champlain, and followed by Courcelles, De Tracy, and others in their sallies against the Iroquois. Then it became the course of the leaders of Frontenac's "winter raids" against the English. Again, in the Seven Years' War, it was over this track Montcalm and his generals led the French army in their attacks upon Crown Point, Ticonderoga, and Fort William Henry. Once more, with a brief respite between, this became the war-path of Montgomery upon his invasion of Canada, and capture of Forts St. John and Chambly, when he went to unite with Arnold at Quebec in a forlorn attack upon that noted stronghold. Over this way, too, passed, on their warlike journeys, Baron Dieskau, Johnson, Abercrombie, and Burgoyne. When at last peace settled her white wings silently and gently over this fair corner of country, the train of home-makers found here an attractive path to civil pursuits rather than to those of carnage.

Chapter XXII

Canada's "White City"

IF Montreal fails to present the bold, grand, picturesque features of Quebec, it is not without its charms of a gentler nature, with a story older and as romantic as that of her sister. Connecting the traditions of Hochelaga to the history of the present metropolis, it becomes the oldest town in Canada. It was here, longer ago than the legends of its people can show, that a populous village existed, or rather, as it seems, collection of villages. Cartier visited this primitive settlement on a beautiful autumn day in 1535. The people were probably Hurons, but when Champlain arrived, upon his first voyage up the river, the inhabitants had vanished, the rude dwellings and fortifications had crumbled to dust, and another tribe of men wandered about the deserted town, with

A SPILL ON THE TOBOGGAN SLIDE.

THE ICE PALACE, MONTREAL, 1885.

nothing to mark the site of the ancient capital. Happily this has been found, through the excavations made for the foundations of some of the modern buildings, to have been where Sherbrooke Street runs toward Metcalfe, nearly opposite the McGill grounds. A tablet now marks the place.

The St. Lawrence along this portion is seen in one of its happiest moods, and, with the Ottawa, forms an island thirty-two miles in length and a little over ten miles in width. The surface is moderately level, overlooked, like a watcher always on duty, by that peerless hemisphere, Mount Royal. In the days of its forest and foliage, it must indeed have been a primeval paradise, where the bronze-hued inhabitants of Hochelaga, and yet other towns antedating that, came and went in wanton freedom, with no greater care to vex them than the shade of the passing hour, and who left no more enduring monuments than footprints in the sand. May not the day come when the same shall be said of the existing race, in spite of their granite pillars, which are but the sands of eternity?

In Montreal there is plenty of room—no call, as in Quebec, for narrow, crooked streets winding up steep rock-sides, nor for one town built to overlap another. But each, in its way, had a purpose. Why, had there been no rock of Quebec, the early history of Canada might have been written in a different language. The approach to "the white city of Canada," as Montreal has been poetically pictured, on account of the large amount of light-grey limestone used in its building material, has been aptly described as

a picture surpassingly beautiful. The solid stone piers and massive warehouses in the foreground, the bright-roofed buildings and glistening church spires in the middle distance, with the noble Mount Royal in the background, delight the artistic sense, and inspire emotions of the keenest pleasure. Viewed from the mountain itself, the picture, while totally different, is none the less attractive. The field of view is greatly extended, and the eye takes in a grand panorama of river and mountain scenery, with the city below in near perspective. Almost at your feet, and excavated from the solid rock in the side of the mountain, is the storage reservoir of the city water-works. Farther down, and sloping away from the foot of the mountain, the streets of the city intersect each other, adorned with public and private buildings, and beautifully shaded with trees and foliage. As far as the vision can extend, to the right and left the sparkling waters of the St. Lawrence are to be seen, a throbbing artery of inland commerce, dotted with shipping, while the distant background is made up of mountain ranges, some of which are in Canada, while dimly outlined on the horizon are the peaks of the Green Mountains of Vermont.

The first object of conspicuous interest to the traveller who approaches by rail from the historic valley of the Richelieu is the famous Victoria Bridge, spanning the south channel of the Mother of Rivers. This structure is nearly two miles long, hung like a dark ribbon sixty feet above the water. With long abutments at the ends, it has twenty-four spans 242 feet in length each, and a link in the middle 330 feet long. This bridge, considered at the time (1860) a great feat of engineering, was conceived by the Hon. John Young, of Montreal, designed by Robert Stephenson of England, and built by the Grand Trunk Railway at a cost of about $7,000,000.

Nearly opposite the city is one of the fairest islands of the St. Lawrence, Helen's Isle, perpetuating the name of Champlain's young wife—who was only twelve when he married her. This is now a favourite resort for pleasure-seekers, though for a long period under the old régime it was a French military station. It was here that Marquis de Levis, the last commander of a French army in New France, retired and burned his flags in the presence of his soldiers on the night before the surrender of the colony to Great Britain, and beneath a "weeping elm" signed the articles of capitulation. These pathetic incidents inspired one of Canada's poets to compose his stirring poem, *All Lost but Honour*. This island was once owned by Champlain, purchased by him with his wife's money. It was the scene of the murder by the Iroquois of two young men named Magna and Dufresne, in the summer of 1664,— but one incident of this kind among many. Around Montreal

the landscape is one long page of history and tragedy. Many a pre-historic savage fight must have taken place in the neighbourhood; many a canoe full of painted warriors have crept stealthily along the shores. Round about, many a party of settlers was murdered by the Iroquois in the earliest days of the colony . . . and on Moffat's, or *Île-à-la-Pierre*, Father Guillaume Vignal was slain by an Iroquois ambush during a fierce battle of a quarry in 1659. . . . La Prairie, far over to the south, across the water, was the scene, in 1691, of the celebrated and desperate battle of La Prairie, the first land attack by the British upon Canada.

Longueuil, across the river, can boast of having been the site of the grandest feudal castle in New France during the eighteenth century.   Leaving the fortress-like walls, tower, and chapel to memory, where they have existed for a long time, we will return to the city, which, with the exception of Quebec, has the most favourable situation of the cities of the St. Lawrence. Over six hundred miles from the outlet of the river it has a fine harbour, though before 1850 a vessel drawing more than eleven feet of water could not come up thus far.   But this has been changed in the last half-century, and a channel over twenty-seven feet deep has been dredged, so the largest ships from the Atlantic Ocean now moor at its piers.   It is a creditable fact, that only two years after Fulton had launched his first steamboat, in 1807, Mr. John Molson launched the first steamboat on the St. Lawrence.   This is recorded by a tablet bearing the following inscription : " To the Honourable John Molson, the Father of Steam Navigation on the St. Lawrence.   He launched the steamer ' Accommodation,' for Montreal and Quebec service, 1809.'

Montreal is built upon a series of terraces marking the different margins of the river ; the streets are well paved, and the buildings imposing and substantial. Had this city no other attraction, its public buildings would insure it more than passing notice. Foremost among these are its churches, first of which stands Notre Dame, with its twin towers rising to the height of 220 feet, one boasting of a chime of bells second to none in the North-

land, and its mate, the huge *Gros Bourdon*, which weighs
24,780 pounds the largest suspended bell in America.
This magnificent house of divine worship, with the exception of the cathedral standing on the site of the
ancient Aztec pyramids of Mexico, is the largest church
building in America, and has a seating capacity of about
fifteen thousand persons.   It was built in 1829 after a
Gothic style adapted to French taste, and has become
the leading temple of a race.   Perhaps the most imposing and impressive scene to be witnessed in Notre
Dame is the midnight mass.   Under the mystic influence of devout strains of sacred music, at that solemn
hour when the human heart is most easily swayed by
surrounding incentives, with all the beauty and solemnity of the building displayed at its best, in the presence
of its fifteen thousand worshippers, there is nothing to
equal this grand, pathetic, picturesque ceremony,—not
even in that form of religious worship which is so
grandly beautiful in this respect.   Notre Dame is a
place to thrill the soul, and leave an impression that
may never be effaced.

Other churches have their attractions in their adornments of statuary, fine paintings, noble interior finish,
or historic setting.   As has been mentioned, the original church in Montreal was builded of bark and inclosed
by fortress walls.   This was suceeded in 1656, by the
first Parish Church, which stood on the north corner
where St. Paul and St. Sulpice streets now cross.   That,
in turn, has been supplanted by others, to be removed

as the city grew and the ground became needed for
Notre Dame Street.　Pausing, upon a warm summer
day, where St. Sulpice and Notre Dame streets meet,
in front of the church, and feeling a cool breath of air,
which it is claimed is always blowing here, the following
legend is retold by the old resident :

The Devil and the Wind were walking down Notre
Dame Street, when the church was being built, and upon
seeing its graceful outlines rise before him, the former
exclaimed : " What is this ?　I never saw it before."
" That may be true." replied the Wind.　" I dare you
to go in there."　" You dare me to do that, do you ?"
cried the Devil, with a smile.　" I will do it if you will
promise to wait here until I come out."　" I will," replied the Wind.　So his majesty went in.　He has
never come out yet, and the Wind is still waiting for
him at the corner.

Under the pavements of Notre Dame Street, in
front of where the old Parish Church stood, a fitting
tomb indeed for such a wild nature, lie the bones of
Kondiaronk, *le Rat*, the Huron Chief, mention of whom
was made when he " broke the peace " between the
French and the Iroquois.　It is said he fell dead in the
midst of a burst of eloquence while addressing the
allied forces of Hurons and French gathered in council
at this spot.

Another place of interest on Notre Dame Street is
the site of the old Récollet Gate, bearing this tablet,—
and you will observe that memorials are plenty in

Montreal, to the credit of her citizens :—" Recollét Gate :
By this gate Amherst took possession, 8th September,
1760. General Hull, U. S. Army, twenty-five officers,
three hundred and fifty men, entered prisoners of war,
20th September, 1812."

Montreal has many squares and public parks worthy
of description. Foremost among these must be numbered that place designed to commemorate the heroic
deed of Maisonneuve, as described in another chapter.
This is properly the heart of the great city, where more
and deeper interests centre than elsewhere, the multi-
tude moving to and fro under the beautiful figure of
that early hero, who does not look down upon them in
bronze with greater calmness than he displayed during
the critical period of founding the first settlement, when
he showed himself master of the dangerous situation.
The statue was designed by a native sculptor, Louis
Hébert, and represents the hero in the French costume
of that day, the right hand holding the *fleur-de-lis* of
his fatherland. The granite pedestal has this inscription : " Paul de Chomedy de Maisonneuve, Foundateur
de Montreal, 1642." The fountain upon which it rests
has four bas-reliefs, showing the following scenes and
actors : Maisonneuve killing the Indian chief ; the
founding of Ville-Marie ; the fate of the heroic Lambert
Closse, who began to fret because he was not killed
fighting the heathen, but who finally met such a death
defending the gate at St. Lambert Hill ; last, but not
least, the fall of the heroic Daulac, with his brave

companions at Long Sault on the Ottawa. The four corners have each a life-size figure in bronze : a colonist, a colonist's wife, an Indian, the dog Pilote, and a soldier.

Omitting mention of the other beautiful squares, every one of which deserves description, it will not do to forget that ideal park, the beautiful crown of a beautiful city, Mount Royal, the noble lookout which attracted Cartier as he came up the river, which drew like a magnet to its summit the sturdy Champlain, and which a little later was climbed to its crest by Maisonneuve with the huge cross in his arms he had vowed to set up in thankfulness for the escape of the colony from flood and famine. Like that huge " Punch Bowl " overlooking the beautiful capital of the Hawaiian Islands, Honolulu, Mount Royal is really the shoulders of a volcano with its head blown off. It was in prehistoric ages, when it belched forth its molten floods and wrote its daily history in letters of fire upon the sky, a high mountain, with one foot planted on St. Helen's Island and the other far back toward the hoary Laurentides. It now lifts its dismantled body 900 feet above the sea, and 740 feet above the river. It covers about 450 acres, and the last purchase of private owners by the city was made in 1860. No better description of its view can be given in as many words than that of the poet :

Changing its hue with the changing sky,
The River flows in its beauty rare ;

DOMINION SQUARE, MONTREAL.

From a photograph by W. Notman & Son, Montreal.

VIEW OF MONTREAL FROM MOUNT ROYAL.

From a photograph by W. Notman & Son, Montreal.

While across the plain eternal rise
  Boucherville, Rougemont, and St. Hilaire.
Far to the westward lies La Chine,
  Gate of the Orient long ago,
When the virgin forest swept between
  The Royal Mount and the River below.

Upon the one hand we look down upon the busy, prosperous city of commerce and inland trade in its very substantial form, and not as the devout Jeanne Mance saw it, when

God, lifting for her the veils of space, showed to her, while yet in France, in a divine vision, the shores of our isles, and the site of Ville-Marie at the foot of the Mountain and on the shore of its great River.

To the north the *Rivière des Prairies*, a branch of the Ottawa, winds downward, while above the island rests that jewel of the uplands, the Lake of Two Mountains.

Coming back we reach Jacques Cartier Square, where once stood the St. Francis Gate. As we stand upon this hallowed spot, the unhappy fate of the four Iroquois warriors who perished here rises vividly before our mind. Let it be repeated in the words of an eye-witness, and, while it is not pleasant reading, it will possibly impress us with the fact that not all of the barbarism belonged to the untutored race, and that men in sacerdotal robes sometimes were more human than divine. Let the narrator tell his story:

When I came to Montreal for the first time it was by the St. Francis Gate, and as I was speaking to a friend, I became distracted because of a large crowd that I saw on the *Place des Jésuites*. Thereupon my comrade said: "Upon my word, you have come just in time to see four Iroquois burned alive. Come on as far as the Jésuites, we'll see better." It was immediately in front of their door that this bloody tragedy was to take place. I thought at first they would throw the poor wretches into the fire; but upon looking on all side I saw no faggots for the sacrifice of victims, and I questioned my friend about several small fires which I saw certain distances apart from each other. He answered me: "Patience; we are going to have some good laughing." For some time it was no laughing matter. They led out these four wild men, who were brothers, and the finest looking men I have even seen in my life. Then the Jésuites baptised them and made them some scanty exhortations; for, to speak freely, to do more would have been "to wash the head of a corpse." The holy ceremony finished, they were then taken hold of and submitted to punishments of which they were the inventors. They bound them naked to the stakes stuck three or four feet in the ground, and then each of our Indian allies, as well as several Frenchmen, armed themselves with bits of red-hot iron, wherewith they broiled all parts of their bodies. Those small fires which I had seen served as forges to heat the abominable instruments with which they roasted them. Their torture lasted six hours, during which they never ceased to chant of their deeds of war.

Similar scenes to this were enacted in Quebec and elsewhere, so the pity is not wholly a one-sided affair. We find the streets of the older section of the city redolent with memories of a stormy past. Down there is a stone marking the spot where Cartier landed in 1535. On the site of the present custom-house the gallant Champlain, the founder of New France, established a trading post in 1611, which he named *Place Royale*. At the corner of St. Peter and St. Paul streets was the house in which La Salle lived in 1668, two years after he came to Montreal. On the corner of the street by the Parish Church was for a time the home of another noted explorer of the Mississippi, Daniel de Grésolon, Sieur Dulhut, or Du Luth. Before leaving France in 1668, he was a soldier in the King's Guard. He passed three years in the solitude of the wilderness, and in 1688 came to Montreal to live. The city of Duluth was named for him. On Notre Dame Street, just east of St. Lambert Hill, is another tablet which tells its own story : "In 1694, here stood the house of La Mothe, the founder of Detroit." Near by were the homes of Frazer, Henry, Mackenzie, and other great fur-traders, who governed the great North-west before the vanguard of civilisation had yet reached the country. Below Longueuil was the seigniory of Pierre Gauthier de Varennes, Sieur de la Verandrye, the discoverer of the Rocky Mountains in 1742, and who did a great service for Canada by his explorations. Where the Bonsecours Market is, was the mansion of Baron Longueuil, where the Intendant Bigot stayed when in Montreal. Put by the magic mirror. We cannot stop to see them all !

So far we have talked of sites and memories of famous buildings. Now let us visit one that is still standing in good preservation, the oldest public building in the country, erected in the days of Louis XIV., the Château de Ramezay. It is doubtful if there is another building in America around which cluster so many associations of bygone days, so many shades of historic figures, so many scenes of social and political life, not

only in the times of French supremacy, but all along
the pathway of English dominion. To begin at the
beginning, as Knickerbocker did in his *History of New
York*, this ancient edifice was builded by Claude de
Ramezay, the eleventh Governor of Montreal, in 1705,
just two hundred years ago. It was very appropriately
raised in what was then the heart of the most fashionable and important part of the town. Standing upon a
slight elevation, scarcely to be noticed now, it had a
plain view of the river-front. Among its neighbours it
numbered such illustrious dwellings as the abodes of
Baron de Longueuil, D'Aillebouts, D'Eschambaults,
Madame de Portneuf, the widow of Baron Bécancourt.
Its owner was one of the most prominent men of his
age, holding one important public position after another
for forty years. He had come to the valley of the St.
Lawrence in 1685, in his twenty-eighth year, in the suite
of Governor Denonville. He was a lieutenant under
De Troye of the marine troops. Two years later he
had become colonel, and in 1703 he was made Governor, holding that high position until 1724. During
the attack of Phips against Quebec, he had hastened
hither with eight hundred men from Montreal. He
not only performed a gallant part in the defence of
the city, but won for his prize the heart and hand
of a fair daughter of Quebec, Mademoiselle Marie-
Charlotte Deny, who belonged to one of the oldest
and noblest houses of Canada. Another connected
with that exciting experience, De Vaudreuil, also, later,

Governor, was equally fortunate in winning a bride almost before the ships of the New Englander had disappeared behind the Point of Orleans.   It seemed like the irony of fate that a son of the first should be the one to open the gates of Quebec to the English in 1759, and a son of the latter should perform a similar unpleasant service in Montreal a few months later.

During the *régime* of Governor de Ramezay the château was ablaze with the glory of the times.   Here met many an illustrious assembly, consisting not only of the Governor-General, the Intendant, and their suites, but the leading military and political spirits of that stirring period.   Here were held the councils of war, and here were considered the terms of peace.   Here many of the early discoverers bade their last adieu to friends and patrons before setting out on their long and uncertain voyages, and from here went forth expeditions into the wilderness in the interests of the fur-trade.   Upon their return were the plans perfected for those annual fairs which were both a curse and a blessing to Montreal.   Hither came the Indian with his grievances, the *voyageur* with his complaints ; and here was given to the plague-stricken, during the sorrowful reign of the pest, in 1721, the kindly, sympathetic attention which won the love and respect of the people for the courteous Governor and his amiable wife.   Not only were the nobleman and his consort sure to find a cordial and courteous welcome within the château, but the humble red man and his squaw met with the same genial treatment from the noble De Ramezay and his family.

After the death of De Ramezay, in 1724, the property remained with his heirs until 1745, when they sold it to *la Compagnie des Indes*. It then became the headquarters of the fur-trade until 1760, upon the capitulation of the city to the English. According to the treaty, however, the company was allowed to hold the château for a period longer. In 1764, it was sold to William Grant, who paid sixty thousand livres in the discredited money of the country to be redeemed by the French Government. Ten years later, Grant leased the property to the Government for the residence of the Lieutenant-Governor, and for the Governor-General when in Montreal.

Soon after this, 1775–76, the château became the headquarters of the Continental army under Montgomery, when Canada hesitated between espousing the cause of the English colonies or that of their King. The British of Canada engaged in the fur-trade looked favourably upon the plot, while a large percentage of the French, not yet reconciled to their change of masters, naturally sympathised with the colonists whose watchword was liberty. General Schuyler, in command of the army of New York, had been instructed to invade the St. Lawrence valley, but falling ill he was succeeded by Montgomery. Colonel Ethan Allen, connected with Schuyler's army as a volunteer, was sent upon a mission of investigation to Montreal, and was captured on the

THE CHÂTEAU DE RAMEZAY, MONTREAL.

From a photograph by W. Notman & Son, Montreal.

KITCHEN IN THE CHÂTEAU DE RAMEZAY, MONTREAL.

From a photograph by W. Notman & Son, Montreal.

25th of September, to be sent to England as a prisoner of war, where he was retained until May 3, 1778, when he was exchanged.

The English having but a small force in Montreal at the breaking out of the American Revolution, Governor Sir Guy Carleton withdrew to Quebec, and, upon the arrival of General Montgomery, the citizens capitulated. On the morning of the 13th of November, 1775, the Continental army marched triumphantly into the city by the Récollet Gate, the château was made the headquarters of the army, while Montgomery stayed at a house on the corner of St. Peter and Notre Dame streets owned by a merchant named Fortier. Upon being ordered upon that ill-fated expedition to unite with Arnold in an attack upon Quebec, Montgomery left General Wooster in command. He was succeeded by Arnold, who was in command at the time of the arrival of the American Commissioners sent to negotiate terms of compromise with the people.

These commissioners, Benjamin Franklin, Charles Carroll of Carrollton, and Samuel Chase, held their councils in the château, in the room where this is written. But, by this time, a feeling of indignation against such a movement had been aroused by the priests and more loyal British. Reinforced at Quebec, Carleton came up the river with such an army that the American Commissioners were glad to beat a retreat. Among those who came with the commissioners was a printer brought by Franklin, whose name was

Fleury Mesplet. There was no printer in Montreal at that time, and Mesplet set up his cases and hand-press in the basement of the château. Upon the return to Philadelphia of Franklin, Mesplet soon after began to publish the *Gazette*, a weekly newspaper, which is still issued, the oldest paper in this part of Canada.

In 1778, the château became the property of the British Government, and during the troublesome period of insurrection, when a special council was appointed by the Governor to succeed the regular officials that withdrew, it became the meeting-place of this council, 1837–41. Pending the decision of new legislation the seat of government was removed to Kingston, but in 1845 Montreal again became the capital, and the château the headquarters of the Government.

The passage and adoption of the Rebellion Loss Bill, which compensated those who had fought against the Government as well as those who stood loyally by it, raised such a storm of indignation among the English-speaking people of Montreal, that the Governor-General, upon leaving the château after sanctioning the bill, was pelted with stones, and other missiles not so severe to the flesh but more offensive to the nostrils. During the exciting period the Parliament Buildings were burned to the ground. This caused the removal of the Government to Ottawa, and the château was no more the headquarters of its officials.

But its usefulness was not past, for it was used as a court-house during the reconstruction of the present court building. In 1849, it began to be occupied by the Jacques Cartier Normal School, the first established in Canada, and it was kept here until about 1875, when a new building was erected for the school. Then a medical branch of the Laval University of Quebec was opened in the château ; and later, it was occupied as an annex to the court-house for his Majesty's court.

In 1893 the Government, concluding that it had no further use for the venerable building, began negotiations with the city of Montreal for its change of ownership, which was soon afterwards effected. Then the Numismatic and Antiquarian Society of Montreal, seeing the special fitness of the ancient structure for its headquarters, finally obtained possession in 1895, and to-day have on exhibit here one of the finest, if not the finest, collections of historical works, portraits of noted individuals, and museum of relics in the country. Surely a happier or more fitting fate could not have befallen it. With walls of Montreal granite, grey and white, long and rambling, after the architecture of the days of Louis, the old landmark is happily located, in a fine state of preservation, with every prospect of a beautiful old age. Happy Château de Ramezay! would that others of our historic buildings might share as appropriate a fate !

Within, one treads upon the footprints of generations gone the way of dust, and breathes the atmosphere of departed spirits. Attended by the courteous curator, whose fund of historic lore seems without end, or one of his efficient assistants, the visitor passes from room to room with ever-increasing veneration and that feeling one might have who comes as an intruder upon sacred scenes.   This apartment was the family sitting-room, where the original owners of the building possibly passed their happiest hours in those troublesome days. There was the reception-room, the council-chamber, the old hall where so many antagonistic visitors mingled in peaceful companionship under the benign influence of De Ramezay.   There stood the wily Huron, over near the deep-set window, while he pleaded in wild, pictur-esque language, half spoken, half acted, the cause of his unfortunate race.   Here stood the fiery Vaudreuil, as he made reply.   And from a chair standing just over there rose the witty De Ramezay, smoothing the rug-ged way to peace by his clear, forceful logic.   Franklin's chair must have stood about where you stand, when, with his associates, he undertook to win over Canada to the American cause, as he had France.   It was here the unfortunate Montgomery stood, as he consulted with his officers only the day before he went to fight and fall for a tablet on Quebec rock.   Here, too, came Arnold, with his sun at its meridian and the dark clouds of dis-honour not yet risen on his horizon, to stand up for his people and his country.   Others came and went, as noble as these.

Following down the dark stairway, with its broad steps, we come to the old kitchen, long and stately, with its stone-ledged windows, and huge old fireplace

at the farther end, where burned many a giant of the
forest.   What feasts have been prepared here !   What
roasts of venison !   Those were hardy days, when men
ate the substances that made them tough and stalwart.
You see that door over there near the corner ?   Behind
that was the wine vault, larger than this big kitchen,
and from which came more life and vivacity, too.   Ay,
from thence came the enemy that robbed the eloquent
Huron on the next floor of the peace that he demanded,
and did more than all else to ruin his race.

Fifteen thousand volumes, books and pamphlets,
have been collected, and relics and curios in large numbers.   A section that cannot fail to interest is the Por-
trait Gallery, from whose walls look down upon the
beholder a vast company of celebrated actors in scenes
of American history.   Foremost among these are Columbus, the discoverer of America ; Cartier, the Columbus of Canada ; Champlain, the chivalrous knight of
civilisation ; Jean Baptiste le Moyne de Bienville, born
1680, died 1768, founded New Orleans, and was Governor of Louisiana for twenty-seven years ; a brother of
the latter, Sieur Pierre le Moyne d'Iberville, born 1661,
died 1706, founder and first Governor of Louisiana ;
Daniel Marie Hyacinthe Lienard de Beaujeu, born
1711, died 1755, commander of the army of *Belle Rivière*
(Ohio), whose troops won the battle of Monongahela
against Braddock, both of the commanders falling in the
fight, as Wolfe and Montcalm fell on the Plains of Abraham four years later ; Lacorne St. Luc, Knight of the

Order of St. Louis, and a man of note under the old
régime ; Chevalier de Levis, born 1720, died 1787, who
so ably succeeded Montcalm, and won the "second battle of the Plains," but was not able to hold it; Louis
Joseph de Saint Veran, Marquis de Montcalm, born
1712, killed on Mount Abraham, 1759.   Then there are
Guy Carleton, Lord Dorchester, born 1725, died 1808,
who fought with Wolfe on the Plains of Abraham, and
with Murray at Ste. Foye, and was Governor-General
of Canada for twenty years; General James Murray,
who succeeded Wolfe as commander of the British army,
and who has the credit of suggesting the plan of scaling
the heights at *Anse du Foulon ;* General James Wolfe,
born 1726, shot September 14, 1759, by his victory on
the Plains of Abraham, the virtual conqueror of New
France ; Charles Cornwallis, Marquis Cornwallis, born
1738, died 1805, Major-General of the British army
until his surrender to General Washington at Yorktown,
October 19, 1781 ; François de Montmorenci de Laval,
born 1622, died 1708, first Roman Catholic Bishop of
Canada, and a most able and zealous prelate; Jacques
Marquette, born 1637, died 1675, one of the most illus-
trious missionaries and explorers of Canada, who, with
Louis Joliet, discovered the Mississippi, June 17, 1673 ;
Le Jeune, the Father of the Jesuit missions in New
France, born in 1592, came to Canada in 1632, preached
Champlain's funeral oration in 1635, was first of the ten
Superiors of the Church, wrote nine of the *Relations,*
returned to France in 1650, and died in 1664 ; Father

Jean de Brébeuf, of the Society of Jesus, born 1593, died from tortures inflicted by the Indians, 1649, the most illustrious of the martyrs of New France; Gabriel Lalement, Jesuit missionary, born 1610, perished by the side of Brébeuf in the Huron country, in 1649, whose bones, with those of his companion, were brought to Quebec for burial; Reverend Père Isaac Jogues, born 1598, was massacred by the Mohawks October 18, 1646, and was the first apostle to the Mission of Martyrs; Charles Carroll of Carrollton was one of the commission to meet at Château de Ramezay, in 1775, and was one of the signers of the Declaration of American Independence in 1776, dying November 14, 1832, the last of the famous group; Major Robert Rogers, Chief of the New England Rangers, who organised and trained the raw militia into soldiers of the forest, capable of meeting in their own tactics of warfare Montcalm's Indian infantry. But the list is too long to complete, and we must quit the old château and its illustrious guests with reluctance.

Montreal had a population in 1760, at the close of French government, of about 3000 people; in 1809 this number had reached 12,000. To-day it makes a grand total of 350,000 souls. This great number is composed of three race divisions, the larger portion being French, and comprising about 200,000; the English-speaking portion, with a strong Scottish element in its make-up, numbers about 100,000; while the third party, comprising the Irish Roman Catholic extraction, has about 50,000 in numbers.

Montreal, the queenly Maid of the St. Lawrence, has a bright future. Nature, as well as man, intended her for a great and powerful metropolis. Situated, as she is, midway between the ocean and the great Central West, with its growing centres of population and commerce, and upon the noblest waterway in America, she will continue to grow, to prosper, and to rule the progress of Canada.

> Sprung of the saint and the chevalier,
>   And with the scarlet tunic wed ;
>   Mount Royal's crown upon thy head,
> And past thy footstool, broad and clear,
>   St. Lawrence sweeping to the sea :
>   Reign on, majestic Ville-Marie !

VICTORIA SQUARE, MONTREAL.

From a photograph by W. Notman & Son, Montreal.

AN OLD WINDMILL ON LOWER LA CHINE ROAD, MONTREAL.
From a photograph by W. Notman & Son, Montreal.

Chapter XXIII

Climbing the Rapids

THE number of passengers who pass up the St. Lawrence at this section is small compared to the crowds that come down. This is due to the generally accepted idea that it is a dull journey up to Prescott, from Montreal, covering the distance of the falls, while the excitement and novelty of "shooting the rapids" has given its own peculiar charm and attraction to the downward ride. But if it takes a night and a part of two days to climb the distance made in a few hours coming down, there is an interest and a fascination in this upward trip which the other does not outrival.

Moving where Cartier led nearly five hundred years ago, the steamer, at the upper end of the harbour, enters the La Chine Canal, by means of which man has overcome the obstacles that a great river has thrown across its passage, those selfsame obstacles that defied and baffled both Cartier and Champlain, eager as they were to climb to the regions beyond. The first explorer, after ascending the river as he judged about two leagues, and coming to the foot of the rapids, says :

> We took counsel to go as far as possible with one of the boats, and the other should remain there until we returned, so we doubled the men in the boat so as to beat against the current of the said rapid. And after we had got far from our other boat, we found bad bottom and large rocks, and so great a current of water that it was not possible to pass beyond with our boat.

It was then decided to run ashore, and follow up the bank to learn the extent of the rapids, finding a beaten path along which the natives had passed in their journeys up and down the river, carrying their canoes. It is not easy at this period of good roads and rapid transit to appreciate the vexatious delays and perils accompanying the early traveller, whose only way of progress was the sedgy streams of the primeval forest, and only means of conveyance the birchen skiff propelled by his own arm. Abounding with rapids, as most Canadian rivers are, blocked with ice in winter, or robbed of their volume by the droughts of summer, there were not many days in the journeys of the early voyageurs when they did not have to check their advance, shoulder their baggage and canoe, and tramp on foot around the impassable places of the waterway. Not infrequently these carrying-places continued for miles, even leagues, over broken spurs of mountains, or through dismal valleys overrun with parasitic vines and crumbling growths reeking with the sweat and slime of ages.

Perhaps no more plain or sympathetic account of such journeys has been given than is to be found in the letters of Jesuit missionaries, who of all others were the best fitted to judge. One of these,[1] in describing his trip up the St. Lawrence, says:

> What detracts from this river's utility is the waterfalls and rapids extending nearly forty leagues,—that is from Montreal to the mouth of Lake Ontario,—there being only the two lakes I have mentioned (Lake St. Francis and Lake St. Louis) where navigation is easy. In ascending these rapids it is often necessary to alight from the canoe and walk in the river, whose waters are rather low in such places, especially near the banks. The canoe is grasped with the hand and dragged behind, two men usually sufficing for this. . . . Occasionally one is obliged to run it ashore, and carry it for some time, one man in front and the other behind—the first bearing the one end of the canoe on his right shoulder, and the second the other end on his left. . . . It is necessary to land and carry all the baggage through woods or over high and troublesome rocks, as well as the canoes themselves. This is not done without much work ; for there are portages of one, two, and three leagues, and for each several trips must be made, no matter how few packages one has. I kept count of the number of portages and found that we carried our canoes thirty-five times, and dragged them at least fifty. I sometimes took a hand in helping my Savages ; but the bottom of the river is full of stones so sharp that I could not walk long, being barefooted.

Something of the deprivations, as well as perils and hardships of these journeys, is shown in another place, quoting from the same authority, in speaking of the Huron mission, which

lasted more than sixteen years, in a country whither one cannot go

[1] The *Jesuit Relations* and allied documents.

with other boats than of bark, which carry at most only two thousand livres of burden, including the passengers—who are frequently obliged to bear on their shoulders, from four to six miles, along with the boat and the provisions, all the furniture for the journey; for there is not, in the space of seven hundred miles, any inn. For this reason we have passed whole years without receiving so much as one letter, either from Europe or from Kebec, and in a total deprivation of every human assistance, even that most necessary for our mysteries and sacraments themselves,—the country having neither wheat nor wine, which are absolutely indispensable for the Holy Sacrifice of the Mass.

Further light is thrown upon the manner and association of the native companions of these humble followers of that faith which made of them priests of the wilderness :

To conciliate the Savages, you must be careful never to make them wait for you in embarking. You must provide yourself with a tinder-box or a burning-mirror, or with both, to furnish them fire in the daytime to light their pipes, and in the evening when they have to encamp; these little services win their hearts. You must try and eat at daybreak unless you can take your meal with you in the canoe; for the day is very long if you have to pass it without eating. The Barbarians eat only at Sunrise and at Sunset, when they are on their journeys. . . . To be properly dressed you must have your feet and legs bare; while crossing the rapids you can wear your shoes, and, in the long portages, even your leggins. . . . It is not well to ask many questions, nor should you yield to your desire to learn the language. . . . You must relieve those in your canoe of this annoyance. . . . Each one will try, at the portages, to carry some little thing, according to his strength; however little one carries, it greatly pleases the savages, if it be only a kettle. . . . Be careful not to annoy any one in the canoe with your hat; it would be better to take your nightcap. There is no impropriety among the savages.

These Indian trails were aptly called by the missionaries "roads of iron," thus but faintly suggesting

the fatigue and suffering falling to the lot of him whose
fortunes led him to traverse the way already pressed by
thousands of feet that failed to leave a single monument
along the way. Many of these portages became noted
meeting-places, where different members of the scattered
tribes met by agreement or by accident for a night's
bivouac; or sometimes they became the battle-ground
of rival clans, an example of this kind being still pointed
out in the north, beyond the Saguenay, where the hosts
of Mamelons suffered almost entire annihilation. Usually they became scenes of rejoicings and wild excitement after a long, hard struggle to reach the place
before the westering sun should take its final plunge
into the "sea of space" on the far-distant horizon.

The La Chine Canal was begun in 1821, and though
at first but five feet deep and twenty-eight feet wide at
the bottom, widening toward the top until it was forty-
eight feet, it was a long time in building compared to
the way such work is done to-day, and many vexations
and unlooked-for perplexities arose in the path of the
constructor. Since then it has been enlarged and
strengthened, until now it is capable of taking up to the
placid waters of Lake St. Francis the big steamers that
draw fourteen feet of water. The performance is very
simple, this outwitting the current too swift to be braved.
It is easy to fancy, from the glimpse that one gets now
and then of the river in the distance, that an extra toss
of indignation is given by the swirling waters as they
sweep downward in sight of us escaping so easily their

rage.   This may be only the dream of a dreamer.   It is not a point for argument.

Now the portage path has been transformed into a link of silver, and the steamer glides gently into its narrow canal whose high walls lift their granite sides over our heads.   A massive gate bars the way, holding in leash the mass of water above.   Then another gate is closed below us, and we are imprisoned between the barriers.   Men spring to the levers upon the platform of the upper gate.   The ponderous structure is seen to move ; it rises !   The flood-like water everywhere surges through the narrow opening, increasing in volume as the aperture grows.   Our prison is being flooded, and as the tide rises we are lifted slowly, until, somewhat to our surprise, we are on a level with the pond that a few minutes before had threatened to swallow us.   The men spring to their task again ; the gate swings ajar, and we move proudly forward into another reception hall await-ing us, another gate to confront us ; the one we have passed to be closed behind us ; another filling of the basin, and we ride another step higher.   In this simple, yet majestic way we climb, lock by lock, the rapids of La Chine !

What is true of these rifts applies to the rapids of Split Rock, where we are lifted bodily eighty-two feet in three locks, of the Long Sault, and of all inter-mediate falls.   It is clearly a case of nature outwitted and baffled by man.

From these locks we enter the celebrated Lake St.

Louis, whose shores Champlain described as bordered with woods of chestnut, groves of walnut trees, and extensive meadows fringed with grape-vines. Upon the one hand we pass the town of La Chine, founded by La Salle soon after he reached Montreal. It was he, too, who first selected the site of Chicago as a trading post at the time of his wanderings in the region of the Illinois. Nearly opposite, as the crow flies, on the south bank of the St. Lawrence, stands the Indian hamlet of Caughnawaga, which name means "praying Indians." It was here that many captives from New England, during the border wars, were brought before the red captors, who delivered them over to the French at Montreal or Quebec. Among others to be held here was the young daughter of James Johnson, whose narrative has been already quoted. Afterwards she was immured in a nunnery at Montreal, from which her father found it impossible to release her, so she was never reunited to her family. Her case was not a solitary one, as many another bereaved New England family had sad occasion to know.

The shores of Lake St. Louis are among the beauty spots of the St. Lawrence. Winding its way reluctantly down from the northlands, the stately Ottawa joins hands, as it were, here with the "river from the west." Immediately our attention is called to a remarkable phenomenon of two rivers running side by side in the same channel without mingling. Other rivers may imitate this attempt, but nowhere is such a marked

distinction shown as here, in the deep green of the St.
Lawrence and the pronounced brown of the Ottawa.
The latter, it has been boldly asserted, gets its hue from
the great forests of fir and hemlock covering its headwaters. I do not vouch for this. I even doubt it. But
I do claim that if a seven-league ruler were laid upon
the water of Lake St. Louis and the boundary marked
with a magic pencil, the line between these rivers
could not be more clearly defined ; and they run in
this close companionship for nearly fifty miles before
they blend into the deep azure of the Lower St. Lawrence. Who can say there is not in this display of jealousy a trait common with humanity, and that the lordly
Ottawa remembers yet the not very distant day when it
and not the Upper St. Lawrence was the outlet of the
Great Lakes ? Preposterous as it seems at first thought,
the geologists offer good proof of the truth of this.
Furthermore, they tell us that before this period the
waters of those great inland seas, larger then than now,
found an outlet by the Mohawk valley and the Hudson
River. Prior to that period they flowed toward the
Gulf of Mexico from an outlet at the site of Chicago.
The next change, that now seems inevitable, is a return
to this ancient route, when the St. Lawrence will be
robbed of its glory. But ere that day dawns another
race may come to shoot its rapids, and another tongue
to tell its history.

The next series of steps in the stairways of the
rapids is the Soulanges Canal, leading from the foot of

Cascade Rapids to Couteau Landing, connecting Lake St. Louis with Lake St. Francis. This is of more recent construction than the other sections, and is one of the finest sets of locks in the country, lighted and operated by electricity. Originally a canal on the south bank, the Beauharnois, overcame the difficulty of navigation on this portion of the river. It was during the passage of the rapids here that a division of General Amherst's soldiers was lost.

The steamer glides gracefully out from the last lock upon the breathless bosom of Lake St. Francis just as the setting sun touches with its magic pencil, tipped with crimson, silver, and gold, the perennial green of the landscape and transparent azure of the river. If Japan is famed for its beautiful sunrise, and there is no scene where the radiance of the morning light is reflected with greater glory than on the highlands of the Nikko district; if Tibet, the "roof of the world," is the favourite tenting-ground of the great round moon's legions of light, dancing with fantastic glee upon the ascension of their queen, then the St. Lawrence deserves especial honours for the glory of its sunsets. Certainly, nowhere are the curtains of twilight drawn with a more delicate hand, and nowhere are the lights and shades blended with happier effects. The river lies bathed in silver and silence. The broad green meadows repose under the tremulous drapery of a June atmosphere. The forest on the highlands, its foliage made up of a hundred hues, glorifies each quivering beam with its own especial charm; and the kingly pine, that has looked out upon thousands of sunsets like this, as if dreaming of childhood's brighter days, suddenly takes on for a moment a cheerful brightness, and then swiftly flings aside its stolen blush to assume its native gloom. Through the great mullioned window of the West stream the lambent flames of evening. As if the sun would linger long over such a fair scene, he opens again and again the eye that has grown heavy with watching, and when at last the green upon the meadow, the purple upon the forest, the umber upon the bank, and the silver upon the river have been vanquished by the overmastering darkness, we, who watch and wonder, half expect that he will re-appear for a farewell good-night.

The next place of importance on the north bank is the bustling town of Cornwall, and here are the last series of locks, six in number, and the canal twelve miles long, completing the grand ascent of the river, which had a total fall between here and Montreal of 206½ feet. These canals have a navigable depth of fourteen feet. The 45th parallel here intersects the St. Lawrence, so the river is no longer entirely Canadian, the line dividing Canada from the United States crossing here, as well as making the division between the two provinces of the Dominion.

Nearly opposite Cornwall is the interesting village of St. Regis, an Indian town. Amid its grove of trees and cluster of houses stands the church having a bell that possesses a peculiar and pathetic interest to the descendants of the New England colonists, as well as those of Canada. This bell, after being captured from the French by an English cruiser, was taken to Salem, Massachusetts, and thence to Deerfield. Upon being informed that their bell was located here the Indians rallied and went upon a raid against the town. Surprising the inhabitants they massacred nearly fifty, and took back to Canada with them over a hundred captives, and the bell, which now hangs in the St. Regis church.

The boat comes to the end of its trip at Prescott, where the passengers going farther up the river, as nearly all are, must change to one of the more palatial steamers that ply between this town and Toronto. These latter, on account of their size, cannot pass the locks. The first large boat to attempt the passage of the river below here was the *Ontario*, built at Niagara about 1840. She proved to be very speedy, and was purchased by men at Montreal for a mail boat between that city and Quebec. The trade closed, the next thing was to get the boat down to Montreal, no craft anywhere near its size having attempted to run the rapids. The best pilots then on the river, two Indians known as "Old Jock" and "Old Pete," were secured for the hazardous undertaking, the owners promising them one thousand dollars each if they accomplished their enterprise successfully. The manner in which they made this initial voyage is best described by that old veteran of the Upper St. Lawrence, Captain Johnston :

First, a crib was made forty feet square, with pine floats ten feet apart, with stakes ten feet long driven in each square, project-ing downward. When all was ready some Indians were sent to the foot of the rapids and some were stationed in the trees on the side of the rapids. Several Indians towed the crib to the head of the rapids with their canoes and let go of it. Then every Indian watched the course it took as the crib sped on its way with the cur-rent of the stream. When it reached the foot of the rapids the crib was turned over, and it was found that none of the stakes were broken. That was a positive indication that there was water enough to run the *Ontario* through. The Indians then boarded the steamer. Each Indian piloted the *Ontario* as far as he had observed the crib's course. The only white man on board was the engineer, who also, I was told, received one thousand dollars. This story I got from "Old Jock," who used to pilot us, and who ran us through the La Chine Rapids nine times without mishap.

In this way, in 1843, was the first steamer taken down the rapids, and a descendant of one of these pioneer pilots now guides with a trusty hand the steamer of to-day that follows in the track of the *On-tario*. The next steamers to follow this course were the *Canada* and *America*, in 1858 or 1859, according to the authority above quoted. It is said that only one white man undertook to run the La Chine Rapids in those early days, and his name was Roebuck.

Prescott is a stone-built town, with a great distillery and brewery and two iron foundries, and a population of about four thousand. It was named for General Prescott, and has on the east the bastions of Fort Wel-lington, named for the Iron Duke. Prescott is filled with historic memories, and has many places of interest to the historian. Among these is the little church, said to be the oldest Methodist church in Canada, where

THE METHODIST CHURCH AT PRESCOTT.

Founded by Barbara Heck. Her grave is marked by a cross.

THE OLD WINDMILL AT PRESCOTT.

Barbara Heck, one of the founders of that faith in the valley of the St. Lawrence, held meetings. In the little yard is her grave, marked by a plain marble slab. Other spots of interest are the old blockhouse, still in a good state of preservation, and filled with memories of warlike days ; and the old windmill, which the Government has since converted into a lighthouse.

This ancient landmark figured conspicuously in the closing scene of what has been somewhat derisively called "the patriot war," one of the most foolish and insane projects ever set on foot by men burning for notoriety. The scheme seems to have originated among some fanatics of Northern New York, and had for its purpose the overthrow of the Canadian Government. This was during the period mentioned in the description of Château de Ramezay, and the burning of the Parliament Buildings in Montreal. In the summer of 1837, the leader of the so-called "reform party," William Lyon McKenzie, with General Van Rensselaer, established a station on Navy Island in the Niagara River, having a force of three hundred men. It was claimed that the Government committed wrongs equal to those the British had inflicted upon the American colonists, but the leaders of the "patriots" only demanded restitution and recognition. Untoward events, however, were soon to turn the tide of politics into more warlike channels. A small steamer, called the *Caroline*, was employed in taking passengers and freight between the island and Buffalo, and this one night was

boarded by a company of British soldiers, fired, and
sent adrift over Niagara Falls. This act inflamed the
" patriots," and one William Johnston, of evil repute,
became the acknowledged leader. He fortified himself
upon an island within the United States line. His
daughter Kate became the trusted informant for Johnston and his band of rebels. On the night of May
30, 1838, Johnston and his followers, disguised as Indians and armed with muskets and bayonets, boarded
the Canadian steamer, *Sir Robert Peel,* while *en route*
between Brockville and Toronto with twenty passengers and a large amount of money to pay off the troops
in the Upper Province. The night was dark and rainy,
and with the watchword, " Remember the *Caroline,*"
the " patriot" band ordered the passengers and crew
to take to the boats, following which they set fire to
the steamer and left her to her fate. The sunken hull
is still to be seen where she went down. Johnston
then made a personal declaration of war, and it became
evident the Canadian Government had got to take de-
cisive action to check the threatened invasion. The
result of this matter was the landing at Prescott of a
force of the " patriots," under command of one Von
Schoultz, who had entered into the struggle with ill-
conceived idea of what it meant. This company took
possession of the old windmill, and were routed only
when thirty-six of the British soldiers and nineteen of
the rebels had been killed, besides many wounded on
both sides. Most of the " patriot" leaders had now

deserted the cause, and this ended the outbreak. Several of the insurgents were hanged, among them Von Schoultz, whose fate was a most unhappy one, as it did not appear that he had really understood the crime he was committing. He left a legacy of ten thousand dollars for the benefit of the British families of those who had been killed. The ill-advised affair had even a wider influence, as it involved several prominent American politicians in the mêlée on account of the decided action they took against some of those in New York who sympathised with the "patriots." President Van Buren lost many votes on account of it, while General Scott believed that he lost the Whig nomination for the Presidency owing to the fact that he had been instrumental in putting down the rebellion.

During the Fenian insurrection in 1865–66, Prescott was again the scene of warlike excitement, when the Fenian forces encamped here upon the eve of the intended invasion of Canada. Happily these and many other disturbing scenes have passed into memory, and the quiet old town lies dreaming of the day when she shall awaken to the possibilities nature has promised her.

Chapter XXIV

The Gateway to the West

Mission of La Presentation—Ogdensburg—Brockville—Romance of the Thousand Islands—A Daughter's Devotion to a Father—Carleton Island—" Lost Channel "—Memory of a Bonaparte—Origin of the Feud between the Iroquois and the Algonquins—Legend of the League of the Five Nations—Tradition of Hiawatha—Cooper's " Station Island "—Gananoque—" The Place of the Deer "—A Poet's Tribute—Kingston, the Limestone City—Conclusion.

THE St. Lawrence is about a mile wide between Prescott and the city of Ogdensburg. The latter place is builded near the site of the Onondaga mission, established by the French in 1749, at the mouth of the Oswegatchie[1] River. Its founder was a Sulpician, named Francis Picquet, and, despite the attack of Mohawks, flourished so well that in two years a sawmill was erected here. It was given the name of La Presentation, and created considerable uneasiness among the English already at Oswego. An Indian runner, appearing suddenly at the latter place, said : " As I came through the forest I heard a bird sing, and he sang that a great many Indians from his castle, and many others from the Five Nations, have gone to Swegage." This mission was maintained until 1760. The Indians and their descendants continued to live

[1] Indian term, meaning " place where the water flows around the hills."

338

about here until 1806, when a part of them went to St. Regis, and the balance to Onondaga upon the demand of the landowners. Over the door of the State arsenal building is a block taken from a stone structure that once stood near the site of the present lighthouse, which has the following inscription :

"In nomine Dei Omnipotentis
Huic habitationi initia dedit
Frans. Picquet.   1749."

While the Treaty of 1783 fixed the St. Lawrence River as the boundary line between the United States and Canada, the English continued to occupy Oswegatchie as a trading station, "to protect their interests," as they claimed. This created great dissatisfaction on the part of the Americans, but it was not remedied until the "Jay Treaty" stipulated that all English posts in the United States should be abandoned on or before June 1, 1796. Immediately after, Mr. Samuel Ogden, who had obtained a controlling interest here, commenced to improve the place, which has continued to prosper ever since. It was named in his honour.

So this modern city stands upon the ruins of an ancient town, whose inhabitants mainly belonged to that vanished people who were the Romans of America. As Ogdensburg is to-day a great railroad centre, where two main lines meet, even before the building of La Presentation mission this place was an important position, where the old Indian trails of the Mohawk and

St. Lawrence valleys crossed, the course of these being closely followed by the iron horse of modern travel.

At the foot of the Thousand Islands, upon the Canadian shore, stands the beautiful city of Brockville, with something like ten thousand inhabitants. The first settlers of this town were United Empire Loyalists, who came here soon after the close of the American Revolution, which left them outlaws in their own country. All through the war of 1812–15, this town was the scene of exciting interest, and was captured by an American force, under command of a Captain Forsyth, of Ogdensburg.

From this fair city, with its pictured rock, speaking to us in the art of a vanished hand of savage superstition and reparation, we come to where lie

> New meadows white, where daisies grow,
> Near where St. Lawrence whispers low;
> Near sylvan dells, where Nature smiles,
> Earth's paradise, the Thousand Isles.

There is poetry in the name, romance in all that clusters about the scene hallowed with a thousand historic memories. Here Cooper, our own Scott, found inspiration for his greatest novel, and here another of their gift might find material for a series of American Waverly novels whose interest would not be less than those of Scottish loch and land.

He would find here mighty fortresses built by no human hand, castles made more secure by natural bulwarks than moat or barbican could make them, hidden by bays in which a fleet might hide, channels three hundred feet deep winding between wooded islands and secure waterways. Ellen's Isle, made famous by the Wizard of the North, is reproduced here in a hundred forms, and Loch Katrine has scores of rivals at our very door.

Scarcely one of the islands that dot the unruffled surface of the lake,

> As quiet as spots of sky
> Among the evening clouds,

does not have its tradition, mellowed by the passing years, of love and war, heroism and intrigue, plot and sacrifice. No fairer example of filial devotion is shown than in the character of brave Kate Johnston, who stood by her father so loyally during his exile while engaged in the "patriot war." "The Devil's Oven," the secluded isle where he found concealment for over a year, still belongs to one of her descendants, for she was happily married when she had succeeded in securing her father's pardon for any misdemeanour he may have committed. He became a lighthouse keeper, while she was loved and respected for her devotion to him through the dark days of his outlawry.

Carleton Island during the War of the American Revolution was the most important post above Montreal. This was a refuge place for the Tories of New York, New Jersey, and Pennsylvania. Here the renowned chief of the Six Nations, Thayendanagea, had his rendezvous. Many councils of war were held, and many a bloody raid had its birthnight here. Among these may be mentioned the heartrending massacres of Wyoming and Cherry Valleys, the Cedars and Stony

Arabia, while from this island sallied forth the band of avengers who made their terrible midnight attack upon Deerfield, Massachusetts, for the rescue of the bell of St. Regis.   Lying in the course of the old Indian trail from the Long House of the Iroquois to the waterway leading to the vale of the Hurons and the Ottawa beyond, it was also crossed by the canoe-path of the St. Lawrence and Ontario.   The early French explorers named it *Ile aux Chevreuils*, or " Isle of Roebucks." Realising the importance of its situation, it was a favourite resort for both the French and English until, just before the beginning of the eighteenth century, the British erected upon the crest of the bluff overlooking the American channel a fortress known as Fort Haldimand, and also as Fort Carleton.   Not very many years since, the traveller up and down the river could see the dismantled chimney.   Now the island has become the beautiful resort of summer pleasure-seekers, and only fragmentary tales remain of those thrilling days of frontier wars.

One of the most romantic incidents of this portion of the St. Lawrence is ths story of the Lost Channel, which is connected with the French and Indian War of 1756–63.   Lord Amherst, in command of the English troops, was *en route* from Oswego upon his expedition against Montreal.   Quebec had capitulated, and though De Levis, in command of the French troops, was playing a bold hand, it was not believed he could hold out much longer.   Murray was already moving up

VIEW OF THE THOUSAND ISLANDS FROM DEVIL'S OVEN.

From a photograph by W. Notman & Son, Montreal,

BELOW THE " RIFT," THOUSAND ISLANDS.

From a photograph by W. Notman & Son, Montreal.

the St. Lawrence toward Montreal, Colonel Haviland was hammering at the defences on the Richelieu, and with Amherst's naval and military force of ten thousand strong victory seemed certain. The only French stronghold between Oswego and Montreal at that time was La Presentation, known to the English as Fort Levis. This was the same station mentioned in the description of early Ogdensburg.

As Lord Amherst was moving gaily down the Lake of the Thousand Islands, his fleet consisting of two armed vessels, the *Mohawk* and the *Onondaga*, and a number of boats, the lookout of the latter ship discovered a bateau carrying a party of French soldiers putting out from Deer Island, since renamed Carleton Island. The captain gave swift pursuit, at the same time signalling the *Mohawk* to follow. A lively race ensued, and after going several miles, before the *Onondaga* could get within range of the French boat, it disappeared down a narrow channel between a large island and a group of smaller islands. Unwilling to give up the chase the *Onondaga* followed, and when about midway of the channel the vessel received a whole broadside from the wooded banks of the islands hemming it in. It then became evident that the whole affair had been planned to entrap the unwary English. The decks of the war-ship were literally swept with the leaden hail of the concealed French and Indians; but the English returned this fire so fast and furiously that the allied forces were completely routed. It now became necessary to find the way out, and for this purpose a boat was despatched to find a passage. Another party, under the command of the coxswain, named Terry, was sent with a message to Captain Fordham of the *Mohawk* to return to the main channel. This duty Coxswain Terry performed, but after he left the *Mohawk* to return to the *Onondaga* neither he nor his crew were ever heard of. The latter ship succeeded in finding her way out, and waited a league below until the *Mohawk* came along. Then it was learned that Terry and his men were missing. Though they were anxiously awaited, and boats were sent out to find them, nothing was ever learned of their fate. It was supposed they had got bewildered in the intricate windings of the waterways between the islands, and, unable to find the channel followed by the *Onondaga*, had fallen into the hands of the enemy. Whether that was true or not, the place has been known ever since as "The Lost Channel."

When satisfied that Coxswain Terry and his crew were not to be found, Lord Amherst resumed his descent of the river, stopping on his way to capture La Presentation, the torch being applied to the dismantled walls of the fort. As the war-ships sailed away, only the charred ruins and a solitary chimney were left to mark the spot. The latter stood for many years as a landmark, giving to the island upon which it had been erected the name it still bears, "Chimney Island." The expedition reached the upper end of Montreal Island, at La Chine, in safety, and, co-operating with Murray and Haviland, effected an easy victory over De Levis and his depleted ranks.

Associated with these charming waters, gemmed with their diamonds cut from fairyland, is the memory of a Bonaparte, a brother of the great Napoleon. The romantic story of this exiled nobleman, who desired to be known in this country as Count de Survilliers, and his connection with the history of this region is interesting enough, but too long, to be given here. He was afforded no greater pleasure than in skimming these "ribbons of water" in pursuit of his favourite pastime, fishing, while he was a constant visitor at Cape Vincent, where a kindred spirit had taken up his abode. Not far away is that beautiful lake, a favourite resort of his, which still bears his family name, and which, with its sparkling surface and isles scattered with a prodigal hand over its glassy surface, reproduces in miniature the grand archipelago of the "Lake of the Thousand Islands."

The list of "memory isles" might be continued almost indefinitely if one desired. As this region is to-day the boundary line between two great countries, so it was for unnumbered years the border-range of two of the most powerful clans of the dusky brotherhoods inhabiting the ancient wilds of America. Upon the north and the east roamed, lords of forest and river, the haughty Algonquins, noted as the greatest hunters of the land. To the south of Manatoana (the Thousand

Islands) dwelt, in the valleys of its rivers and lakes, the Iroquois, who lived by fishing and cultivating the soil. They boasted of great fields of tasselled corn and large apple orchards, and looked with disdain upon the excitement of the chase. If of different tastes and habits, these people of the wilds lived side by side in harmony for many a changing season.

Upon certain times it had been the practice for the young men of the two families to hunt and fish together, it always being the rule that whichever party should kill the fewer of the game animals, or spear the fewer fish, should skin and dress the fruits of their united efforts. Usually the Algonquins were the fortunate ones. In fact, it became looked upon as a certainty that the Iroquois were to do the "squaw" work, while the others enjoyed the running to earth of the noble game. Thus the former began to decline a sport that really did not fall to their lot. Occasionally they would join in the chase to please their neighbours, and upon one of the last hunts, when the Algonquins had boastfully declared that the young Iroquois would have little to do but care for the game they brought down, the mighty hunters of the St. Lawrence valley went forth to slay the unwary victims of the wilderness. But somehow now their vaunted skill failed them. Though the woods ran thick with tempting game, they followed their quest in vain for three days. Then the Iroquois, elated over the failure of their rivals, though they had been careful not to betray this feeling, offered to try their hand. The Algonquins readily agreed to this, thinking no better result would fall to their lot, and that such a failure would compensate for the wounds upon their own honour. Their disappointment may be imagined when the Iroquois, looked upon as women on the hunt, came in with an abundance of game.

The Algonquins sullenly held their peace, but, their pride, sorely wounded, they vowed among themselves to have revenge. That night, while the tired hunters slept, every one of them was slain. The murderers denied their deed, and it was a long time before the friends of the dead learned the truth. Then they mildly asked that justice should be done the slayers. A council was called, but the Algonquins evaded the matter of a settlement, and tried to satisfy the others with honeyed words. This failed of its purpose. Aroused to a fierce pitch of indignation, the Iroquois proved that they were warriors as well as " squaw-men." By the fires of their prophets, by the honour of their women, by the sign of the Great Spirit, they swore they would never rest—they nor their children, even to the last generation—until the last Algonquin had been swept from the earth. This explains the origin of that terrible feud which existed between these rival races at the coming of the white men, and which continued to rage, drawing into its toils the French and the English, all through the long, dark years of border warfare. If given as a story, there seems to be a foundation of truth beneath it.

In this connection it may not be out of place to say that the origin of the legend relating to the formation of the League of the Iroquois, so beautifully described by Longfellow in his immortal poem of *Hiawatha*, belongs to this realm of lakes and islands, though the poet gives no hint of this. It was upon the calm blue waters of the Lake of a Thousand Islands that the two young men of the Onondaga nation were gazing, when they saw, as if in a vision, the white canoe driven over the water by the strong arm of the river god, who proved to be, upon nearer approach, an old, but venerable, man. With a single oar he sped his light canoe toward them, not so much as a murmur of the wind breaking the silence as he approached, his brow fixed in deep thought. He did not seem to notice them until he had reached the shore, and, drawing up his majestic form to a great height, exclaimed aloud that name which told them beyond doubt that he was the deity who reigned over the waters and their inhabitants. He then invited them to go with him upon a voyage over the river, showing them many wonderful sights they had not dreamed of, and when promising to clear the sedgy channels environing the charming plots of land, he warned them of the approach of war, and counselled a union of nations. He even, through these young men, called a council of the different tribes, and during the meeting of that assembly was formed the League of the Five Nations, which became so famous. His mission accomplished, Hi-a-wat-ha, as he chose to be known, paddled his snowy canoe out upon the lake, to disappear as mysteriously as he had come.

The admirer of Cooper's interesting tale of *The Pathfinder*, while aware that the author does not attempt to describe the exact spot, locates the culminating scenes of his story upon what he calls " Station Island." According to the historical facts that are woven about it, there is little doubt of its being one of the " Admiralty Group," located in the Canadian channel above Gananoque. The time was toward the close of the French and Indian War, when the English were stationed at Oswego, the French at Fort Frontenac, now Kingston, and controlling the river. The supplies of the latter came up the St. Lawrence from Montreal, and it was prudent that the English should keep a sharp lookout for these provisioned bateaux and the arrival of any troops that might be sent into these waters. In order to carry out their purpose the British actually established places of concealment. This idea is corroborated by Mr. J. R. Haddock, who says, in speaking of the situation of Cooper's island :

It is evident that this very group of islands (Admiralty Group) would be the one chosen for such a hiding place for several reasons. First, it was nearer Oswego; second, the chances of recapture were lessened; third, the opportunity of watching the approach of a fleet of bateaux unseen. If the hiding place had been chosen in the Lower or Naval Group, the chances of a recapture would have been materially increased. On " Station Island " a lookout could be kept on the river below, so that the French on the mainland could be watched; so that the island itself could hardly be distinguished from those by which it was surrounded. One island in this group fulfils the conditions, and there is not another among all the Thousand Islands that does; and hence the presumption that the island is here, and that it borders on the Bostwick Channel.

Nearly opposite here, upon the Canadian shore, is the pretty town of Gananoque, with a population of between four and five thousand. It is situated at the mouth of a small river by the same name, which was an Indian term meaning, it is claimed, "The Place of the Deer." The first settlers were loyalists, who came here from the State of Connecticut at the close of the American Revolution. One of them, Sir John Johnson, was commander of an organisation known as "Johnson's Royal Greens." He received a grant for the territory now including the village in conjunction with Colonel Joel Stone, who became its most enterprising founder. Gananoque is now aptly styled the Birmingham of Canada, its water-power and commercial advantages fully entitling it to this distinction.

And now after our round trip of nearly two thousand miles, from Ontario to the ocean and back again, we find ourselves approaching the place from which we started, "where the lake and the river meet." In paying a last look upon the beautiful scene we are reluctantly leaving the tender tribute of Cremazie, the sweet-voiced singer of Canada, comes to mind:

When Eve plucked death from the tree of life, and brought tears and sorrows upon the earth, Adam was driven out into the world to mourn with her, and taste from the bitter spring that we drink to-day. Then the angels on their wings bore the silent Eden to the eternal spheres on high, and placed it in the heavens; but in passing through space they dropped along the way, to mark their course, some flowers from the Garden Divine. These flowers of changing hues, falling into the great river, became the Thousand Isles, the paradise of the St. Lawrence.

AMONG THE THOUSAND ISLANDS.

From a photograph by W. Notman & Son, Montreal.

Within sight of this happy retreat at the head of the St. Lawrence River, with Lake Ontario upon one hand and the Great Cataraqui or Rideau River upon the other, stands Kingston, connected to Ottawa by rail and canal; to the west by the lakes; to the east Montreal, Quebec, and the ocean, by rail and river St. Lawrence, it is the most happily located city in Canada. While the attractions of both Quebec and Montreal are not to be forgotten, this would seem to combine the favours of the others.   As a military station it stands next to Quebec, while its harbour is deep, commodious, and well protected.

The early explorers and defenders of the valley of the St. Lawrence showed keen foresight in their selection of outposts, and scarcely one played a more important part in the border wars than Kingston, first known in the days of its founding by La Salle as Cataraqui, and then as Fort Frontenac.   The last name still clings to the county, but even the name of the fort that he built, which was destroyed by the English in 1758, to be rebuilt soon after, was renamed Fort Henry. When Carleton Island, first selected as a military station, came within the American lines, Kingston was chosen as the stronghold for the English, and it has since gained the name of the Sandhurst, or the West Point of Canada.   But with its Martello towers and martial atmosphere clinging to it, the Limestone City is far more than a military school or a place of defence. Upon the separation of Canada into two provinces,

Kingston became the first capital of the province of Ontario, or Upper Canada, as it was then called. During the period of the United Provinces of Upper and Lower Canada, 1841 to 1844, the legislature met here.

Considerable shipbuilding has been done, and it has become a great grain depot. At the time of the War of 1812, the Duke of Wellington advised the construction of a route to Montreal independent of that by the St. Lawrence, and the outcome was the Rideau Canal, built at a cost of nearly four million dollars. This connected Kingston to Ottawa, but the railroad some time since relegated the canal to the use of pleasure travel. It winds through one of the most picturesque sections of the country.

This city is also a great educational centre, and its colleges are of national importance. Among these may be mentioned the Queen's University, School of Art, Science Hall, Royal Medical College, School of Gunnery, School of Mining, and several others deserving of notice. Considerable manufacturing is done here, and altogether it would appear as if the city should be larger than it is, having about twenty thousand inhabitants.

Here we bid, not adieu, but *au revoir*, to the noble St. Lawrence, typical of the wonderful swing and freedom of nature. We see evidence of this everywhere. We see it in its vast volume of crystal water, now gathering its forces for a plunge down some mighty incline; anon smoothing its ruffled bosom before one of those great mirrors suggestive of the source whence it has

brought its offering.   But whether driven by rapids, or
loitering by some sleepy lake, it ever maintains its hold
upon the grand, the immense, the sublime.   Never does
it degrade its dignity, or militate its majesty.   Winding
between the green banks of some pastoral region, sinister sentinels of rock-walls, by city gates, or open country, it ever displays its cheerful brightness, reflects the
deep azure of the northern sky, and sweeps on with
magnificent mien, as if conscious of its gigantic work of
draining half a continent, of carrying to the sea in its
great drinking-horn one-third of all the fresh water on
the globe.

Index